The Canary Islanders of Louisiana

The Canary Islanders of Louisiana

Gilbert C. Din

LOUISIANA STATE UNIVERSITY PRESS
Baton Rouge and London

Copyright © 1988 by Louisiana State University Press
All rights reserved
Manufactured in the United States of America

10 9 8 7 6 5 4 3 2 1

Designer: Sylvia Loftin
Typeface: Palatino
Typesetter: Focus/Graphics
Printer: Thomson-Shore, Inc.
Binder: John H. Dekker & Sons, Inc.

Library of Congress Cataloging-in-Publication Data

Din, Gilbert C.
    The Canary Islanders of Louisiana / Gilbert C. Din.
        p.   cm.
    Bibliography: p.
    Includes index.
    ISBN 0-8071-1383-2 (alk. paper)
    1. Canary Islanders—Louisiana—History. 2. Louisiana—History.
3. Immigrants—Louisiana—History. 4. Louisiana—Emigration and
immigration. 5. Canary Islands—Emigration and immigration.
I. Title.
F380.C22D56 1988
976.3—dc19   87-29941
                                                                CIP

The paper in this book meets the guidelines for
permanence and durability of the
Committee on Production Guidelines for Book Longevity of the Council on
Library Resources.∞

For Judy

Contents

Illustrations

Preface

The arrival of the Spanish ship *Santísimo Sacramento* in New Orleans, with its cargo of Canary Islander immigrants, in late 1778 began a new chapter in the history of Louisiana's ethnic minorities. Eventually, nearly two thousand Canary Islanders stepped foot in Louisiana, and a somewhat smaller number settled in several locations in the bayou country. Mostly poor and illiterate small farmers, they struggled long and hard against nature as well as against man in order to survive. Soon numerous Americans and Frenchmen—mainly Acadians—overwhelmed the province and state. But, owing largely to isolation and Louisiana's poor educational system, economy, and class-ridden society, many of the Canary Islanders preserved their identity and a good part of their culture through the nineteenth century. Not until the present century did the breakdown of their principal strongholds in St. Bernard Parish and in the small communities of Bayou Lafourche occur. That has facilitated the assimilation of large numbers of Canarians into the state's main culture.

Because of the smallness of the original group of Canary Islanders that arrived in the eighteenth century and the lack of substantial infusions of additional people of Hispanic heritage in the nineteenth and twentieth centuries, Canarians have had only limited influence on other people in Louisiana. Their small numbers have worked against any kind of cultural imperialism, although there have been persons of Canarian culture without Spanish surnames. But by and large, the more numerous Americans and Acadians have influenced the Canary Islanders far more than they, in turn, have been influenced. Moreover, most of the original group of Canary Islanders did not think in terms of preserving their identity and culture, and instead intermarried freely with other cultural groups. Only where they practiced endogamy did their culture survive.

The present study of the Canary Islanders in Louisiana makes no pretense at being exhaustive or definitive. The Canarians have in the past attracted little attention and few investigators. Earlier works, all since World War II, have centered on language and folk literature. As a consequence, this history is explorative since it tries for the first time to trace the Canary Islander experience in Louisiana over the past two hundred years. Its emphasis is on history rather than on culture. Spanish records as well as nineteenth- and twentieth-century accounts, until about 1940, have had little to say about the Canarian customs. This is unfortunate because it means that much of the Canarian cultural past in Louisiana is now probably lost forever.

This study focuses primarily on the Spanish-surnamed Canarians and on the two areas in Louisiana where their impact was most profound, St. Bernard Parish and Bayou Lafourche (Ascension and upper Assumption parishes). I have used the terms *Canary Islander, Isleño* (which means "Islander" and is a name still in use in the Canary Islands), and *Canarian* interchangeably within the Louisiana context. While, in St. Bernard Parish, residents preserve the word *Isleño*, the term disappeared from usage on Bayou Lafourche in the nineteenth century. The people in the latter location have tended to refer to themselves as Spaniards or Spanish. Accent marks for Spanish names are used in the text only through the Spanish era. They have not been kept by the Isleños (except for the tilde in that word). Also, the pronunciation of Spanish names has sometimes changed, not to mention the spelling. Perhaps the best example of the change in pronunciation is *Nunez*, which has dropped the accent mark (stress) and the tilde (which gives the *n* a "ny" sound, as in *canyon*, from the Spanish *cañon*). *Nunez* is now pronounced "NOO-nes" while the Spanish pronunciation is "NOO-nyes."

The appendix contains the names of the Canary Islanders who boarded the first five of nine ships to take the immigrants to Louisiana. Of the other four ships, only two reached Havana. A third was captured by the English, and the survivors continued on to Havana via Puerto Rico; and the fourth sailed to Caracas, Venezuela. In 1783, many of the Canary Islanders in Havana embarked two ships to bring them to

Louisiana, and their names are reproduced in the appendix. The names on these lists, excluding those of a few persons who died or deserted, represent the overwhelming majority of the Canary Islanders who arrived in Louisiana.

I am indebted to many people for help in making this study possible. Among Canary Islander descendants, I wish to single out Louise Molero O'Toole, Mrs. B. M. Rodriguez, Juanita Harwell Sparks, and W. L. Serpas, Jr., all of Louisiana. The staffs of the Archivo General de Indias, Seville, Spain; the New Orleans Public Library; the Louisiana Historical Center; the Louisiana State University library, particularly the Louisiana Room; and the Fort Lewis College Library were most helpful. Francisco Morales Padrón of the University of Seville and the Cabildo of Las Palmas de Gran Canarias made possible a trip to Las Palmas to attend the V Coloquio de Historia Canario-Americana in 1982. William deMarigny Hyland introduced me to St. Bernard Parish for the first time. St. Bernard Parish historian and Isleño Frank Fernandez made me aware that some modern-day Canarians are attempting to preserve their cultural heritage. In Durango, Judy Sutliff provided valuable assistance in the preparation of the manuscript. Finally, Ronald R. Morazán read the manuscript and helped me to avoid pitfalls in Louisiana history after 1803, which until recently was terra incognita for me.

The Canary Islanders of Louisiana

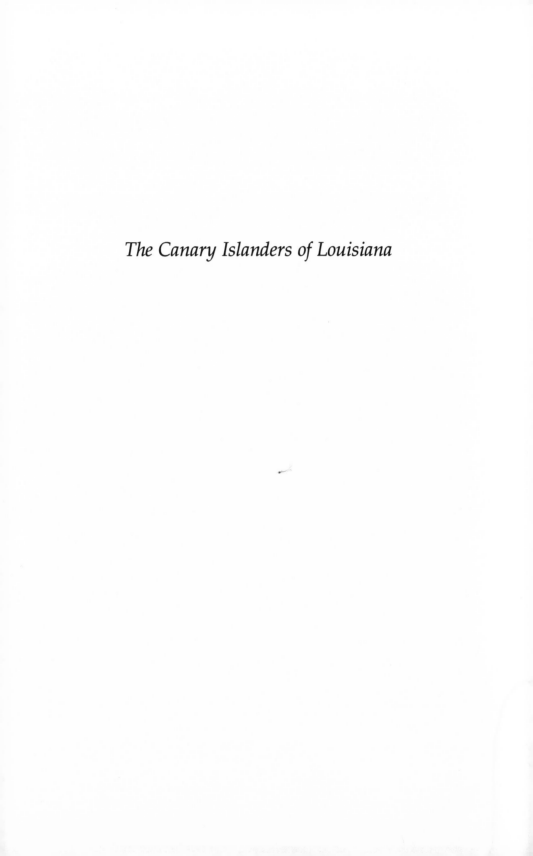

One

The Origins of Louisiana's Canary Islanders

The homeland of the Isleños, the Canary Islands, has been known for three thousand years. But, until 600 years ago, knowledge of the islands consisted more of legend than of fact. Before the time of Christ, a few primitive Mediterranean sailing vessels venturing into the Atlantic Ocean found the "Fortunate Isles." Writers of those expeditions left only fragmentary accounts of what the sailors saw. Thereafter, for well over a thousand years, outsiders had little contact with the islands despite their location of only between one hundred and five hundred kilometers west of the coast of Morocco. Once Europeans rediscovered the islands about the fourteenth century, however, knowledge about them increased, and contact was never again lost. The islands' natural beauty and mild climate attracted and enchanted outsiders, but all too frequently they came to exploit both the people and the resources. While the islands appeared to be a paradise to outsiders, the inhabitants often endured privation and misery. Consequently, from the time of the discovery of the New World, a steady stream of Canarians embarked on Spanish ships to seek a better life in the Western Hemisphere.

The archipelago of the Canaries consists of seven main islands, Tenerife, Gran Canaria, Gomera, La Palma, Hierro, Fuerteventura, and Lanzarote, having a total area of 2,807 square miles (less than 6 percent of the size of Louisiana). Some geographers believe that the islands, really mountain peaks jutting out of the Atlantic Ocean, are a prolongation of the Atlas Mountains of North Africa, while others, more romantically, speculate that they are the remains of the lost continent of Atlantis. The islands, however, owe their origin to volcanic activity. From the Miocene

1

epoch of thirty million years ago to as recently as 1971, the islands have experienced volcanic eruptions, which have produced their rugged, mountainous surface. Plains are almost nonexistent, and agriculture today exists only where the land has been terraced. The rich volcanic soil permits crops to flourish where sufficient rainfall or irrigation is available.[1]

Lack of water is a serious problem for most of the islands. The average precipitation is approximately 14 inches, but it is not distributed evenly. The western islands of Tenerife, La Palma, Hierro, and Gomera, located farthest out in the Atlantic and possessing the highest elevations, receive the most rain, with La Palma—the green island—surpassing all others with 26 inches. At the other end of the archipelago, Lanzarote and Fuerteventura, nearest the Sahara Desert and lower in elevation, receive a scant 5.5 inches. Not surprisingly, these last two islands have small populations and deserts. Even Gran Canaria, which is slightly more to the west and higher in elevation than Lanzarote and Fuerteventura, has an arid appearance on much of its surface.[2]

The geographic zones of the islands are an important characteristic. Elevation determines the climate and the crops grown on the islands. From sea level to 650 feet, the temperature ranges from 66° to 75° F, and precipitation averages 8 inches annually. At this low elevation, the ocean prevents the temperature from rising or falling excessively. Bananas, dates, sugarcane, and subtropical plants abound. Many of the trees and plants brought by the Spanish government in colonial days from the mild regions of the Western Hemisphere are found in this zone in botanical gardens or even growing naturally. From 650 to 2,000 feet, the temperature ranges from 61° to 73°, and Mediterranean-type vegetation predominates. It is a cool and pleasant climate that permits vineyards, citrus orchards, and other fruit trees. Rainfall varies from 8 to 19 inches, usually with the northern and western sides of the islands receiving the greater amounts. From 2,000 to 5,000 feet, the temperature drops to a colder 54° to 61°, while rainfall increases. Nineteen to 39 inches fall. Clouds form from the humid air, and dew is deposited on the vegetation. Wheat, barley, potatoes, and chestnuts are the crops grown. Only the islands possessing high mountains, such as Tenerife, La Palma, and

1. Pedro Hernández Hernández (ed.), *Natura y cultura de las Islas Canarias* (4th ed.; Santa Cruz de Tenerife, 1982), 22–27.

2. *Ibid.*, 35–36. On the geography of the Canary Islands, see Telesforo Bravo, *Geografía general de las Islas Canarias* (Santa Cruz de Tenerife, 1964). In addition to the seven major islands, there are several *islotes*, or small islands of little value; they are Montaña Clara, La Graciosa, Alegranza, Lobos, Roque del Este, and Roque del Oeste.

Gran Canaria, have the next zone, which ranges from 5,000 to 9,000 feet. Since the zone is often above the cloud cover, rainfall diminishes to approximately 16 inches. Here the Canary pine grows, and agriculture is not practiced. The temperature occasionally drops below freezing, and the mean temperature is a brisk 48°. A final zone extending from 9,000 to 12,000 feet is found only on the island of Tenerife, where the often snow-covered Pico de Teide rises majestically. It is the highest point in the Canaries and on a clear day can be seen from neighboring islands. Because that zone is above the tree line, only a sparse alpinelike vegetation grows.[3]

The ancient natives of the Canary Islands were the Guanches, who lived in a Stone Age way of life. While the term *Guanche* is properly used only for the former inhabitants of Tenerife, it has been commonly applied to all of the prehistoric population of the islands. The Guanche language, which is related to the ancient idioms of North Africa, has disappeared except for a few words. The Guanches never developed writing. These earliest inhabitants of the Canary Islands have been described as robust, fair skinned, and handsome. They largely dedicated themselves to a pastoral life, caring for their goats, sheep, and pigs. They also practiced a limited agriculture, growing wheat and barley, among other foodstuffs. Although a number of Guanches lived in huts, caves sheltered the majority from the elements. Adult Guanches dressed in skins or grasses sewn together, while the younger people went about naked. On the larger islands, the Guanches had a king called *mencey* or *quanartem*, held land in common, and lived peacefully with one another except for occasional fights over the theft of animals. Their primitive weapons were mainly sticks, spears, and stones. They developed a system of government that included judges and laws. Their religion consisted of belief in a single god, and they carefully buried their dead after embalming the bodies. In the late nineteenth century, anthropologists unearthed and examined large numbers of Guanche mummies and skeletons.[4]

The origin of the Guanches has mystified scholars. Recent studies classify the people into two groups called Cro-Magnon and Mediterra-

3. Hernández Hernández (ed.), *Natura y cultura de las Islas Canarias*, 32–34; Enrique Romeu Palazuelos *et al.*, *Las Islas Canarias* (Madrid, 1981), 11–20.

4. Hernández Hernández (ed.), *Natura y cultura de las Islas Canarias*, 156–99; Romeu Palazuelos *et al.*, *Las Islas Canarias*, 32–39; Luis Diego Cuscoy, *Los guanches* (Santa Cruz de Tenerife, 1968); and Ernest A. Hooten, *The Ancient Inhabitants of the Canary Islands* (Cambridge, Mass., 1925).

nean. The Cro-Magnon type is described as broad faced, robust, long headed (dolichocephalic), and fairer than the Mediterranean type. The Mediterranean type is described as long faced, delicate, and having a short, broad skull (brachicephalic). Skeletons of these two physical types have also been found among the prehistoric populations of northwest Africa, where the Guanches undoubtedly originated. However, not all of the islands' inhabitants went there at the same time. Perhaps between 2500 and 1000 B.C., the first people arrived in the Canary Islands. Some writers have speculated that the increased aridity of North Africa drove the people there. Newcomers, probably in fewer numbers, went to the islands between the sixth and ninth centuries after Christ fleeing from the Arab conquerors of North Africa. How both of these groups reached the islands remains a mystery inasmuch as the Guanches of the fifteenth century did not know the use of boats. In an effort to explain this, it has been suggested recently that many of the Canarians were originally Berbers living in Mauretania, North Africa, under Roman dominion. They rebelled unsuccessfully against their rulers, and the Roman Senate punished them with deportation to the Canary Islands. Although the Romans deposited the rebels without ships, the Romans thoughtfully provided grain and animals. Later, shipwrecked sailors periodically washed up on the islands' shores and added to the cultural diversity of the inhabitants. Fifteenth-century Spanish chroniclers noted that the natives possessed different cultures not only among the several islands but even on the same island.[5]

Before the time of the Romans, stories circulated in the Mediterranean about islands existing beyond the "Pillars of Hercules" (the Straits of Gibraltar). These stories were veiled in mist, and little was definitely known about the islands. Possibly Greeks, Phoenicians, and Carthaginians visited them. Not until the days of the Roman Empire does information become more certain. King Juba II of Mauretania, who reigned between 25 B.C. and A.D. 25, reported to the Roman emperor about an expedition he sent to investigate the islands. His explorers sighted several of the "Fortunate Isles," and their description left no doubt that the islands were the Canaries. They related seeing no humans but encountering ferocious dogs. King Juba named the islands

5. Hernández Hernández (ed.), *Natura y cultura de las Islas Canarias*, 144–53; Romeu Palazuelos *et al.*, *Las Islas Canarias*, 28–32; John Mercer, *The Canary Islands: Their Prehistory, Conquest, and Survival* (London, 1980), 17–24; Ilse Schwidelzky, *La población prehispánica de las Islas Canarias* (Santa Cruz de Tenerife, 1963).

for the dogs, *canine* in Latin being *canaria*. Contrary to common belief, the well-known songbirds derive their name from the islands rather than giving it to them. After the Roman era, the islands disappeared from recorded history for nearly a thousand years.[6]

Following the collapse of the Roman Empire, the Muslims of the Arabian Peninsula expanded through the Mediterranean, conquering North Africa and Spain by the early eighth century. Muslims are known to have made several visits to the Canary Islands. For example, the Arab captain Ben-Farroukh was there about 999. Later, Xerif-el Edrisis wrote about another expedition that went to the islands in 1170. In the late thirteenth century, as Muslim power waned in Spain, European ships explored in the Atlantic.[7]

The Genoese appear to have first arrived on the islands in 1291. A half century later, in 1341, the Portuguese followed them, sent by King Affonso IV under Angiolino del Tegghia. The next year Majorcans called at the islands. Many of these voyages, sponsored by merchants, acquired positive information about the Canaries and no doubt encouraged other navigators to go there. From the fourteenth century on, as Europeans ventured farther into the Atlantic in their improved ships, contact with the islands increased. This contact initiated a sad era of exploitation, as the Europeans often sacked and enslaved the natives. In 1390 one such expedition hit Lanzarote hard, but it avoided Tenerife when the island's volcano, Teide, erupted. Guanches were sold as slaves in Seville before 1400 and in Valencia about the same time. The nefarious practice continued throughout the fifteenth century.[8]

The conquest of the Canary Islands occupied most of the 1400s. Jean de Bethencourt, a Norman French adventurer, began the subjugation and Christianization of the islands for Castile in 1402. The invaders soon established colonies on Fuerteventura, Gomera, and Hierro. The conquest of Gran Canaria, Tenerife, and La Palma proceeded more slowly and lasted until 1496. The reasons for the slowness of the conquest were several: a strong resistance by the natives; the conquerors' lack of financial resources; and the poverty of the islands, which did not make their subjugation profitable. Portugal also opposed the presence of

6. Salvador López Herrera, *Las Islas Canarias a través de la historia* (Madrid, 1971), 82–83.
7. *Ibid.*, 84–87.
8. Buenaventura Bonnet y Reverón, *Las expediciones a las Canarias en el siglo XIV* (Madrid, 1946); Miguel Angel Ladero Quesada, *Los primeros europeos en Canarias (Siglos XIV y XV)* (Las Palmas, Gran Canaria, 1979); and Charles Verlinden, *The Beginnings of Modern Colonization* (Ithaca, N.Y., 1970), 33–51.

Castile in the islands. The rivalry between the two Iberian kingdoms lasted until 1479, when Castile defeated Portugal in war. The Treaty of Alcaçovas of that year at last confirmed Castile's right to the Canary Islands.[9]

In the next seventeen years, the conquest of the islands was completed. Under Isabel and Fernando, the Catholic Kings of Spain, Castilian nobles defeated the remaining Guanches. Among the nobles were the members of the important Herrera-Peraza family, which employed its own resources in dominating the islands. The Catholic Kings bought out the Herrera-Peraza claims to Gran Canaria, La Palma, and Tenerife but recognized the family's feudal rights over the other four islands. The descendants of the Herrera-Peraza family would rule those islands for the next three hundred years.[10]

Changes occurred rapidly in the Canaries in the fifteenth and sixteenth centuries. European immigrants settled in the islands, enslaving or mixing with the Guanches. Nobles seized the best agricultural lands, holding them in large estates while the common people provided the labor. The system of land tenure produced a stratified society that hurt the lower classes. Commerce and agriculture developed on the islands, helped in some measure by the discovery of the New World. Spanish ships often stopped last at the islands before crossing the Atlantic. Christopher Columbus himself called there on all four of his voyages across the ocean. The Canary Islands also served as a trial laboratory for political and economic institutions Spain transferred from Europe to its new American colonies. Throughout the Spanish colonial period, the islands were closely linked to the New World.[11]

The Spanish conquerors of the Canaries often treated the gentle, peaceful Guanches in the most barbaric manner. They were killed in wars or enslaved and sold in Spain. Often the natives preferred death or suicide to servitude. The conquerors diluted the purity of the Guanches by mixing freely with them. Nevertheless, despite all the factors that reduced the Guanche population, at the end of the sixteenth century

9. Joseph F. O'Callaghan, *A History of Medieval Spain* (Ithaca, N.Y., 1975), 538, 557. Chronicles of the conquest are in Francisco Morales Padrón, *Canarias: crónicas de su conquista* (Seville, 1978).

10. Rhea Marsh Smith, *Spain: A Modern History* (Ann Arbor, 1965), 117; and the two works of A. Rumeu de Armas, *España en el Africa atlántico* (2 vols.; Madrid, 1956), and *La política indigenista de Isabel la Católica* (Valladolid, Sp., 1969), which is mostly on the Canaries.

11. See Francisco Morales Padrón, *Sevilla, Canaria y América* (Las Palmas, Gran Canaria, 1970).

two-thirds of the islands' inhabitants consisted of Guanches. Furthermore, most authorities today are of the opinion that the basis of the existing Canary Island population is still principally Guanche and that many of the Cro-Magnon and Mediterranean type characteristics survive among the present inhabitants.[12]

After the conquest of the Guanches, fighting continued in the Canaries because of raids made by Spain's enemies. The powerful Ottoman Turks harried the islands from North Africa in the sixteenth century. Although the defenders successfully parried many attacks, others caused considerable damage, killing and enslaving the defenders. Of the islands, Lanzarote and Gomera suffered the most, and fishermen were often enslaved when corsairs seized their vessels. Jarife, the king of Fez, briefly occupied Lanzarote in 1569 and 1586. England, Spain's traditional enemy for 250 years, also raided the islands periodically. Sir Francis Drake and Sir John Hawkins unsuccessfully assaulted Las Palmas on Gran Canaria in 1595. In 1656 Admiral Sir Robert Blake attacked Santa Cruz de Tenerife with a fleet of thirty-six ships, inflicting much harm. In 1743, during the War of Jenkins' Ear, Admiral Sir Charles Winston menaced the islands. Horatio Lord Nelson attempted the most notable of all English attacks only to suffer his only defeat off Tenerife by the Spanish navy in 1797. After the battle, Spanish officials graciously permitted Nelson, who lost an arm in the fight, to have his wounds treated on shore.[13]

Those years of intermittent warfare disrupted the economic life of the islands, which was essential for the welfare of the inhabitants. Economic conditions were always precarious, and the islands suffered repeatedly from numerous calamities. Drought, epidemics, volcanic eruptions, plagues of locusts, famines, and a shortage of manpower in the sixteenth and seventeenth centuries all hurt the economy. A man-made problem was Spanish governmental restrictions on the islands' trade. Sixteenth- and seventeenth-century curbs on trade often meant economic hardship for the inhabitants. Not until well into the eighteenth century did the government ease the restrictions.

The most important crops and products of the Canary Islands were those that were successfully exported. The first major export crop was

---

12. Jocelyn Nigel Hillgarth, *The Spanish Kingdoms, 1250–1516* (London, 1978), 86; Manuela Marrero Rodríguez, *La esclavitud en Tenerife a raíz de la conquista* (La Laguna, Tenerife, 1966).

13. Hernández Hernández (ed.), *Natura y cultura de las Islas Canarias*, 253–55.

sugar. The growing of sugarcane on the wetter islands required large estates and considerable capital, and it utilized manpower only seasonally. Provisioning ships sailing to the New World was a significant activity in the sixteenth century. Export items included wine, cereals, and fruits, many of which went to England. The English market rose to paramount importance in the seventeenth century, and trade continued legally in peacetime and illegally in wartime. But after 1723 the balance of trade shifted to favor the English since they reduced their purchases of Canary Island wine, sugar, tobacco, flour, fish, lard, and wood while they increased their sales of textiles. The loss of the English wine market to Portugal by the mid–eighteenth century, coupled with low export prices in general, produced a serious economic crisis in the islands. Tenerife, the most populated island (14,710 heads of household in 1776) and described by contemporaries as a vineyard, perhaps suffered the most. Many of the rural inhabitants lost their jobs and flocked to the towns in search of employment. To add to the woes of the labor force, the large numbers of unemployed workers depressed the job market and reduced wages.[14]

There are few detailed studies of economic conditions in the Canary Islands shortly before the emigrants to Louisiana departed. But those that exist provide an understanding of the reasons that induced most, if not all, of the emigrants to leave. The island of Gomera gives the most information. From the time of the Spanish conquest, nobles who were private landowners predominated and worked the common people as tenants. By the eighteenth century the production of orchil, a lichen that yields a violet dye on which the landlords speculated, monopolized the island's economy. When orchil production was abundant, wheat came in from Tenerife to feed the inhabitants; and when the orchil crop failed, the tenant farmers and their families starved. The other economic activities of the island, livestock raising and silk production, were unimportant. Through the eighteenth century, Gomera's already vulnerable economy declined even more, and the nobles, the only persons in a position to improve it, refused to do so. The deplorable conditions led to social discontent and to opposition of the seignorial system that

14. José Peraza de Ayala, *El régimen comercial de Canarias con Las Indias en los siglos XVI, XVII y XVIII* (Seville, 1977); Victor Morales Lezcano, *Relaciones mercantiles entre Inglaterra y los archipiélagos del Atlántico Ibérico, su estructura y su historia (1503–1783)* (La Laguna, Tenerife, 1970). For population figures of the Canaries, see Fernando Jiménez de Gregorio, "La población de las Islas Canarias en la segunda mitad del siglo XVIII," *Anuario de estudios atlánticos*, XIV (1968), 135.

dominated Gomera. The commoners advocated royal administration of the island instead of private control, the cultivation of vacant lands (*tierras baldías*) by themselves to increase agricultural production, additional taxes on the nobles in order to put more money into circulation on the island (the landlords constantly drained money from Gomera, investing it elsewhere), and economic diversification. But the effort at reform ended in failure, and the Crown joined the nobles to crush an uprising in 1762. Given the conditions on the island, emigration was one of the few alternatives for the people, and more than three hundred inhabitants of Gomera chose to leave for Louisiana.[15]

Somewhat similar conditions prevailed on the island of Tenerife, especially in the La Laguna region. It shared in the general worsening of the economy in the eighteenth century due to the fall of the wine trade, epidemics, drought, invasions of locusts from Africa (in 1755, 1757, 1761, and 1762), and periodic crop failures. Perhaps Tenerife did not suffer as much as the more arid islands of Lanzarote and Fuerteventura, because beggars from these islands went there in search of food. Food shortages in Tenerife, nevertheless, drove home some of the Lanzarote and Fuerteventura people, while others who remained reportedly starved to death. Bad harvests on Tenerife in 1774 and 1778 hurt the production of the population's basic diet of wheat, corn, and potatoes. Censuses of the second half of the eighteenth century reveal the decline of La Laguna's population: in 1755, there were 9,139 inhabitants; in 1769, 8,796; and in 1787, 7,222. Epidemics, food scarcities, a declining birth rate, and emigration shared responsibility. Not until the 1790s, when conditions had gradually improved, did La Laguna's inhabitants again increase in number.[16] Before then, however, many Gomera, Tenerife, Gran Canaria, Lanzarote, and La Palma inhabitants clearly recognized that emigration to Louisiana was preferable to remaining at home.

In emigrating to Louisiana, the Canarians followed a well-trodden path to the New World. From the time of the first voyages across the Atlantic, sailors from the islands shipped aboard vessels bound for the newly discovered lands. Some perhaps joined Columbus on his voyages of exploration. The Spanish government frowned on emigrants leaving

15. Germán Hernández Rodríguez, "La aportación de la isla de la Gomera al poblamiento de la Luisiana, 1777–78," in *IV Coloquio de historia canario-americana (1980)* (2 vols.; Salamanca, 1982), II, 227–45.

16. Mercedes Coderch Figueroa, *Evolución de la población de La Laguna entre 1750–1860* (La Laguna, Tenerife, 1975), 19–64. See also Francisco Morales Padrón, "El desplazamiento a las Indias desde Canarias," *Revista Museo Canario*, XXXV–XXXVI (1950), 1–24.

in the sixteenth century, when the islands' population was still relatively small and subjected to Muslim attack. By the late seventeenth century, however, the Crown allowed Canarian families to settle in Puerto Rico, Santo Domingo, and Cuba. It even encouraged them by requiring a certain number of families, often five, to go for every hundred tons of commerce permitted with the Caribbean colonies. In 1718 the Crown ordered fifty families yearly to emigrate to the New World. Canarians soon sailed for Buenos Aires, Puerto Rico, Trinidad, Montevideo, and Texas. Later in the century they also went to the Caribbean, Florida, and Venezuela. Isleños settled eventually in virtually every Spanish colony in the New World. They dreamed of "hacer América"—striking it rich in the Americas. In the words of historian Francisco Morales Padrón, the average Canarian "from the moment he acquire[d] the use of reason long[ed] for America (the New World) as his true homeland."[17]

The emigration of the families, nevertheless, disturbed the noble landowners, who resented losing their work force. On the island of Gomera, they deplored the recruitment of emigrants for Louisiana. The island's cabildo protested to the local audiencia and claimed that the most robust agricultural workers were leaving and that their departure resulted in fewer cultivated fields. Moreover, permitting them to leave left the island defenseless. No doubt much of what the cabildo asserted was an exaggeration since it represented the interests of the landlords, who, if a labor shortage developed, might be forced to pay higher wages. The Crown refused to heed their complaints and allowed the emigration to the New World to proceed.[18]

The sending of Canary Island settlers to Louisiana resulted in large measure from the Spanish wish to protect and populate the huge, virtually empty province. Despite French ownership of Louisiana for approximately two-thirds of a century, its population was tiny. France had entered the Mississippi Valley for the first time from Canada with the voyage of exploration down the Mississippi River of Louis Joliet and Père Marquette in 1673. They stopped before reaching the Gulf of Mexico, and Réné-Robert Chevalier, Sieur de La Salle, finally found the

17. Francisco Morales Padrón, "Las Canarias y la política emigratoria a Indias," in *I Coloquio de historia canario-americana (1976)* (Seville, 1977), 212–30. The quotation is on p. 230. See also, by the same author, "Colonos canarios en Indias," *Anuario de estudios americanos*, VIII (1951), 399–441.

18. Hernández Rodríguez, "La aportación de la isla de la Gomera al poblamiento de la Luisiana, 1777–78," 229, 243–45. A total of 85 families, consisting of 393 persons, was recruited in Gomera for Louisiana.

river's mouth in 1682. La Salle soon tried to establish a colony on the Mississippi, but his plans floundered when his ships on the Gulf of Mexico missed the "Father of Waters" and landed in Texas. There most of the settlers perished, as did La Salle, killed by one of his own men in 1687. Alarmed by French activity on the gulf, which for nearly two hundred years had been a Spanish lake, Spain rushed soldiers to establish a base at Pensacola and ordered troops and settlers into east Texas. The Spaniards worried about French desires to open trade with Texas and New Spain, to subvert the Indians, and to penetrate across the North American continent to the Pacific Ocean.[19]

Spanish apprehensions, however, were for the most part unfounded. The French constituted anything but a serious threat in the early years of colonizing Louisiana. Pierre Le Moyne d'Iberville established the first French settlement at Biloxi on the Gulf Coast in 1699 and started another at Mobile in 1702. The first years of the eighteenth century coincided with the War of the Spanish Succession, and Louisiana almost died aborning. The settlers and soldiers found life on the gulf arduous, death constantly lurking about, and themselves poorly suited to colonization. Aid from France arrived irregularly during the war, and the ships never seemed to bring sufficient food. Attempting to improve conditions, the French government granted Antoine Crozat a fifteen-year concession for the development of the province in 1712, but he failed as badly as had the government. Although Crozat agreed to send two shiploads of colonists yearly, he did not live up to the contract. When he surrendered Louisiana in 1718, the same year that New Orleans was founded, the province had a population of only four hundred. John Law's Company of the West succeeded Crozat, and Louisiana fared somewhat better, receiving thousands of white settlers and black slaves. But many of the whites came ill-prepared for the primitive conditions in the Louisiana wilderness, and they succumbed to disease and hardship in unusually large numbers. Nevertheless, the influx of colonists added to the existing settlements and started new ones.

Following the bursting of Law's "Mississippi Bubble" in the 1720s, Louisiana settled down to a quarter of a century of slow growth. A

19. There is no single study on the French era in Louisiana. Covering the early years, however, are the four volumes of Marcel Giraud, *A History of French Louisiana*, Vol. I: *The Reign of Louis XIV (1698–1715)*, trans. Joseph C. Lambert (Baton Rouge, 1974); Vol. II, *Années de transition (1715–1717)* (Paris, 1958); Vol. III, *L'Epoque de John Law (1717–1720)* (Paris, 1966); Vol. IV, *La Louisiane après le système de Law* (Paris, 1978).

sluggish economy and vexing Indian wars hindered faster development. By 1750 Louisiana's population had risen to about five thousand whites and perhaps two thousand slaves. Although this population represented a substantial improvement, the colony remained an enormous financial burden on the mother country. When France lost Canada to England in the Seven Years' War, there seemed little purpose in retaining Louisiana. France, consequently, offered the province to Spain in payment for the Iberian nation's valiant, if futile, late entry in the war and as compensation for the Spanish loss of Florida to England. Spain initially resisted the offer, realizing only too well that the colony was a huge liability. Reluctantly, Spain accepted Louisiana in order to prevent the English from acquiring it and threatening the other Spanish colonies on the gulf—Texas and Mexico.[20]

When Spain obtained Louisiana in 1763, its tiny population had risen to only approximately eleven thousand people, less than half of whom were white. In the first years Spain owned the province, it made only modest attempts to increase the number of inhabitants. In 1766 the first Spanish governor, Antonio de Ulloa arrived. He continued to aid the Acadians, who had been entering the colony for the past several years, with free lands, shelter, rations, tools, seeds, and medical care. In 1768, acting upon Ulloa's suggestion, the Spanish government allotted 25,000 pesos annually for assisting immigrants in Louisiana. But General Alejandro O'Reilly, who came to the province the next year to suppress the French Creole rebellion that ousted Ulloa, frowned on expenditures for new settlers. As a result, aid to immigrants declined.[21]

In the 1770s, under Governor Luis de Unzaga, the Spanish Crown reduced funds for Louisiana and in a variety of ways neglected the colony. The drop in expenditures was but one of the problems. Spain could not provide the province with an adequate commerce, and Louisiana remained constantly in need of a subsidy from Mexico in order to stay afloat financially. Meanwhile, the British in West Florida, a possession acquired in 1763 at the end of the Seven Years' War, carried on clandestine trade with the Louisiana inhabitants. From Manchac and Baton Rouge, and on floating warehouses and ships on the Mississippi, British merchants supplied the Louisiana inhabitants with nearly all

20. Herbert Eugene Bolton and Thomas Maitland Marshall, *The Colonization of North America, 1492–1783* (New York, 1920), 275–88, 395–402.
21. Gilbert C. Din, "Early Spanish Colonization Efforts in Louisiana," *Louisiana Studies,* XI (1972), 31–49.

their needs, bought the produce that Spain did not want, and extended credit to the impecunious planters. The British posed no overt threat to Louisiana until the mid-1770s, when a new situation arose.[22]

By 1776 two important changes had occurred. Clashes between British soldiers and colonials erupted in the English colonies of North America in 1775, and war became general the next year when the thirteen colonies declared their independence. Spaniards in Europe and in the Mississippi Valley worried that the conflict might involve them as well. The second development was the appointment of José de Gálvez as Spanish minister of the Indies. Gálvez adopted vigorous measures to increase Spain's defenses in its American colonies, including Louisiana. In July, 1776, Minister Gálvez appointed his thirty-year-old nephew, Bernardo de Gálvez, as colonel of the Fixed Louisiana Battalion and soon after also named him governor of the province. That same summer José de Gálvez received the Memoria of Francisco Bouligny, a captain in the Louisiana battalion then on leave in Spain, that advocated greater military defenses, improving Louisiana's economy, a closer relationship with the Indians, and an increase in Spanish settlers to the province in order to augment the loyal population and to further its Hispanization. The minister included a number of the Memoria's recommendations in his instructions of November 25, 1776, to the new governor.[23]

Upon assuming the governorship on January 1, 1777, Bernardo de Gálvez inaugurated an active administration with the consent and support of his uncle. When the British high-handedly seized several Spanish boats on Lake Pontchartrain in May, Gálvez retaliated by capturing eleven British ships or floating warehouses engaged in illicit trade on the Mississippi. The British then dispatched a warship to New Orleans to demand the return of their property and threatened the city's destruction if the Spaniards did not comply. The governor held his ground but immediately issued a plea for assistance. The captain general of Cuba rushed troops to reinforce New Orleans' tiny garrison. Aware that Louisiana now faced greater danger from West Florida as the British poured in more troops, the Spanish Crown started a slow buildup of soldiers, artillery, and munitions in Louisiana. It ordered the creation of a second battalion for Louisiana, upgrading the Fixed Louisiana Battal-

---

22. *Ibid.*
23. Gilbert C. Din (ed. and trans.), *Louisiana in 1776: A Memoria of Francisco Bouligny* (New Orleans, 1977), and "Spain's Immigration Policy and Efforts in Louisiana During the American Revolution," *Louisiana Studies*, XIV (1975), 241–57.

ion to a fixed regiment. For the second battalion, the Crown authorized the recruitment of seven hundred soldiers in the Canary Islands, with preference being given to married men. The wives, children, and close relatives of the recruits would be transported to Louisiana for permanent settlement at royal expense. The immigrant-soldiers and their families would achieve several objectives for the Crown: the enlargement of military defenses, the promotion of commerce and industry, and an increase in Spanish population in the colony. The enlistment of the recruits soon was underway in the Canary Islands.[24]

24. Gilbert C. Din, "Protecting the *'Barrera'*: Spain's Defenses in Louisiana, 1763–1779," *Louisiana History*, XVIII (1978), 183–211.

Two

The Journey to Louisiana

By the royal order of August 15, 1777, the Spanish Crown commanded the governor and commandant general of the Canary Islands to enlist seven hundred men for service in Louisiana. The government expected to recruit and transport the volunteers within a short period of time. No doubt it envisioned the start of the Hispanization of the province, and it foresaw a continuous flow of Spanish settlers to Louisiana. That did not occur, however, and the Canary Islanders constituted the only large influx of Spanish civilians into Louisiana.[1]

Almost as soon as the royal order arrived in Tenerife, the cabildo of La Laguna raised its opposition in a meeting on November 12, 1777, and later it attempted to block the recruitment. Despite the opportunity that would be given to many lower-class islanders to escape the deplorable conditions in which they lived, the cabildo claimed that the local work force was depleted and the population declining. That assertion, however, appears to have been untrue, and the overall number of inhabitants was actually increasing. Since the cabildo could not legitimately prevent the enlistment of soldiers and the departure of their families, it next attempted to circumvent the royal decree by recruiting beggars and vile persons rather than the decent soldiers the Crown specified in its order. Royal officials also thwarted that effort.[2]

1. Royal order to the governor and commandant general of the Canary Islands, San Ildefonso, August 15, 1777, and royal order to Matías de Gálvez, San Ildefonso, August 15, 1777, Archivo General de Indias (Seville), Audiencia de Santo Domingo, legajo 2661 (hereinafter cited as AGI, SD, leg.).
2. Miguel Molina Martínez, "La participación canaria en la formación y reclutamiento del batallón de Luisiana," in *IV Coloquio de historia canario-americana (1980)* (2 vols.; Salamanca, 1982), I, 135–58, esp. 137–38.

Matías de Gálvez, the king's lieutenant in the Canary Islands, brother of José and father of Bernardo, received the charge to recruit the soldiers and families. He issued instructions for enlisting the immigrant-soldiers for Louisiana in late 1777. The volunteers needed to be between 17 and 36 years of age, at least 5 feet ½ inch tall, robust, and without noticeable imperfections or vices. Mulattoes, gypsies, executioners, and butchers—the last two by either profession or punishment—could not enlist. Although not stated explicitly, the Crown expected the Canarian families to remain in Louisiana permanently. For joining the army, the volunteer would receive 90 *reales* (11¼ pesos), half to be paid upon signing on and the other half upon reaching New Orleans. Each recruit received a daily wage of a half peso while awaiting transportation to Louisiana. Persons finding recruits were compensated according to the height of the soldiers: 15 *reales* for a recruit 5 feet ½ inch tall, 30 *reales* for a recruit 5 feet 2 inches tall, and 45 *reales* for one over 5 feet 3 inches tall. The height requirement was similar to the army's and indicates that Spain's population then—and probably that of much of Europe—was not tall.[3]

Several persons perpetrated fraud by inducing friends to enlist in order to receive the monetary compensation; those bogus recruits later deserted before the ships left Santa Cruz de Tenerife. A few poor families also enlisted to obtain the daily wage the emigrants enjoyed while waiting passage, and then vanished on the eve of the ships' sailing. On several occasions the wife and children fled when the moment for departing arrived, leaving the husband to sail alone.[4]

Several months after beginning work, Matías de Gálvez received a promotion to captain general of Central America. By April, 1778, he charged Lieutenant Colonel Andrés Amat de Tortosa, an engineer stationed on Tenerife, to complete the task. Before departing, however, Gálvez issued new orders for the recruitment that differed from the

3. Matías de Gálvez to José de Gálvez, Santa Cruz de Tenerife, October 24, 1777, AGI, SD, leg. 2661, and enclosures. Two Spanish articles discuss the recruitment of the Canary Islanders: Molina Martínez, cited in note 2, and Pablo Tornero Tinajero, "Emigración canaria a América: La expedición cívico-militar a Luisiana de 1777–1779," trans. by Paul E. Hoffman and published as "Canarian Immigration to America: The Civil-Military Expedition of 1777–1779," *Louisiana History*, XXI (1980), 377–86. Tornero Tinajero's article is incomplete and argues that the recruitment of the Canarians hurt the development of the islands.

4. Andrés Amat de Tortosa to Bernardo de Gálvez, Santa Cruz de Tenerife, June 5, 1779, Archivo General de Indias, Papeles Procedentes de la Isla de Cuba, legajo 119 (hereinafter cited as AGI, PC, leg.). See also Amat's accounting of expenses of February 29, 1780, in *ibid*.

earlier instructions in several respects. Volunteers could now be only five feet tall, and the bachelor recruits from throughout the archipelago were to be gathered in Santa Cruz de Tenerife until they departed. Roll call would be taken each night in order to detect desertions as quickly as possible. Married volunteers could remain at home with their families until the time for sailing neared. They were then to assemble in Santa Cruz.[5]

The recruits for Louisiana appear to have come from five of the seven islands. According to one investigator, Hierro, a thinly inhabited island, and Fuerteventura, where official opposition to recruitment was strong, yielded no volunteers. Tenerife, meanwhile, supplied nearly 45 percent of the recruits; Gran Canaria less than 40 percent; and Gomera, Lanzarote, and La Palma the remainder. After Gálvez left the Canaries in early 1778, a number of officials, probably closely connected to the landowners of the islands, tried to stop the recruiting, claiming that they were losing their labor supply. Even the new commandant general of the Canaries, the marqués de Tabalosos, joined the opposition and attempted to discredit Amat. The lieutenant colonel nevertheless persevered and, between April, 1778, and May 31, 1779, recruited the 700 soldiers, who with their families, totaled 2,373 Isleños.[6]

While the enlistment continued, Amat searched for vessels to transport the emigrants. The contracts he negotiated with the owners of the nine vessels hired contained numerous similarities. The Crown agreed to pay thirty pesos per passenger, except for those on the two ships *Santa Faz* and *El Sagrado Corazón de Jesús*, whose owners accepted the reduced fare of twenty-eight pesos. Nursing infants went free of charge if they numbered fewer than ten per hundred passengers. If there were no nursing babies, the shipowners agreed to allow six adult passengers per hundred to travel at no expense. The ship captains pledged to treat the passengers well and to provide them with decent food, a chaplain, a

5. Matías de Gálvez to José de Gálvez, Santa Cruz de Tenerife, March 27, 1778, AGI, SD, leg. 2661. The royal appointment of Matías de Gálvez as captain general of Central America is dated January 27, 1778. He wrote out instructions on how to carry out the recruitment to his replacement, Andrés Amat de Tortosa, and to the other officials in March, 1778.

6. Molina Martínez, "La participación canaria en la formación y reclutamiento del batallón de Luisiana," 142–46. Molina Martínez does not mention the 393 Isleños from the island of Gomera. For Gomera, see Hernández Rodríguez, "La aportación de la isla de la Gomera al poblamiento de la Luisiana, 1777–78," 245. Tornero Tinajero, in "Canarian Immigration to America," 384, erroneously states that the recruits came only from Tenerife, Gran Canaria, and Lanzarote.

surgeon, a pharmaceutical chest, and aromatic herbs. Unless emergencies occurred, the ships were to sail directly to New Orleans or Havana. If an emergency required a ship to stop, the Crown assumed responsibility for the passengers while on land, but the captains bore the cost for ship repairs and the crew's wages.[7]

Amat wrote into the contracts elaborate instructions for feeding the Isleños while on board ship. The passengers were to prepare their food in groups of ten, with a different person acting each day as mess corporal (*cabo de rancho*). The passengers would receive two hot meals daily, consisting of meat or fish in the morning and pottage (*menestra*) in the evening. For the sick there was soup, and for the crying children biscuits. The ships went well stocked with food and beverage, including biscuits, or hardtack, flour, beef, pork, salted fish, peas, garbanzos, rice, barley, potatoes, olive oil, vinegar, eggs, onions, garlic, pumpkins, cheese, olives, honey, dried fruit, sugar, wine, coffee, tea, and chocolate. In addition to staples and perishables, live animals—sheep, goats, pigs, and chickens—also went on board in order to provide the passengers with fresh meat. Finally, the ships carried a supply of wood for making fires to cook with, and a large quantity of water.[8]

Only three months after Amat began the enlistment of the Isleños, the first ship with immigrants sailed from the Canaries for Louisiana. Because of Amat's careful record keeping, more information is available on the departure of the vessels from Santa Cruz than on their arrival in Havana or in New Orleans. According to Amat's information, the packet boat *Santísimo Sacramento* departed on July 10, 1778, carrying 125 recruits, of whom 53 had families, for a total of 264 passengers. Two army officers, Francisco Bonet and Francisco Manuel de las Caxigas, who joined the Louisiana regiment, had charge of the immigrants. Nearly all nine of the ships had officers or subalterns who oversaw the Isleños. The second ship, the polacre (a three-masted vessel) *La Victoria* of Captain Andrés Orange, left on October 22, with 292 persons. Of the 88 recruits, 63 had families. Antonio Palao, soon to become a cadet in Louisiana, had command of the immigrants. The third vessel, the frigate *San Ignacio de Loyola*, sailed on October 29, with 423 persons. The

7. The contracts negotiated between Amat and the ship captains to transport the recruits and their families are in AGI, SD, leg. 2661.

8. Molina Martínez, "La participación canaria en la formación y reclutamiento del batallón de Luisiana," 150–51, lists the foodstuffs and beverages specified for *El Sagrado Corazón de Jesús*, which was probably typical for all the ships.

115 recruits it carried, under the orders of Sublieutenant Martín Palao (Antonio's father), had 95 families. The fourth ship, the packet boat *San Juan Nepomuceno* of Captain Domingo Morera, departed on December 9, with 202 passengers. Among its 53 recruits under distinguished soldier Josef Herrera, 48 had families. The fifth ship, the frigate *Santa Faz*, weighed anchor on February 17, 1779, with 406 immigrants under militia sublieutenant Pedro Venero del Castillo. It contained 102 soldiers, of whom 90 had dependents. Nearly four months elapsed before the sixth ship, the frigate *El Sagrado Corazón de Jesús*, sailed on June 5 from Santa Cruz, with 423 passengers. The vessel's captain, Manuel de Monsión, and the distinguished soldier Joaquín de Vera were in charge of the Isleños.[9]

On May 31, 1779, shortly before the *El Sagrado Corazón de Jesús* departed, Amat dispatched a status report to José de Gálvez of his work thus far. Including those on board the sixth ship, Amat had sent to Louisiana 2,010 Isleños. Of this number 600 were soldiers, 444 of whom had families. Another 100 soldiers with 75 families remained in the Canaries awaiting transportation.[10]

Their wait became prolonged when war broke out between Spain and Britain. It delayed the convoy bound from Cádiz to Havana via Santa Cruz. When the last immigrants eventually left the Canaries in 1780, they went only as far as Cuba, where they sat out the war. Many of these Canarians for various reasons never resumed the journey to Louisiana. The Canary Islanders stranded by the war in Santa Cruz and in Havana suffered hardship, and a substantial number of them spent time in local hospitals. The summer season was particularly dangerous in both ports, and hospital entries soared during those dreaded months. A number of Isleños died in Cuba, particularly infants. Meanwhile, those who waited in Santa Cruz for ships to sail to Louisiana also endured privation, inadequate housing, and disease. The families from Gomera allegedly suffered the most since they lacked their customary food, *pan de Gelecho*. Several soldiers succumbed to disease and left their families

9. *Ibid.*, 153–55. AGI, SD, leg. 2661 contains numerous documents of Amat detailing the number of recruits, their names, and the ships on which they sailed. AGI, PC, leg. 119 has letters from Amat to Bernardo de Gálvez between 1778 and 1782, which have information on the soldiers, enlistment papers, amounts of money advanced to each ship captain, the contracts, and money supplied to the recruits and their families. See in particular Amat to Bernardo de Gálvez, Santa Cruz de Tenerife, February 17 and June 5, 1779.

10. Amat, "Estado," Santa Cruz de Tenerife, May 31, 1779, AGI, SD, leg. 2661.

with neither support, home, nor relatives to turn to. Amat did what he could to mitigate their suffering, even permitting some of the women and children to join the families of relatives who were about to sail or had already departed. Other widows and orphans received assistance to return to their native islands.[11]

After the war began, Amat waited anxiously for the convoy to arrive from Cádiz in order to send the remaining emigrants. But as the months stretched out and expenses mounted, he decided to dispatch the remaining 99 recruits and their families, 368 persons in all, on three small vessels. Two brigantines belonged to Bartolomé Montáñez—the *San Carlos*, which carried 47 recruits, 159 persons in all, under Sergeant First Class Josef Martínez Rubio; and the *San Pedro*, with 35 recruits and a total of 119 passengers, under Corporal Juan Jardín. The brig belonging to Francisco Suárez de Miranda, the *Nuestra Señora de los Dolores*, carried only 17 recruits, 89 passengers in all, under Lieutenant Esteban Botiño de Echevarría. Of those three ships, only the *Nuestra Señora de los Dolores* made the voyage safely to Havana. For reasons unknown, the *San Pedro* dropped anchor at La Guaira, the port for Caracas, Venezuela; and its passengers seem never to have gone to Louisiana. Meanwhile, the English captured the *San Carlos* in the Caribbean and brought its passengers to Tortosa. Only with difficulty did they reach Havana via Puerto Rico.[12]

Almost as a footnote, three additional passengers, wives of soldiers, sailed from Santa Cruz for Louisiana in May, 1784, on board the *San José*, under the care of Lieutenant Miguel de la Vega. They had deserted on the eve of the sailing of their husbands' ships in May, 1780. They later repented their rash behavior, and went to Louisiana after the war ended. By June 27, 1784, they were in Havana. From there de la Vega, who proceeded to Mexico, sent the women to New Orleans with the documentation for the expenses that Amat had incurred in recruiting and dispatching the Isleños.[13]

Of the ships that sailed from Santa Cruz with immigrants, the

11. Documents listing hospital stays in Havana are in AGI, PC, leg. 689, and in Santa Cruz de Tenerife, in Amat to Bernardo de Gálvez, Santa Cruz de Tenerife, February 29, 1780, AGI, PC, leg. 119.

12. Amat to Bernardo de Gálvez, Santa Cruz de Tenerife, May 8, 1780, and Bernardo de Gálvez to Amat, Havana, February 23, 1782, AGI, PC, leg. 119; Francisco Varela, "Relación de los reclutas y familias prisoneras . . . ," Havana, December 29, 1780, AGI, PC, leg. 689.

13. Amat to Bernardo de Gálvez, Santa Cruz de Tenerife, May, 1784, AGI, SD, leg. 2662.

Santísimo Sacramento, which left in July, 1778, reached Havana in September, where it stopped owing to sickness on board. Six recruits had died in crossing the Atlantic, and many others were too ill to continue. After taking on supplies, the ship departed in October for Louisiana, leaving behind 14 recruits and their families. The *Santísimo Sacramento* arrived in New Orleans on November 1. The second ship to depart from Tenerife, *La Victoria*, made the voyage directly to New Orleans. Its journey appears to have been more fortuitous since none of the 88 recruits on board died. It reached its destination on January 14, 1779. Meanwhile, the *San Ignacio de Loyola*, which also traveled directly to Louisiana, entered the Mississippi River on January 9. By January 15, the recruits who had reached Louisiana numbered 314; of them, 176 married soldiers had dependents. The married men had families too large for them to support with their daily wage of 12 *reales* (one and a half pesos). Governor Gálvez therefore decided to use all of the married men as agricultural colonists; their only military obligation would be to serve in the militia units where they settled. The costs, however, of providing them with housing, rations, farm implements, clothing, and many more items would be considerable.[14]

In the first half of 1779, Isleños continued to arrive in New Orleans. Although the documents do not state specifically when they came, the *San Juan Nepomuceno* and the *Santa Faz* were in Louisiana by early July. On July 7, Governor Gálvez reported that, to date, a total of 1,582 immigrants had come. They represented the passengers of the five ships that left Santa Cruz between July, 1778, and February, 1779, discounting deaths, desertions, and the sick left behind in Havana. Of the 1,582 immigrants, 153 were bachelor recruits, 329 married recruits, and 1,100 dependents. Although Gálvez had hoped to form a second battalion with the Isleños, he could only fill the vacancies in the first battalion, and that with the aid of 133 soldiers recruited in Mexico and 106 dragoons from Cuba.[15]

Only the *Santísimo Sacramento* of the first five ships to sail stopped in Havana. The sick Isleños it left behind probably continued to New Orleans at a later date on board the steady stream of ships that were

14. Bernardo de Gálvez to Diego José Navarro, New Orleans, October 26, 1778, AGI, PC, leg., 1232; Navarro to Gálvez, No. 118, Havana, October 6, 1778, AGI, PC, leg. 1; Bernardo de Gálvez to José de Gálvez, New Orleans, January 15, 1779, AGI, SD, leg. 2547.
15. Bernardo de Gálvez to José de Gálvez, New Orleans, July 7, 1779, AGI, SD, leg. 2662.

ferrying artillery, munitions, and soldiers to Louisiana for the military buildup then underway. Spain expected to become involved in the conflict going on between England and its colonials in North America. By 1778 France had declared war on England, and the probability of Spain entering the struggle grew with each passing day. The sixth ship with Isleños, the *El Sagrado Corazón de Jesús*, reached Havana on July 25, 1779, about the same time that news came of Spain's declaration of war on England. The captain general of Cuba, Diego José Navarro, decided to detain the passengers until he heard from Governor Gálvez in New Orleans. Only recently Gálvez had written to him about the growth of British troops in West Florida. Now, with hostilities declared, Louisiana did not appear to be the place to send immigrants since Gálvez expected fighting there. Navarro recognized Britain's superior strength in Pensacola, its bastion on the Gulf of Mexico, and the danger posed by English forts on the Mississippi at Natchez, Manchac, and Baton Rouge. He had worked to improve Spanish defenses in New Orleans, but the preparations had moved forward slowly. He removed the Isleños from the ship and housed them in Oquendo, adjacent to the Santuario de Nuestra Señora de Regla. He assigned Sublieutenant Francisco Varela to look after them. Noting that seventeen of the recruits were bachelors and without obligation to continue to Louisiana, he offered them the opportunity to enlist in the Havana dragoons. Eight of them accepted. Navarro planned to send an additional four recruits to Louisiana at the first opportunity as part of the reinforcements to assist Gálvez. Five other recruits from the ship deserted in Havana within two weeks after arriving. When, in October, Governor Gálvez approved the detention of the *El Sagrado Corazón de Jesús* passengers, it started a four-year sojourn for them in Cuba, and many never completed the journey to Louisiana.[16]

Unfortunately, there is no complete accounting of the Canarians from the ships *El Sagrado Corazón de Jesús*, *Nuestra Señora de los Dolores*, and *San Carlos*, who stayed in Cuba during the war. Spanish officials did not compile a full explanation of what happened to them. The only information extant comes from accounting-house records of the money paid to

16. Bernardo de Gálvez to Diego José Navarro, New Orleans, October 16, 1778, AGI, PC, leg. 1232; Diego José Navarro to Bernardo de Gálvez, Havana, July 27 and August 10, 1779, AGI, PC, leg. 1. See "Relación," Havana, February 6, 1779, AGI, PC, leg. 1, for eight Isleños who had remained behind in Cuba and who were then sailing to New Orleans on board the *Volante*.

the families, and they provide meager details about some of the families. Record keepers paid scant attention to the births and deaths of dependents, registering only their numbers and not their names. The death or desertion of recruits attracted more attention.[17]

Despite their incomplete accounts, the records reveal in gross measure the fate of many of the Canary Islanders in Cuba. Because Isleño parents were young, they frequently brought children with them to Cuba, and more were born during their stay. Disease and death came all too often, especially to the young. A few accounts closed when all the members of the family perished or the surviving members acquired a new status. In several instances, the father of the family succumbed, the mother remarried, and the children, if they were of age, either married or joined the army. When both parents died, sympathetic families adopted the orphans. Fortunately, the tragedies that ended accounts were few.[18]

The depletion of the Isleño ranks also came from desertions. Sometimes only one member of a family fled, usually the father or mother, but more often the entire family surreptitiously abandoned its lodgings to blend in with the Cuban population. Over half of the family desertions occurred shortly before the ships sailed for Louisiana in 1783. A third group of Isleños who remained in Cuba received official permission to do so. Often the army recruit, the father, was judged physically unfit (inútil) for military service or for the arduous occupation of farmer. The authorities also granted Isleño girls who married Cubans permission to stay behind, although several Cuban husbands accompanied their wives to Louisiana as colonists.[19]

A major reduction in the number of Canary Islanders going to Louisiana occurred in early 1782, when 36 families, 145 persons in all, from the El Sagrado Corazón de Jesús departed to settle in Pensacola. After Bernardo de Gálvez conquered Pensacola in May, 1781, the English civilians had departed, leaving the town almost vacant. The Isleños took over abandoned English houses, where they lived for the next three years. The Canarians found life difficult in Pensacola. Lacking funds, the government failed to settle them on the land or to assist them in the

---

17. AGI, PC, leg. 689 contains the family accounts of the Isleños who were delayed in Cuba by the war.
18. Ibid.
19. Ibid.

same manner as in Louisiana. In 1783 Commandant Arturo O'Neill of Pensacola recommended to Intendant Martín Navarro of New Orleans to settle the families on the Escambia River, where they could raise livestock and dairy cows. In time, he reasoned, they could provide the Pensacola garrison with fresh meat and become completely self-sufficient. The government, however, ignored O'Neill's advice and left the families idle in town, consuming rations and burdening the royal treasury. The Isleños also suffered because they received assistance irregularly. In 1785, weary of their plight, the families petitioned the commandant for authorization to settle in Cuba. Before the end of the year, they returned to the island. It does not appear that this group of Canary Island immigrants ever went to Louisiana.[20]

The ranks of the Isleños in Cuba decreased by perhaps 250 persons or more; if the passengers on the San Pedro, which went to Venezuela, are counted, the figure rises to over 370. Those who waited patiently for the war to end found transportation to New Orleans in the summer of 1783, when the government hired two ships. The first group of 40 families sailed from Havana on July 28, on board the frigate Margarita. They reached the mouth of the Mississippi at Balize on August 17. Two days later, the packet boat Santísima Trinidad under Captain Borja, with 25 additional Isleño families, arrived. The two ships brought a total of 263 persons, who represented the bulk of the immigrants who had sat out the war in Cuba. However, they were not the last to leave Havana; a final group of immigrants went to Louisiana in December. It consisted of six families, mostly deserters and the sick who had been left behind, on board the sloop Delfín. Henceforth any additional Isleños who went to

20. AGI, PC, leg. 689 has a list of the families that went to Pensacola based on the families on board El Sagrado Corazón de Jesús. For their stay in Pensacola, see Arturo O'Neill to Martín Navarro, Pensacola, March 28, 1783, and Bernardo de Gálvez to O'Neill, Guarico, October 26, 1782, both in AGI, PC, leg. 595A; Luis de Unzaga to O'Neill, Havana, October 24 and 25, and November 15, 1785, AGI, PC, leg. 85; Juan Ventura Morales to Martín Navarro, New Orleans, October 11, 1782, AGI, PC, leg. 608A. Probably a few Isleños remained behind in Pensacola in 1785. In 1820, thirteen Canary Islanders in a population of 441 lived in Pensacola. See Jack D. L. Holmes, "Pensacola: Spanish Dominion, 1781–1821," in James R. McGovern (ed.), Colonial Pensacola (Pensacola, 1972), 97. Possibly, a number of the Isleños who returned to Cuba soon resettled in east Florida. See Vicente Manuel de Céspedes to the Marqués de Sonora (José de Gálvez), St. Augustine, May 12, 1787, in Arthur Preston Whitaker (ed.), Documents Relating to the Commercial Policy of Spain in the Floridas (Deland, Fla., 1931), 55.

Louisiana from Cuba did so as individuals, and government records did not single them out.[21]

How many Canary Islanders actually reached Louisiana cannot be determined precisely. As nearly as can be calculated, almost 2,000 Isleños arrived at their final destination. Not quite 1,600 were on board the first five ships that reached New Orleans by July, 1779. After the war with Britain ended, perhaps as many as 300 more immigrants crossed the gulf from Cuba. These two groups of settlers made up the nucleus of the original Canary Islanders of Louisiana, and from them the present-day descendants can trace their ancestry.[22]

Of concern to the Fixed Louisiana Regiment was the cost of transporting the Isleños to Louisiana and their maintenance while they were in Santa Cruz de Tenerife and in Cuba. Inasmuch as Amat de Tortosa originally recruited the men for army service, the Louisiana regiment bore the responsibility for paying their expenses until they arrived in New Orleans or were released from their obligation. For several years after the war ended, accounting officials in New Orleans labored to liquidate the debts resulting from the enlistment of the Canarians.

In Santa Cruz, Amat stated that his costs to the end of February, 1780, had amounted to 856,722 *reales*. That figure, however, did not include the total expense of the ships nor the maintenance of the recruits and their families until the last ship with them sailed in May, 1780. Although Amat sent the expenses as each ship sailed, the later vessels did not reach New Orleans, and the Louisiana officials did not receive the documentation. After the war, letters flowed back and forth across the Atlantic to determine what the Louisiana regiment owed. In 1783 the cost of the first five ships to sail was set at 204,297 *reales*, which was in addition to Amat's expenses. In the same year Sublieutenant Francisco Varela, charged with caring for the Isleños in Cuba, stated that the 65 families had cost 56,968 pesos to maintain. That sum did not include the expenses for the other families in Cuba. When the New Orleans officials inquired about those accounts, they learned that Varela had left for the

21. Joseph Petely to Martín Navarro, Balize, August 17 and 19, 1783, AGI, PC, leg. 608B; Martín Navarro to José de Gálvez, New Orleans, September 25, 1783, AGI, SD, leg. 2609. Sidney Villeré (comp.), *The Canary Islands Migration to Louisiana, 1778–1783* (Baltimore, 1972), 88–94, has incomplete and erroneous names of the passengers on the *Margarita* and the *Santísima Trinidad*.

22. The names of the Isleños who sailed on the first five ships can be found in AGI, SD, legs. 2661 and 2662, but the documents do not note the names of the recruits who died on the voyage.

Canary Islands to recruit soldiers and immigrants for Cuba. In 1784 Amat sent what he considered to be a complete tally of his expenditures for the Isleños, including the amounts advanced to each ship captain who sailed from Santa Cruz. For unexplained reasons, the New Orleans accounting house found his figures unsatisfactory.[23]

During the next two years, a lull occurred in straightening out the accounts. In 1786 Juan Ventura Morales, in charge of immigration expenses, raised the question again. The issue also arose as to who should be charged with the expenses, the Louisiana regiment or the Division of Immigration, since the soldiers with families had not remained in military service. Moreover, the matter of the *San Pedro*, which had gone to Venezuela, continued unresolved. Should the Louisiana regiment bear the expenses for the recruitment and voyage or not? Nor had it yet been resolved what to do about the costs for the families that had not gone to Louisiana from Cuba. In 1786 Louisiana officials again requested information from Amat in the Canaries and complained to Spain about his failure to carry out his duties. The complaint to the court resulted in the royal order of February 14, 1787, that Amat settle the accounts.[24]

Whether Amat received the royal order is not known, but he replied to the New Orleans inquiry in April, 1787, stating that he was endeavoring to supply the needed information. Almost simultaneously, however, Amat received a new assignment in Mexico as the political and military commandant (intendant) of the city and province of Guanajuato, and he soon sailed for Mexico. While at his new post, Amat appears not to have done further work on the accounts up to 1790, when tragedy struck. At that time, Amat lost his sanity, and authorities incarcerated him for his own safety. Despite the precaution, he died about 1791 from self-inflicted wounds.[25]

The efforts to determine the full cost of recruiting and transporting

23. [?] to Amat, New Orleans, March 1, 1783, AGI, PC, leg. 119; Martín Navarro to José de Gálvez, New Orleans, September 25, 1783, AGI, SD, leg. 2609; Miguel de la Vega to [Martín Navarro?], Havana, June 27 and July 8, 1784, AGI, PC, leg. 11.

24. Morales to Martín Navarro, March 11, 1786, and Morales *minuta*, May 12, 1786, both in AGI, PC, leg. 606; Martín Navarro to José de Gálvez, New Orleans, June 16, 1786, AGI, SD, leg. 2610; Estaban Miró to the Marqués de Sonora, No. 55, New Orleans, October 30, 1786, and royal order to the governor of Louisiana, El Pardo, February 14, 1787, both in AGI, SD, leg. 2657.

25. Amat to Miró, Santa Cruz de Tenerife, April 28, 1787, with Miró to Amat, New Orleans, October 30, 1786, enclosed, AGI, PC, leg. 119; David A. Brading, *Miners and Merchants in Bourbon Mexico, 1763–1810* (London, 1971), 241.

the Canary Islanders seem to have failed. No total figure has been located in the Spanish archives. The expenses were considerable, and an estimate of a quarter of a million pesos appears plausible. But as enormous as that amount seems, the cost to assist the immigrants in their settlement in Louisiana rose to several times the original expenditure to take them there. Those expenses began with the arrival of the first Isleños in New Orleans in late 1778.[26]

26. As an example of the extraordinary expenditures caused by the Isleños, 185,000 pesos was added in 1782 to the 40,000 pesos budgeted annually for settling immigrants (Martín Navarro to José de Gálvez, January 13, 1783, AGI, SD, leg. 2609).

Three

The Tragedy of Galveztown

In November, 1778, the first Canary Islanders, the passengers of the *Santísimo Sacramento*, stepped foot on Louisiana soil. They and the others who followed represented the first significant number of Spaniards, other than soldiers and officials, to come to the province since it became Spanish in 1763. Governor Bernardo de Gálvez used the Isleños to found four settlements, two on bayous above New Orleans and two below the city on opposite banks of the Mississippi. He placed them on vacant lands and at locations that would afford the city with some protection. Although Gálvez expected the settlements to thrive and quickly become independent of government support, this did not happen. Thrust upon Louisiana's bayous and lowlands and at the mercy of the elements, the settlements required considerable assistance. Moreover, two of the sites were not suitable, thus assuring their failure.

The arrival of the first Canary Islanders dismayed Governor Gálvez. He had expected more soldiers than dependents, and he realized immediately the impossibility of keeping the married recruits in the regiment because of their large families. He decided to employ all the immigrant-recruits as settlers only, and on November 12 or 13, he traveled upriver to investigate possible sites for their establishment. On his reconnaissance tour, he first stopped at Bayou Lafourche, where he found excellent vacant lands. A tiny community already existed at the head of the bayou, founded about 1770 by Acadians. From there he journeyed to Bayou Manchac (Iberville River) on the Mississippi's east bank. It and the Amite River separated British West Florida on the north, or left, bank from Spanish Louisiana on the south, or right, bank. The so-called Isle of Orleans lay on the right bank as well. Gálvez followed Bayou Manchac eastward for roughly fifteen miles to its juncture with the Amite River, where the streams flowed together in an easterly direction to Lake Maurepas. By November 22, he reached the junction, where an embryonic settlement had recently been formed, composed of Anglo-American refugees from the warfare in the English Atlantic colonies. Gálvez praised the high banks on the right side and looked upon the region as eminently suitable for the Spanish settlers. Probably to win the governor's goodwill, the Anglo-Americans named their settlement Villa de Gálvez, or Galveztown, a name that the governor adopted. He favored the two sites of Bayou Lafourche and Galveztown because they would act as sentinels and help to safeguard Spanish lands against the English in adjacent West Florida. By December 10, Gálvez had returned to New Orleans, and a month later he briefly reported the results of the journey to José de Gálvez.[1]

Almost nothing is known about the Isleños while they waited in New Orleans for lands. No doubt Governor Gálvez wished to transfer them to the countryside as quickly as possible, but they had to wait until he selected sites and collected supplies. Evidence suggests that many Canary Islanders, perhaps more than 20 percent, did not move to the agricultural settlements and that a few other Spaniards joined those who did. Four Canarian communities began almost simultaneously: Galveztown and Valenzuela (Lafourche Interior) upriver, and St. Bernard and Barataria below New Orleans. Of the documentation in the Spanish archives, more exists on Galveztown than on the other settlements. Despite the government's efforts to make Galveztown thrive in the face of numerous hardships, it barely survived the Spanish era. The poor location compelled the colonists to try to abandon it on several occasions. But only when Spain no longer ruled Louisiana did the

---

1. [Bernardo de Gálvez] to José de Gálvez, New Orleans, January 15, 1779, AGI, PC, leg. 2351; Bernardo de Gálvez to José de Gálvez, New Orleans, January 15, 1779, in Lawrence Kinnaird (ed.), *Spain in the Mississippi Valley, 1765–1794* (3 parts; Washington, D.C., 1949), Pt. I, 326–27; [Bernardo de Gálvez] to Francisco Bouligny, New Orleans, November 12, 1778, and Galveztown, November 22, 1778, both in AGI, PC, leg. 2358. On November 1, 1778, 177 recruits arrived from the Canary Islands; there were 6 widows whose husbands, who were recruits, had died. For a contemporary description of the Galveztown location, see Thomas Hutchins, *An Historical Narrative and Topographical Description of Louisiana and West Florida* (facsimile of 1784 ed.; Gainesville, Fla., 1968), 60–61. Until now the only study of Galveztown has been the biased article by V. M. Scramuzza, "Galveztown, a Spanish Settlement of Colonial Louisiana," *Louisiana Historical Quarterly*, XIII (1930), 553–609. It represents the bulk of his 1924 M.A. thesis at Louisiana State University, Baton Rouge.

Map drawn by Sylvia Loftin

South Louisiana and the Canarian settlements

Lake Borgne

Lake Pontchartrain

New Orleans

St. Bernard Parish

Lake Maurepas

Amite River

Bayou Manchac

Galveztown

Baton Rouge

Donaldsonville

Valenzuela

Bayou Lafourche

Mississippi River

Isleños leave the settlement that had brought them poverty, misery, and death.

When Governor Gálvez returned from his inspection trip in December, 1778, he left Sublieutenant Francisco Collell at Galveztown as commandant and in charge of settling the Isleños. Collell prepared for their arrival by laying out house lots in Villa de Gálvez, selecting and clearing lands for crops, and starting the construction of houses. The houses were to measure 32 by 16 feet (512 square feet), be wooden, and have a gallery on one side. On December 31, Gálvez informed Collell that the first group of settlers would soon be sent. Collell in turn asked the governor for farm implements, food, and other essentials for aiding the colonists. He hired slaves belonging to Gilberto Antonio de St. Maxent, Gálvez' father-in-law, to assist the immigrants. Gálvez wanted the settlers to begin agricultural work immediately in order to be able to feed themselves by year's end.[2]

On January 19, the first 14 Isleño families, 54 persons in all, reached Galveztown. They came from New Orleans via Lakes Pontchartrain and Maurepas and up the Amite. This water route remained the preferred way for communicating with New Orleans. Collell sheltered the colonists temporarily in a warehouse and in several rented houses until he finished their dwellings. The second group of Canarians came on February 14 and also consisted of 54 persons. While continuing work, Collell observed the English, who were building their own settlements and increasing their troops on the Mississippi. He asked Governor Gálvez to erect a fort at Galveztown for the settlement's protection. At the end of March, 12 more Isleño families of 53 people came, and in April, Gálvez sent 50 additional colonists. By then the Spanish settlers numbered 211. They continued to go to Galveztown until more than 400 had arrived.[3] In addition to the Isleños, the Galveztown district received small numbers of other people who went to live there voluntarily.

On April 1, Collell reported to Gálvez on the recent rains and the rise

2. Francisco Collell to Bernardo de Gálvez, Galveztown, December, 1778, AGI, PC, leg. 2351; Collell to Gálvez, Villa de Gálvez, January 15, 1779, in Kinnaird (ed.), *Spain in the Mississippi Valley*, Pt I, 322–25. See also [Gálvez] to Collell, New Orleans, January 5, 1779, AGI, PC, leg. 2351, and [New Orleans], January 5, 1779, AGI, PC, leg. 1.

3. Collell to Gálvez, Galveztown, January 22, April 1, 1779, AGI, PC, leg. 2351; Collell to Gálvez, Galveztown, February 16, 1779, and Gálvez to Collell, New Orleans, January 29, 1779, both in AGI, PC, leg. 1; [Gálvez] to Collell, New Orleans, April 8, 1779, AGI, PC, leg. 112; "Yndice de las familias Ysleñas qe. han de establecer la Nueva Población de Galveztown," Libro Maestro, AGI, PC, leg. 568. See also Antonio Acosta Rodríguez, *La población de la Luisiana española (1763–1803)* (Madrid, 1979), 140–41.

of the Amite River. The waters rose perilously close to the banks and were an omen of what was to come. Although the governor thought the lands high, he had visited the region in a dry season. He did not notice that swamps, bayous, and rivers ringed the settlement. Collell also appealed again for food, as he did in almost every letter to the governor. He particularly lacked rice and peas, which the Isleños loved. By late March or early April, Galveztown acquired its first priest, Father Francisco López, who had recently arrived from Spain. He took his meals with the commandant but slept in a corner of the barracks' gallery. In the opposite corner, he installed a makeshift chapel.[4]

That same spring, the first of the marriages between Spanish soldiers and the daughters of Isleño families took place. Corporal Fabián Ramos of Castilla la Vieja in Spain asked permission to marry the seventeen-year-old daughter of Juan Viera, María del Buen Suceso, of Aguimes in the Canary Islands. Collell approved the match, but he needed the governor's consent, which Gálvez soon sent. The date of the marriage is missing. In early 1782, Fabián and María became the parents of Antonio Josef, who might not have been their first child. Over the years, they had seven known children, four sons about whom nothing else is recorded and three daughters who all married, two at the age of fourteen and the other at twenty. Gálvez and the subsequent governors of Spanish Louisiana favored unions such as those of Corporal Ramos and, later, one of his daughters, who also wedded a soldier, because they served to increase the colony's Spanish population. Most if not all of the soldiers who married local women settled down to become permanent colonists and probably merged with the Isleño population.[5]

As the Galveztown settlement began in the spring of 1779, Collell exhorted his people to greater efforts in order to produce a harvest in the fall. He had them plant corn, rice, beans, potatoes, peas, flax, and even wheat. He continued the construction of the houses although the lack of materials periodically held him up. By May he had completed several structures. That month, two families of ten more Isleños arrived, bringing with them additional supplies, medicines, and foodstuffs. Collell remained constantly in need of nearly everything—money, food,

4. Collell to Gálvez, Galveztown, April 1, 1779, AGI, PC, leg. 2351.
5. Collell to Gálvez, Galveztown, April 23, 1779, AGI, PC, leg. 1; Catholic Diocese of Baton Rouge, *Catholic Church Records, 1770–1803* (Baton Rouge, 1980), 615. By 1793 the Ramos family had four living children: Theresa, María, Modesto, and Juana (Marcos DeVilliers, "Población de la Villa de Galvez-Town y su Districto, Año de 1793," Galveztown, August 16, 1793, AGI, PC, leg. 27A).

utensils, seeds. He could, however, report on May 20 that the village plaza had been cleared of vegetation except for tree roots. Twenty houses now stood, although they still lacked shingles for roofing.[6]

Collell also kept Gálvez posted on British activities in West Florida. As summer approached, the likelihood of war with Britain increased. In preparation, the English sent troops, arms, and supplies to their Mississippi outposts. Governor Gálvez, on the other side, strove to improve Louisiana's defenses, too, and he authorized the formation of two militia companies at Galveztown—one of Isleños, in which Antonio Díaz served as lieutenant; and a second of Anglo-Americans. The governor provided them with two cannons and sixty fusils.[7]

Before the war arrived, however, the Galveztown Isleños began to suffer from the worst blow that any of the Canarian settlements experienced. Diseases hit the community, claiming numerous lives. Five persons first came down with fever in the spring. By April six children and one woman had died of scabies (*sarna*). Apprised of the sicknesses, Gálvez dispatched surgeon Antonio Demar to attend to the ill. After examining his patients, Demar requested medicines consisting of wine, honey, oil, vinegar, aguardiente, and chickens; and mattresses for a hospital. Despite his efforts three more children died of *sarna* and diarrhea, while three others fell sick with fever. In May conditions worsened. In two weeks death claimed seven children, and ten more people were sick, two of them seriously. In the last month, however, five infants had been born.[8]

As summer arrived, the mortality rate at Galveztown soared. During July and August, twenty-four additional persons died. Collell blamed the sicknesses on the lack of fresh food, and he purchased supplies from neighboring settlements on the Mississippi. He attributed two new diseases, dropsy and scurvy, to the salted meat in the settlers' diet. Illness became so general that Collell lamented that the settlers' houses resembled miniature hospitals and that their gardens had fallen into neglect. He wrote to the governor pathetically, "I am sad that I cannot do anything about it." In the last month, six men and seven children had died, and four more were in danger. To add to their misery, many

6. Collell to Gálvez, Galveztown, May 1 and May 20, 1779, AGI, PC, leg. 2351.
7. Collell to Gálvez, Galveztown, March 1, May 10, June 27, July 5, August 14, 1779, *ibid.*; [Gálvez] to Collell, New Orleans, May 27, 1779, AGI, PC, leg. 112; Collell to Gálvez, Galveztown, June 15, 1779, in Kinnaird (ed.), *Spain in the Mississippi Valley*, Pt. I, 340–42.
8. Collell to Gálvez, Galveztown, July 26, 1779, AGI, PC, leg. 2351.

colonists still did not have houses; nor had the fort been built—a necessity, since the British continued their military preparations. Gálvez waited until July 10 before granting permission for the construction of the Galveztown fort.[9]

In the midst of sickness and death, war came to Galveztown in late August. By August 23, Collell knew that a state of hostilities existed between Spain and Britain. Governor Gálvez ordered Collell to keep the news secret but at a given moment to cut down trees to block the passage of British boats on the Amite and seize them. Before the Spaniards could act, however, a hurricane struck Louisiana on August 18, sinking Gálvez' boats on the Mississippi. Not until August 24 did the governor give Collell permission to proceed against the English. About six days later the Galveztown commandant and his soldiers and militiamen, including Isleños, carried out the first military action in Louisiana. In all, they seized 7 British vessels of different sizes and took 125 soldiers and sailors prisoner. Collell's men also captured the British post on the Amite, not far above Galveztown, on August 30. The governor, meanwhile, moved up the Mississippi with his men and wrested the forts at British Manchac, Baton Rouge, and Natchez from the enemy. After those victories, Gálvez feared the possibility of a British counterattack from Mobile or Pensacola up the Amite River, and Galveztown became the focal point to thwart such a move. He sent thirty soldiers to reinforce the settlement. Collell reported on September 26 that he had finished the fort and had guards posted on all the neighboring bayous and rivers.[10]

Following his success on the river, Gálvez started preparations for an assault on Mobile. His capture of it in March, 1780, removed the possibility of an English attack on the Mississippi via Galveztown. The governor's vigorous actions threw Pensacola, Britain's bastion on the Gulf Coast, on the defensive, and Galveztown was safe. Once the war

9.   [Gálvez] to Collell, New Orleans, July 10, 1779, AGI, PC, leg. 112; the quotation is in Collell to Gálvez, Galveztown, July 21, 1779, *ibid.*

10.   [Gálvez] to Collell, New Orleans, August 16, 17, and 18, 1779, AGI, PC, leg. 112; Collell to Gálvez, Galveztown, August 23 and 26, 1779, AGI, PC, leg. 132; Scramuzza, "Galveztown, a Spanish Settlement of Colonial Louisiana," 583; Collell to Gálvez, Galveztown, August 30, September 3, 7, and 10, 1779, AGI, PC, leg. 2351; Jack D. L. Holmes (ed.), *Honor and Fidelity* (Birmingham, Ala., 1965), 102; John Walton Caughey, *Bernardo de Gálvez in Spanish Louisiana, 1776–1783* (Berkeley, Calif., 1934; rpr. Gretna, La., 1972), 161. See also "The Capture of Baton Rouge by Galvez, September 21st, 1779," *Louisiana Historical Quarterly*, XII (1929), 255–65; Collell, "Rela[ci]on de los Oficiales, Sargentos, Tambores, Cavos y Soldados . . . ," Galveztown, May 6, 1780, AGI, PC, leg. 132.

had passed it by, the settlement's chief problems became disease, food, and Indians.[11]

The diseases that had ravaged Galveztown in the spring of 1779 continued through the summer and into the early months of 1780. Smallpox claimed the lives of most of the Isleños who died during those months, and it probably contributed to the eventual failure of the settlement. The "Libro Maestro Para Sentar el Cargo a las Familias de La Nueva Población de la Villa de Galveztown" preserves the names of the families settled in Galveztown and records the deaths of the Isleños. Like many other records, it is neither complete nor entirely accurate; but it does provide a good idea of the enormity of the smallpox tragedy. According to the "Libro Maestro," 146 persons died up to January 17, 1780, a large number of them from smallpox. Few families escaped unscathed. Children died in large numbers, particularly newborn infants. Sometimes entire families succumbed. Twice the only family survivor was a male who soon fled from the settlement. The more fortunate families gathered up orphans. Most families lost one to three members. However, Josef Antonio Gonzáles lost his wife and four children, and all seven children of Antonio Pimentel and his wife perished. When winter came, the death rate diminished, but deaths did not cease until early 1780. The loss of life at Galveztown surpassed one-third of the total Isleño population established there.[12]

By spring, 1780, the illnesses had run their course, and the settlers could go on with the task of making Galveztown flourish. The settlers made progress that year, or so Intendant Martín Navarro, in charge of overseeing the new settlements, thought. The crops the colonists planted pleased him, and he hoped for a harvest in order to make them self-sufficient. Navarro also had the unenviable task of paying the colony's expenses and providing Gálvez with money for his military operations; these expenditures made Navarro chronically short of funds. On August 24, 1780, as the harvest neared, another hurricane slammed into lower Louisiana, inflicting tremendous damage on property, level-

11. Caughey, *Bernardo de Gálvez in Spanish Louisiana*, 153–54; Collell to Pedro Piernas, Galveztown, April 19, 1780, AGI, PC, leg. 2.
12. "Libro Maestro Para Sentar el Cargo a las Familias de la Nueva Población de la Villa de Galveztown," 1779, AGI, PC, leg. 568. Acosta, in *La población de la Luisiana española*, 141, gives the number of dead as 161 in a population of 404, or 40 percent. In Antonio Acosta Rodríguez' article, "Overview of the Consumption of Food and Goods by Isleño Immigrants to Louisiana," trans. Paul E. Hoffman, *Louisiana History*, XXI (1981), 299–306, he argues that the government supplied the immigrants inadequately with food, which contributed to their high death rate in Galveztown.

ing the cornstalks, and flooding the fields. Galveztown produced little food in 1780, and government assistance to the infant settlement continued.[13]

In 1781 Galveztown entered its third year of existence, with the settlers still on rations. Collell's explanation was the laziness of some Isleños. He asked the government for rations until they harvested their crops in September, adding that the recipients would pay for the food. Soon after, the colonists penned a memorial to Governor Gálvez, who had returned to Louisiana for the last time shortly after the conquest of Pensacola. They asked for clothing and complained about the settlement's poor location. But Gálvez ignored their hardships, and he refused to consider their petition. By then sixty-seven houses had been built, and five more were under construction. Five arpents of land around the village had also been cleared. That year, after an abundance of water in the two previous years, drought dried up the fields, and the food shortage continued. Collell bought food for the Isleños, explaining to Gálvez that without it they would either die of hunger or abandon the settlement. By May seven persons had already fled. Collell used the opportunity to complain about Galveztown's remoteness, which made everything more expensive. The settlers, he stated, lived in poverty and lacked clothing.[14]

In mid-1781, Captain Antonio de St. Maxent, commandant of Valenzuela and Gálvez' brother-in-law, replaced Collell at Galveztown. The governor personally ordered him to the settlement to recreate the prosperity that St. Maxent had brought to Valenzuela. As Collell departed, he emphasized to the governor the need to assist widows, orphans, and the hospital. Rations had ceased, but the settlers still required food since drought had ruined their crops. Collell now praised the Isleños for working hard that year.[15]

The new commandant, St. Maxent, had done a commendable job at Valenzuela. Much of it, however, was due to a better location, and Galveztown severely tested his ability as major problems persisted.

13. Collell to Gálvez, Galveztown, June [14?], 1780, AGI, PC, leg. 2. Thirty-four houses had been finished, and ten were framed but not completed because of a lack of nails (Collell to Piernas, Galveztown, September 30, 1780, AGI, PC, leg. 113).
14. Collell to Morales, Galveztown, May 1, 1781, AGI, PC, leg. 608B; Collell to Gálvez, Galveztown, June 20, 1781, AGI, PC, leg. 2.
15. Collell to Morales, Galveztown, July 2, 1781, AGI, PC, leg. 608B; [Gálvez,] "Ynstrucción que observará Dn. Antonio Maxent, Capn. del Reximiento de Ynfantería de la Luisiana destinado al mando de la nueva Población de Galveztown," New Orleans, June 27, 1781, AGI, PC, legs. 112 and 606.

Because the settlers lived practically in rags and the government lacked clothing to give them, St. Maxent asked New Orleans in November to provide the Isleños with 250 blankets. The government agreed and also resumed sending rations. Moreover, St. Maxent insisted that the French surgeon, in whom the Isleños had no faith, be replaced. When the German physician Franz Rausman arrived in Galveztown in 1781, twenty-two Canarians immediately sought him out.[16]

In 1782 the settlement fared no better. Heavy rains swelled the Mississippi and flooded all of lower Louisiana. Galveztown and the other settlements, including Valenzuela and Barataria, lost their crops. Indians also suffered agricultural losses that year, and they entered the Galveztown district, searching for food, killing animals, and spreading fear among the settlers. Esteban Miró, who replaced Gálvez as governor in late February, 1782, ordered St. Maxent to placate the natives in their demands for food. Miró acted cautiously; the war dragged on, and he did not want to alienate the natives. Giving food to the Indians meant, however, that expenses increased. Intendant Navarro reported in December that he had spent 185,000 pesos in 1782 on settlements and Indians alone. Since the settlers did not have food, he had to continue rations, or else they would desert Galveztown. He recognized that they lived in poverty and that the Indians aggravated their suffering by stealing everything they could, even breaking into residences and storehouses for corn and potatoes. They ignored St. Maxent's orders to stop.[17]

Rations for Galveztown continued, amounting to fourteen thousand pesos in 1783. The settlers also needed clothes, tools, animals, and medicines. Again that year, the government hoped that the colonists could grow food successfully. Miró gave them permission, if they did, to sell their surplus produce on the Mississippi and in New Orleans, which might net them some money. However, they could not abandon Galveztown.[18]

---

16. Antonio de St. Maxent to Morales, Galveztown, November 8, 1781, AGI, PC, leg. 608B; St. Maxent to Martín Navarro, Galveztown, July 3, 1781, AGI, PC, leg. 603B.
17. Navarro to Bernardo de Gálvez, New Orleans, June 16, 1782, AGI, PC, leg. 83; St. Maxent to Morales, Galveztown, July 16, 1782, AGI, PC, leg. 608B; Navarro to José de Gálvez, New Orleans, December 4, 1782, AGI, SD, leg. 2609; St. Maxent to Piernas, Galveztown, June 16, 1782, St. Maxent to Bouligny, Galveztown, September 24, 1782, and St. Maxent to Miró, Galveztown, December 5, 1782, in Kinnaird (ed.), *Spain in the Mississippi Valley*, Pt. II, 20–21, 59, and 67–68, respectively; Caroline Maude Burson, *The Stewardship of Don Esteban Miró, 1782–1792* (New Orleans, 1940), 49.
18. St. Maxent to Morales, Galveztown, July 21, 1783, AGI, PC, leg. 608B.

Since the death of Father López on September 10, 1779, the Spaniards at Galveztown had been without a resident priest. For the next several years, the padres at St. Gabriel de Iberville on the Mississippi, about fifteen miles away, served them, but the lack of nearby spiritual comfort displeased the devout Canarians. The two priests at St. Gabriel during those years were Fathers Valentín and Angel de Revillagodos.[19]

With the war over in the spring of 1783, the settlement could begin to progress. The population of the Villa de Gálvez was 242 in 1785 and increased modestly to 268 in 1788. Most of those counted were probably Isleños, although Anglo-Americans, Frenchmen, or Acadians, Irishmen, and a few persons of other nationalities also resided in the district.[20]

In December, 1784, and January, 1785, a new smallpox epidemic hit Galveztown. Commandant Francisco Maximiliano de St. Maxent, who replaced his brother Antonio, reported that eighteen persons had died in two months. Because they lacked medicines, the local residents assessed themselves two *reales* each to purchase them, thus raising fifty-one pesos and two *reales*. When Governor Miró heard about the dreaded disease, he hurriedly dispatched a New Orleans surgeon, Robert Dow, to the settlement to prevent the smallpox from spreading. The prompt action of Governor Miró, the able work of Dr. Dow, and good fortune all combined to avert a repetition of the 1779 tragedy.[21]

In 1786 Governor Miró permanently ended rations for the Galveztown residents, reiterating that they could sell their produce on the Mississippi or in New Orleans. Commandant Maximiliano de St. Maxent had permission to allow a few of them to leave to do so, but they could not move out of the district.[22]

In January, 1787, Lieutenant Joseph Petely replaced Maximiliano de St. Maxent as commandant, and he soon provided a new description of the settlement. More than half of the houses had fallen into ruins. Their owners had presumably either died or abandoned the tiny town. Petely recommended sending Acadian families to the district. Because he seemed more responsive to the needs of the Isleños, they beseiged him

19. [Miró?] to St. Maxent, New Orleans, April 10, 1783, AGI, PC, leg. 196; Roger Baudier, *The Catholic Church in Louisiana* (New Orleans, 1939), 196.
20. Charles Gayarré, *History of Louisiana* (4 vols.; 3rd ed.; New Orleans, 1885), III, 240, 251.
21. Maximiliano de St. Maxent to Navarro, Galveztown, January 16, 1785, and Navarro to Maximiliano de St. Maxent, New Orleans, January 21, 1785, both in AGI, PC, leg. 603A.
22. [Miró] to Maximiliano de St. Maxent, New Orleans, September 3, 1786, AGI, PC, leg. 117A.

with their requests. In particular, the lack of spiritual comfort distressed them; they had neither priest, church, nor vessels for the celebration of mass.[23]

At that time a number of inhabitants petitioned the governor for permission to leave Galveztown. Juan de la Roca, whose bad arm impeded his work and forced him and his wife to live from charity, asked to relocate to Havana, where he had relatives. Domingo García had an incurable disease that prevented him from performing agricultural labor; he, too, sought to go to Havana with his wife and two small daughters. It appears that the government granted the two requests.[24]

When Marcos DeVilliers replaced Petely as commandant on May 8, 1787, the Isleños quickly came calling with their petitions. They wanted church ornaments for mass, which they would pay for themselves but only with the produce of their land since they had no money. They asked the government to build them a chapel, and in July, they petitioned for the return of their priest. In April, 1787, Fray Manuel García arrived to serve the village. But he and Commandant DeVilliers quarreled, and García left in a huff. When he returned, Governor Miró exhorted García and DeVilliers to live in harmony and to avoid quarreling. García stayed in Galveztown until November, 1789. The next year Father Bernard von Limpach served the settlement from St. Gabriel.[25]

Petitions to leave Galveztown continued in late 1787 and in 1788. Juan Sánchez Melián wished to leave for "Torno del Yngles" (St. Bernard), where his family lived. Catarina Monsón wanted to join her family at the same location. Sebastián de Niz asked to remove to another district— anywhere was better than Galveztown. Juan Antonio Martínez and his wife, María Antonia Fernández, received permission to leave for an undisclosed destination. St. Bernard was the preferred choice for those departing Galveztown. In December, 1788, DeVilliers painted a distressing picture of the settlement. Many of the houses were empty, and others collapsed into heaps of debris. Those still standing, with neither

23.   Petely to Miró, Galveztown, January 30, 1787, AGI, PC, leg. 13.

24.   Petely to Miró, Galveztown, April 10, 1787, "Statement of Francisco Rausman," April 20, 1787, and "Petition of Domingo García," New Orleans, December 5, 1786, all in AGI, PC, leg. 13.

25.   Marcos DeVilliers to Miró, Galveztown, July 28, 1787, AGI, PC, leg. 13; Felipe Ximénes et al., petition, Galveztown, July 28, 1787, and [Miró] to DeVilliers, New Orleans, August 4, 1787, both in AGI, PC, leg. 132; Baudier, The Catholic Church in Louisiana, 237.

doors nor windows, provided shelter for animals. With such deplorable conditions, still more Isleños received permission to depart in 1789.[26]

Although the Galveztown residents had petitioned the governor for a church in 1787, not until 1789 was a contract issued to build it. Its construction proceeded slowly and only in February, 1791, did Governor Miró send the Capuchin friar Félix de Quintanar to the settlement. On June 4, 1791, Quintanar took charge of the edifice. He remained at Galveztown until 1799. Only one other priest, Fray Domingo Joachín Solano, resided there briefly between November, 1802 and May, 1803. Otherwise, St. Gabriel again served Galveztown.[27]

In 1793 a census revealed that 32 Spanish families, 126 persons in all, lived in Galveztown out of a total 35 Spanish families, 135 persons. The census showed that the Spanish population was declining. Virtually all of the Isleños resided in the decaying town since government policy required them to reinforce the fort's garrison in case of an emergency. Non-Spanish families in the district numbered 52 and consisted of 136 persons. In the early 1790s, new people settled in the district as the Indian menace and earlier diseases no longer constituted problems.[28]

Although Louisiana gained in population and perhaps increased its prosperity, hardships still dogged Galveztown. On August 18, 1793, another hurricane battered lower Louisiana, including Galveztown. Two empty, dilapidated houses collapsed in the storm. The hurricane also demolished the corn fields, damaged the other crops, and killed a number of animals when trees collapsed on them. The storm, another setback in the settlers' efforts to advance, no doubt demoralized them still further.[29]

About this time, Félix de Quintanar complained again that his house had not been built despite Captain Joseph Pauli, the militia captain,

26. DeVilliers to Miró, Galveztown, May 12, December 17, 1787, "petition of Juan Sánchez Melián," Galveztown, August 18, 1787, and approved by Miró, New Orleans, August 28, 1787, all in AGI, PC, leg. 13; DeVilliers to Miró, Galveztown, September 23, December 1, 1788, AGI, PC, leg. 14; [Miró] to DeVilliers, New Orleans, September 17, 1787, New Orleans, January 5, 1788, and New Orleans, October 31, 1788, AGI, PC, legs. 132, 117A, and 119, respectively.

27. DeVilliers to Miró, Galveztown, September 28, 1789, AGI, PC, leg. 115, and February 4, June 4, 1791, AGI, PC, leg. 17; Fr. Félix de Quintanar, petition to the governor, Galveztown, July 1, 1791, AGI, PC, leg. 121; DeVilliers to Governor Carondelet, Galveztown, September 19, 1792, AGI, PC, leg. 25B; Scramuzza, "Galveztown, a Spanish Settlement of Colonial Louisiana," 605; Baudier, *The Catholic Church in Louisiana*, 196.

28. Galveztown census, August 16, 1793, AGI, PC, leg. 27A; DeVilliers to Carondelet, Galveztown, September 17, 1792, AGI, PC, leg. 17.

29. DeVilliers to Carondelet, Galveztown, September 7, 1793, AGI, PC, leg. 27A.

having a contract to do so. Quintanar claimed that the cabin that temporarily sheltered him was uninhabitable; when it rained, water rose to the level of the bed. His repeated pleas for decent quarters fell on deaf ears. Exasperated, in December, 1793, Quintanar issued an ultimatum—he would quit the settlement if his residence was not built. Another year passed before Pauli completed the presbytery for the sum of two hundred pesos.[30]

In late 1793 events that had started in France began to have an effect in Galveztown. The French Revolution had found sympathizers for radical change in Louisiana, particularly in New Orleans. Governor Barón de Carondelet feared that those Jacobins might cause serious problems and perhaps even attempt to seize power. Uncertain of events, he appealed for help from the loyal settlements upriver, and in November, Galveztown sent its militiamen down to the capital, along with other units from rural Louisiana, in a show of strength against the advocates of revolution. The Galveztown volunteers descended the lakes to New Orleans on board DeVilliers' schooner under the command of militia captain Pauli. They stayed only a few days, but long enough to dampen the enthusiasm of the Jacobins.[31]

In 1794 Galveztown suffered renewed calamities as storms inflicted more hardship. Two hurricanes struck the Louisiana coast on August 10 and 21, bringing floodwaters to inundate the settlement. The winds of August 10 damaged the old Galveztown houses, knocking down several of them while high waters flooded the fields and drowned animals. While Galveztown was trying to recover from that misfortune, another hurricane battered the town eleven days later, with stronger winds and deeper waters. More of the "old houses"—which were only fourteen years old—collapsed. After the winds and rains subsided, floodwaters, the worst in the settlement's history, rushed down the Amite. They rose four feet over the river's banks and washed away the planted fields. Every Galveztown family lost property, and food again became a serious concern.[32]

In reporting the twin disasters of August to the governor, Comman-

---

30. Fr. Félix de Quintanar, petition, Galveztown, *ca.* October, 1793, AGI, PC, leg. 27B. Pauli allegedly started work in early November, 1793 (DeVilliers to Carondelet, Galveztown, November 7, December 3 and 6, 1793, *ibid.*).

31. DeVilliers to Carondelet, Galveztown, November 7, 1793, AGI, PC, leg. 27B. See also Ernest R. Liljegren, "Jacobinism in Spanish Louisiana, 1792–1797," *Louisiana Historical Quarterly*, XXII (1939), 6–14; Gayarré, *History of Louisiana*, III, 327–28.

32. DeVilliers to Carondelet, Galveztown, September 10 and 25, 1794, with attachment to the first letter, all in AGI, PC, leg. 30.

dant DeVilliers summarized the dismal record of the past three years. Floods had occurred repeatedly, eating away the river's banks and preventing the settlers from moving about freely. The fort's barracks had collapsed, and the troops slept without shelter. Although Isleños had not died, several of them had become sick. The 1794 storms returned Galveztown to the conditions that had prevailed in its first years, when it suffered repeatedly from the hands of nature. The passage of fifteen years had not improved the quality of life for the Canary Islanders of Galveztown.[33]

On December 25, 1794, Captain Francisco Rivas, former commandant of Manchac, assumed charge of the Galveztown district. A year later, in January, 1796, he reported to the governor that the Galveztown Isleños wanted to leave. They argued that their compatriots at the other settlements possessed greater resources than they did and could sell their produce with greater ease in New Orleans. Although Rivas tried to make them see the reason he perceived for their poverty—they needed to work more assiduously in order to rise above their present misery—they rejected his advice. Likewise, Governor Carondelet was not amenable to letting the Canarians depart. Failing to understand their problems, he wrote Rivas: "It is not right that the King spend money on these lazy and indolent people who are not content in any place except that one in which they are not."[34]

Perhaps Commandant Rivas finally recognized the sufferings of the Isleños in April, 1796. At that time, high waters again wiped out their newly planted fields and inundated their houses for five days. The deep waters in Galveztown allowed pirogues to navigate the streets. In reporting the latest misfortune to Carondelet, Rivas commented that the Spaniards had been working with dedication "until the flood and it [now] explains their sadness and their misery."[35] The new disaster meant continued privation and hardship for those unfortunate colonists.

Later that same year, a detailed military report on Louisiana's defenses by Engineer Juan María Perchet shed additional light on the

33. DeVilliers to Carondelet, Galveztown, September 10, December 20, 1794, both in AGI, PC, leg. 30.
34. Francisco Rivas to Carondelet, Galveztown, December 29, 1794, AGI, PC, leg. 30; Rivas to Carondelet, and the attached petition of Juan Medina, Galveztown, January 8, 1796, AGI, PC, leg. 34; [Carondelet] to Rivas, New Orleans, January 21, 1796, AGI, PC, leg. 129. Rivas found the Galveztown fort badly deteriorated; see his "Relación del Estado . . . ," Galveztown, January 2, [1795], and Carondelet to Francisco Rendón, New Orleans, January 16, 1795, AGI, PC, leg. 2364.
35. Rivas to Carondelet, Galveztown, April 27, 1796, AGI, PC, leg. 33.

Galveztown settlement, if only to emphasize the wretchedness of the Canary Islanders. The December, 1796, report revealed that the community's closeness to the banks of the Amite accounted for its repeated flooding. Waters were then eight feet deep in the swamps that surrounded the fort and settlement. The report mentioned that the settlers could easily abandon the village's few cabins since their lands had never been purchased nor given to them in title. Galveztown's population had declined to 21 families, comprising 109 persons. The report commented about their poverty: "They live in the depths of obscurity and misery . . . the small population barely eking out what is necessary for subsistence, and they are lodged in miserable cabins. The lands that surround this place are little suited for labor and sterile for the progress of agriculture."[36]

This was perhaps the most damning statement that had been made about the suitability of Galveztown. In the eighteen years since Governor Gálvez selected the site, the settlers had lived in dire poverty and suffered with each new misfortune owing to its location. Compelled by the memory of the former governor and by the substantial royal investment, subsequent Louisiana officials kept the Canary Islanders anchored there although experience clearly showed its disastrous location. Another reason for keeping the settlement, however, was the presence of the fort. The civilians constituted a militia that could be called upon in case of an emergency.

Governor Manuel Gayoso de Lemos in 1798 advocated rebuilding the Galveztown fort because he regarded the site on the Amite River as good for intercepting an enemy force that might penetrate the colony via that watery avenue. He rebuilt it later that year. Gayoso's brief administration was filled with concern about Americans pouring into Louisiana, which they were in fact doing. Already, by the Treaty of San Lorenzo of 1795, Spain had abandoned its claim to the east bank of the Mississippi down to the thirty-first parallel, not far above Baton Rouge. In 1799, the year that Gayoso died, he warned the Galveztown commandant not to let Americans settle there and to drive out any who had come.[37]

36. Juan María Perchet, report, December 29, 1796, AGI, PC, leg. 2354.
37. Jack D. L. Holmes, *Gayoso: The Life and Times of a Spanish Governor on the Mississippi, 1789–1799* (Baton Rouge, 1965), 238; Manuel Gayoso de Lemos to the Prince of the Peace (Manuel Godoy), No. 9 confidential, New Orleans, April 19, 1798, Archivo Histórico Nacional (Madrid), Sección de Estado, leg. 3900; Samuel Flagg Bemis, *Pinckney's Treaty: America's Advantage from Europe's Distress, 1783–1800* (rev. ed.; New Haven, Conn., 1960); Matías Hernández to Gayoso, Galveztown, June 2, 1798, AGI, PC, leg. 49; Tomás Estevan to Bouligny, Galveztown, July 27, 1799, AGI, PC, leg. 134.

In the last years of Spanish Louisiana, the final two Galveztown commandants wrote little about the settlement. Sublieutenant Matías Hernández replaced Rivas on October 8, 1797, and about February, 1799, Lieutenant Tomás Estevan relieved Hernández. It is known that a storm described as a hurricane hit Galveztown at 11:00 A.M. on April 18, 1801. It destroyed the old barracks, damaged part of the military kitchen, and harmed many houses. New devastations continued to hurt the settlement and crops. In 1805 the white inhabitants of the Galveztown district numbered only 213, and many of them were not Isleños.[38]

Between 1800 and 1803, Louisiana was in the process of changing hands. Spanish officials surrendered the province in New Orleans on November 30, 1803, to France, but the United States had already purchased it. On December 20, American authorities took charge in New Orleans, and in June, 1804, they assumed command at the Galveztown fort. In retroceding Louisiana to France, the Spaniards retained possession of West Florida, which extended on the Mississippi's east bank from Bayou Manchac and the Amite River northward to the thirty-first parallel. Galveztown was left on the American side of the international boundary. With American ownership over the settlement, the Isleños no longer felt the restraints that had bound them to the site for so many years. Indeed, on December 14, 1803, twenty-nine Canarian families petitioned the Spanish government to leave since they wished to live on Spanish soil. They claimed that they did not want to remain under a foreign power they knew nothing about. They doubtlessly also wanted to reside at a better location. The government momentarily told them to wait to see if Spain regained Louisiana.[39]

In the spring of 1804, the American governor of Louisiana, William C. C. Claiborne, sent Dr. John Watkins to visit the settlements upriver. Watkins reported about the Galveztown settlers: "They are chiefly Spaniards, poor and very miserable." Knowing their restiveness, he encouraged them to remain, declaring that their liberty, property, and

38. Rivas to Gayoso, Galveztown, October 8, 1797, AGI, PC, leg. 50; Estevan to Gayoso, Galveztown, April 3, 1799, AGI, PC, leg. 51; Estevan to Ramón López y Ángulo, Galveztown, April 28, 1801, AGI, PC, leg. 260; Gayarré, *History of Louisiana,* III, 300. Claude Cesar Robin, *Voyage to Louisiana,* trans. Stuard O. Landry, Jr. (abridged ed.; New Orleans, 1966), 98, has the population of Galveztown in 1805 as 213 whites, 8 free men of color, and 26 slaves.

39. Josef Pereira *et al.,* petition, Galveztown, December 14, 1803, AGI, PC, leg. 139; Pedro Cevallos to the Marqués de Casa Calvo, Aranjuez, January 15 and 16, 1805, AGI, PC, leg. 176B. On May 22, 1804, Casa Calvo reassigned Estevan to Baton Rouge ([Casa Calvo] to Carlos de Grand-Pré, New Orleans, May 22, 1804, AGI, PC, leg. 73).

religion would be respected. Despite Watkins' blandishments, many of the Isleños chose to abandon the Galveztown district.[40]

By 1804 a few Canarians were already departing the settlement, and the authorities at Baton Rouge, now Spain's main post on the Mississippi, marked out lots for them in what is today Spanish Town. The demise of Galveztown was underway. Many of the colonists probably remained there through 1804 and 1805, and the principal exodus occurred in 1806. Unfortunately, the details concerning their departure are missing. There is, however, evidence that Isleños entered the Baton Rouge district in 1806. The last recorded church entry at Galveztown was a marriage performed in February, 1807.[41]

It was not long before the village of Galveztown fell completely into ruins. American officials did not use the fort since it had little importance to them, nor did newcomers flock to the district. Major Amos Stoddard, whose book *Sketches, Historical and Descriptive, of Louisiana* was published in 1812, asserted that Galveztown had thirty or forty houses; but Stoddard exaggerated, and he probably never visited the site. Most of the settlement was in ruins by 1810. Several years later William Darby, in his *Geographical Description of the State of Louisiana*, which appeared in 1817, called Galveztown a village of little consequence that contained only a few ruined wooden houses.[42] Although the Isleños departed from the settlement, a number of them remained behind living in the countryside and tending to their lands. Within a few years, several gathered two miles away from their former residence, at a location probably high enough to avoid most floods and with a name that recalled their past, Galvez. That tiny community, unlike its predecessor, has endured to the present.

40.   John Watkins to Governor Claiborne, New Orleans, February 2, 1804, in Dunbar Rowland (ed.), *Official Letterbooks of W. C. C. Claiborne, 1801–1816* (6 vols.; Jackson, Miss., 1917), II, 7; James Alexander Robertson (ed.), *Louisiana Under the Rule of Spain, France, and the United States, 1785–1807* (2 vols.; Cleveland, 1911; rpr. New York, 1969), II, 316. Watkins reported that only 28 families lived in that part of the district.

41.   "Plano de los terrenos destinados para las familias españolas de Galveztown . . . ," Baton Rouge, Fort San Carlos Settlement, December 11, 1804, Archivo General de Indias, Mapas y Planos, Luisiana y Florida, No. 228; Pintado Papers, Vol. I, 94, Pensacola, July 6, 1806, Louisiana State University Archives.

42.   Major Amos Stoddard, *Sketches, Historical and Descriptive* (Philadelphia, 1815), 165; William Darby, *A Geographical Description of the State of Louisiana* (2nd ed.; New York, 1817), 88.

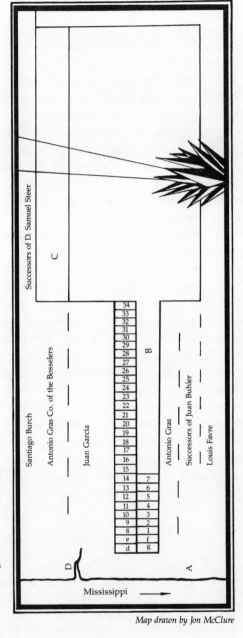

A Reserved land adjacent to fort
B Concession in favor of D. Manuel Gayoso de Lemos, 1,000 arpents
C Antonio Gras purchase
D Bridge

Map drawn by Jon McClure

Numbers 1 to 14—lots for Galveztown families, each measuring 3 arpents, 92 perches, 57 feet

Numbers 15 to 34—lots of 3 arpents, 88 perches, which the governor ordered divided among the same families

d e f g—land for gardens

Modern representation of 1806 map by Vicente Sebastian Pintado, showing lots granted in Baton Rouge to Canary Islander families from Galveztown

Four

Failure and Success: Barataria and St. Bernard

Little information has survived about the Isleños of Barataria and St. Bernard, unlike those of Galveztown. Barataria, the most short-lived of the Canarian communities, has the least in documentation, while St. Bernard, the most enduring of the settlements, also suffers from incomplete records. It is possible, nevertheless, to piece together an outline of their history. Similar to Galveztown, the Barataria and St. Bernard communities began in 1779, but unlike the settlement on the Amite, St. Bernard has survived to the present, while Barataria failed as an Isleño community within four years.

The settlement at Barataria existed from 1779 to 1782. No "Libro Maestro" with the names of its settlers has been found in the Spanish archives. The community began with about 150 Isleños and Andrés Jung as its commandant. In 1779 Jung received supplies to begin the settlement, and José Chalon of Bayou St. John had charge of building the houses. Within a few years, Jung repaired the houses that perhaps hurricanes damaged. The settlement, situated on the edge of Lake Barataria and about a dozen miles below New Orleans, received fewer colonists than the other three. Perhaps some question existed even then about its suitability. Governor Gálvez probably selected Barataria because he wanted a settlement on the Mississippi's west bank to stop invaders from ascending the river or entering Lake Barataria. The site, however, barely rose above sea level and the surrounding marshes. The hurricanes of 1779 and 1780 inflicted severe hardship on the immigrants, and repeated flooding prevented any progress from being made. Soon after Barataria's founding, the Spanish government needed to help it because of "the total loss of [its] planted fields and livestock caused by a crevasse in the river bank which inundated the settlement."[1]

Possibly the flood of late 1779 induced the government to transfer several Baratarian settlers to Valenzuela. By December, Governor Gálvez sent Lieutenant Antonio de St. Maxent, commandant at Valenzuela, to escort a group of Baratarians to his settlement. St. Maxent spent three days in Barataria, where he described the ground as unpropitious as it tended to flood. Although many colonists wished to depart, he took only sixteen families, plus three more from New Orleans. They were the first Isleños to abandon Barataria.[2]

In mid-1781, after his victory at Pensacola, Governor Gálvez reported on the Isleño settlements. In a lengthy letter to his uncle, José de Gálvez, minister of the Indies, he discussed the advances made by the new settlements. The governor minimized the Canarians' hardships. Instead, Gálvez elaborated upon the expected growth of all four communities and his plans to form a fifth at Bayagoulas with the immigrants still in Havana. Because of wartime exigencies, however, he indefinitely postponed the Bayagoulas settlement. Following this report and his permanent departure from Louisiana in July, 1781, Gálvez left care of the settlements to subordinates. As for Barataria, nothing more is mentioned about it in the documentation until August, 1782.[3]

That month Intendant Martín Navarro wrote that the Baratarian families had been receiving rations since January 1 and that they had suffered from floods. He acknowledged that their condition was the same or worse than that of other Canarian settlers. Progress at Barataria seems to have been nonexistent, nullified by the adversity of the elements. By 1782 most of the Isleños were ready to depart.[4]

In September, 1782, a group of Baratarian residents formally petitioned Pierre DeMarigny, the St. Bernard commandant, to allow them to move to his district, with rations for a year and the benefits the other settlers enjoyed. DeMarigny notified Juan Ventura Morales of the New Orleans accounting office, who was in charge of immigration and Indian

1. Morales to Martín Navarro, New Orleans, January 12, 1786, AGI, PC, leg. 606; Edna B. Freiberg, *Bayou St. John in Colonial Louisiana, 1699–1803* (New Orleans, 1980), 272.

2. Antonio de St. Maxent to the governor, Valenzuela, January 4, 1780, AGI, PC, leg. 192; St. Maxent to Morales, Valenzuela, January 4, 1780, AGI, PC, leg. 608A.

3. Bernardo de Gálvez to José de Gálvez, New Orleans, July 19, 1781, AGI, SD, leg. 2548 and AGI, PC, leg. 608A. For Bernardo de Gálvez' later military exploits, see Caughey, *Bernardo de Gálvez in Spanish Louisiana*, 243–47; and Guillermo Porras Muñoz, "El fracaso de Guarico," *Anuario de estudios americanos*, XXVI (1969), 569–609.

4. [Navarro] to Morales, New Orleans, August 6, 1782, AGI, PC, leg. 606.

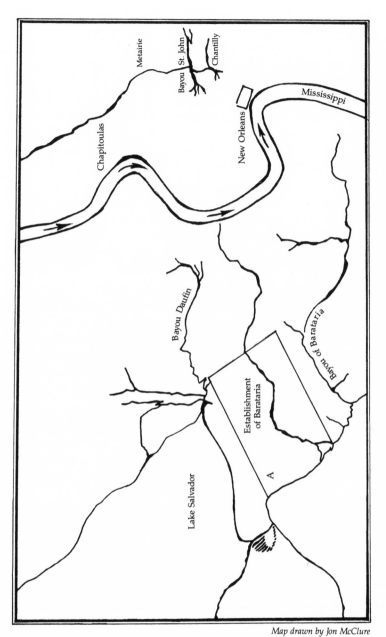

Modern representation of Spanish map showing area purchased to settle Canary Islanders in Barataria (A)

Map drawn by Jon McClure

affairs. The New Orleans officials clearly recognized the unsuitability of Barataria and the deplorable conditions in which the settlers lived. On September 22, twenty-five Baratarian heads of family petitioned Morales directly to move, claiming the infertility of Barataria's soil and their inability to prosper. Intendant Navarro acquiesced and authorized their transfer to Terre-aux-Boeufs with rations until the end of 1783, houses, tools, and clothing. They were to repay the royal treasury when circumstances permitted. To pressure all the Isleños of Barataria to move, Navarro suspended aid to that settlement as of October 31.[5]

By November the Barataria families were crossing the Mississippi to St. Bernard. As 1782 ended, their exodus across the river continued, and it did not cease until early the next year. DeMarigny informed Morales of the need for a surgeon. In New Orleans, Dr. Robert Dow was already putting together medicines to send to them. By March, 1783, Morales sent Surgeon Joseph Petit to provide medical attention for the colonists.[6]

In settling the Baratarians, DeMarigny first constructed twelve houses for them, and he later built at least three more; no doubt still others were put up for them. Approximately 111 persons resettled in St. Bernard, not counting a few late arrivals. The commandant placed them farther down Bayou Terre-aux-Boeufs, beyond the lands given to the first Isleños who settled in 1779. He formed another tiny establishment in order to have them near their lands. Morales sent army sergeant Romano to assist DeMarigny in settling the recent arrivals. The commandant believed that the new families would not require aid after the harvest and that the majority of the other, previously established families of St. Bernard were on the verge of supporting themselves.[7]

By 1783 the Baratarian settlement was vanishing. Most of those who had remained abandoned it later for St. Bernard; among them was

5. Pierre DeMarigny to Morales, Concepción, September 10, 1782; Juan García Raimundo, Antonio Joseph de Armas et al., petition, with Navarro's marginal notation, New Orleans, September 22, 1782; [Morales] to Navarro, New Orleans, November 13, 1782, all in AGI, PC, leg. 608A.

6. DeMarigny to Morales, [St. Bernard], November 28 and December 16, 1782, AGI, PC, leg. 608A. In January, 1783, Intendant Navarro permitted Juan Espino and five members of his family to move to St. Bernard from Barataria (Navarro to Manuel Ramos, New Orleans, January 2, 1783, [Morales] to DeMarigny, New Orleans, March 20, 1783, AGI, PC, legs. 689 and 608A, respectively). A list of Barataria families who moved to St. Bernard is enclosed in Navarro to Morales, New Orleans, January, 1783, AGI, PC, leg. 689. See also Judicial Records, Spanish File No. 31, April 30, 1789, Louisiana Historical Center (New Orleans).

7. [Morales] to DeMarigny, New Orleans, December 30, 1782, AGI, PC, leg. 608A. A voucher for payment for rations supplied to Barataria families amounted to 47,608 reales in 1783 (New Orleans, February 4, 1784, ibid.).

Bernardo Nieves and his family, who moved in December, 1785. Others, meanwhile, left for New Orleans or elsewhere. The few Isleños that stayed behind in Barataria appear to have become independent, and they perhaps derived a living from fishing or raising livestock, rather than from farming. How long Andrés Jung served as commandant at Barataria is unknown, but by the time of his death on September 4, 1784, he was engaged in business elsewhere. Today, little remains that recalls the Barataria community of two hundred years ago.[8]

Of the four Isleño settlements, St. Bernard alone has retained its identity to the present. Little is known about its early years. Only the upper part of the present-day parish had settlers in 1779. The ridges of Bayou Terre-aux-Boeufs, where the Spanish settlement of St. Bernard began, rose a scant few feet above sea level. The bayou, once a channel for carrying the Mississippi's waters to the gulf, had over the past centuries become a refluent stream, used principally when the "Father of Waters" overflowed. Otherwise, its languid current was scarcely discernible. An early-nineteenth-century American traveler described the region in these words: "On the east side of the Mississippi, and about twelve miles below New Orleans, a dry strip of land extends from the river in a direction towards the lakes, where it terminates at the distance of twenty miles. This tongue of land, called *Terre au Boeuf*, is about a mile in width, and divided in the center by a creek or bayou; and, like the Mississippi, is bounded on each side by cypress swamps."[9]

Terre-aux-Boeufs probably derived its name from oxen rather than from buffalo. Its Spanish name, Tierra de Bueyes, seems to confirm this. In the 1720s, shortly after the founding of New Orleans, Frenchmen built several indigo and sugarcane plantations in the area below the city (upper St. Bernard Parish today). When the Canary Islanders arrived, the plantations extended no farther than the head of Bayou Terre-aux-Boeufs. Realizing that Governor Gálvez wanted lands near New Orleans for the colonists, Pierre DeMarigny de Mandeville, whose wife's deceased brother had been married to the governor's wife, Felicité, offered his vacant property at Terre-aux-Boeufs. The settlement on the bayou near New Orleans would allow the immigrants to help defend the city in case of attack. The governor accepted DeMarigny's offer, and the

8. The Barataria district still had 40 inhabitants, 30 of them white, in 1788 (Census of 1788, enclosed in Miró to Domingo Cabello, New Orleans, July 15, 1788, AGI, PC, leg. 1425; [Morales] to DeMarigny, New Orleans, December 12, 1785, AGI, PC, leg. 608A). Most of Barataria's population probably lived near the Mississippi (Freiberg, *Bayou St. John*, 269).

9. Stoddard, *Sketches*, 161.

settlement began in 1779, with DeMarigny becoming its commandant the next year. Perhaps as many as 160 families eventually settled there, with 42 families numbering 168 persons going in the first group.[10]

During the war against Britain, DeMarigny accompanied Gálvez as an army lieutenant in charge of black soldiers in 1779 and 1780 and as aide-de-camp to Gálvez at Pensacola. Perhaps a few St. Bernard Isleños joined Gálvez' army also. Who commanded the settlement in DeMarigny's absence is unknown, but once the French Creole returned from Pensacola in 1781, he again took charge.[11]

In its early years, the Terre-aux-Boeufs community had several names. Spanish officials used *Nueva* (New) *Gálvez* and *Concepción* frequently in documents, although *St. Bernard*, for the governor's patron saint, was also used occasionally quite early. As the 1780s progressed, *Concepción* and *Nueva Gálvez* gradually faded from usage, and *St. Bernard* emerged as the name for the entire district and later the parish.[12]

The Spanish government did not force the St. Bernard immigrants, like those in Galveztown, to huddle together in a single community. The settlement did not have a fort, and the imperative to assist a garrison did not exist. The lands of the settlers were supposed to consist of approximately 3 arpents of bayou front (576 feet) by 40 deep (7,680 feet), but they seem not to have had those measurements. Sometimes individuals received land on both sides of the bayou, and usually the grants were irregular in size. The authorities formed three tiny communities with the colonists, each about a league apart from the others. The Baratarians later created a fourth in 1782. Hurricanes and periodic floods made the life of the colonists difficult. Lakes, swamps, marshes, and the gulf encompassed their lands and often brought hardship and misery. Nevertheless, the waters also teemed with fish, shrimp, crabs, oysters, crawfish, and other maritime delicacies. Perhaps those Isleños with prior knowledge of fishing or familiarity with the sea gravitated to the water and away from agriculture. The majority, however, stayed on the lands as farmers. When not hindered by the elements, their small farms on the banks of Bayou Terre-aux-Boeufs produced vegetables for their own consumption and for sale in neighboring New Orleans. Although the St. Bernard Canary Islanders required rations in their first years and

10. "Relación de la Primeras familias Ysleñas del Establecim.to de Sn. Bernardo," AGI, PC, leg. 568; Public Affairs Research Council of Louisiana, Inc., *Statistical Profile of Saint Bernard Parish* (Baton Rouge, 1973), ii.
11. Holmes, (ed.), *Honor and Fidelity*, 205.
12. Morales to Navarro, New Orleans, March 11, 1786, AGI, PC, leg. 606.

costly housing, animals, equipment, clothing, and many other effects, most of them became self-sustaining by the early 1780s.

Information about St. Bernard is lacking until late 1782. On December 16, Commandant DeMarigny informed Morales that with few exceptions all the settlers could provide for themselves, and the few who could not required rations for only two to three additional months. Morales, a watchdog of the royal purse strings, consulted Intendant Navarro and replied that he could not grant them that favor. The king had agreed to support the families for only one year, and they had now enjoyed rations for four. Since they had recently obtained good harvests, Morales did not believe them entitled to further assistance. He also denied them the clothing they requested because he lacked funds. DeMarigny, however, protested the suspension of rations for four families and for a widow and orphans. Morales and Navarro acquiesced and continued to feed the truly needy. Morales, nonetheless, rejected another request—opening Bayou Terre-aux-Boeufs to the sea—since it required Governor Gálvez' order to earmark funds for such a project. Perhaps by 1782 some of the Canary Islanders wanted to earn their livelihood from the sea or at least to vary their diet. In time many settlers turned to the waters that surrounded them for food.[13]

In 1783 three ships brought the remaining Isleños from Cuba to New Orleans, two in August and one in December. They numbered 67 heads of family and approximately 271 persons. The new arrivals stayed briefly in the city and afterwards settled primarily in St. Bernard, with a small number going to Valenzuela. On Terre-aux-Boeufs they took up residence in the second, third, and fourth tiny communities. Pierre Bailly, a New Orleans carter, made 206 cart trips to transport the families and their possessions, for a cost of 618 pesos. The government supplied the new arrivals well, even lavishly at times, for some of them received a cart and two horses valued at 125 pesos. In the case of Domingo Núñez, whose family numbered 7 persons, supplies included 150 ounces of cloth, 30 ounces of printed linen, 4 hats, 10 plain and 4 silk hand-kerchiefs, 6 pairs of stockings, 16 ounces of cloth of white thread, 4 needle cases, 8 thimbles, 1,000 pins and needles, 3 fusils, 3 pounds of gun-powder, 4 shaving razors, 5 axes, 8 hoes, 2 shovels, 10 ounces of Limburg cloth, 2½ pesos in coin per person, 20 pesos for the purchase of a mare,

13. [Morales] to DeMarigny, New Orleans, March 18 and 20, 1783, with the former enclosing DeMarigny's "Etat du Rattions . . . ," March 17, 1783, AGI, PC, leg. 83; DeMarigny to [Morales], New Orleans, December 16, 1782, AGI, PC, leg. 608A.

and a number of other items. In all, the families that arrived in 1783 received 2,696 ells (*anas*) of imperial linen, 1,590 ells of light or course cloth, 50 blankets of 3 points, and 50 blankets of 2½ points. Merchandise for these immigrants cost 14,807 pesos. The total expenditure, however, was greater. Medicines supplied by Surgeon Joseph Montegut of New Orleans amounted to 343½ pesos. By February 10, 1784, expenses for these families alone had risen to 30,111½ pesos.[14]

A voucher for the payment of 8,100 pesos to Commandant DeMarigny provides a further glimpse of the St. Bernard settlement. He built 78 houses for 100 pesos each, 48 of them at the second, third, and fourth communities, and 30 more houses for 110 pesos each, on the lands belonging to the new settlers. Probably constructed between 1782 and 1784, they contained approximately 500 square feet of living space and resembled those erected in 1779.[15]

Several people who were not Isleños also settled in St. Bernard in 1783. These Spaniards, numbering about a dozen persons, included discharged Spanish soldiers and sailors, and the husbands of Isleño daughters. Intendant Navarro used the opportunity to settle former military men who chose not to return to Spain. The attraction of marriageable Spanish women in St. Bernard probably helped to induce them to remain. Among the bachelors were Carlos Suárez Sola, Francisco Caravallo, Joaquín Gómez, Antonio de Ylliade, and Juan Antonio Cabrera. The husbands of Isleño women included Diego Alfonso, wedded to Angela, the daughter of Sebastián Casorla; Nicolás de Ascención Ramos, married to the daughter of María Suárez; and Juan Pérez, whose wife was the daughter of Nicolás Valentino.[16]

While most of the Havana Isleños of 1783 settled in St. Bernard and Valenzuela, several remained in New Orleans. Patricio Gonzáles and his

14.   Navarro to Ramos, New Orleans, September 12 and 13, 1783; Morales, "Resumen gral. que la Conta. Pral. de Pobln. y Amistad de Yndios . . . ," New Orleans, July 4, 1784; DeMarigny, "Quenta y relación (de las familias) que se han situado en el segundo, tercero, y quarto establecimientos," February 4, 1784; Pierre Ballo, New Orleans, February 2, 1784; "Statement of Pedro Marigny, Lieutenant, of goods supplied to the families of St. Bernard arriving from Havana," February 4, 1784, all in AGI, PC, leg. 689. On the Isleños arriving in 1784, see, for example: [Morales] to DeMarigny, New Orleans, April 12, 1784, AGI, PC, leg. 608A, Morales to Navarro, New Orleans, September 25, 1786, AGI, PC, leg. 606; "Libro para . . . los viberes y efectos que reciven las Familias Ysleñas . . . destinadas a la Población de Sn. Bernardo . . . ," 1783, AGI, PC, leg. 568.

15.   "Libranza en favor de Pedro Marigny," July 10, 1784, AGI, PC, leg. 689.

16.   DeMarigny, "Relación," New Orleans, February, 1784, AGI, PC, leg. 689. Rations cost 32,559 *reales* in 1783 (Navarro to Ramos, with "Lista de Yndividuales a quienes se dará entrada en la Población de Sn. Bernardo con las Demas familias que acaban de llegar de la Hav.a," New Orleans, October 20, 1783, AGI, PC, leg. 603A).

family were excused because he was not a farmer; Bernardo Delgado replaced him. Intendant Navarro also exempted Antonio Esteves, a sailor, but he first needed to give surety, pledging to repay the Crown the total costs of his transportation to Louisiana. He offered to substitute Miguel Ramírez, his wife, and their son for his own family. One can speculate that cases similar to these existed in 1779, when the first Canary Islanders arrived in New Orleans. Two others who left St. Bernard, at least temporarily, were Antonio Flores and Sebastián de Mar, who obtained permission to return to Cuba for eight months to attend to affairs they left pending. In 1785 still others departed from St. Bernard. Juan Alfonso, Juan Morales, and Gregorio Ojeda complained of indisposition (*achaques*) and received permission to go wherever they pleased. The government accounting house in New Orleans required them to supply a complete list of all their animals, goods, and other property. For those who departed for Havana, Morales demanded that they return all the goods they had received, and he arranged free transportation for them to Havana on the packet boat *El Paula*. In addition to these Isleños, a small but steady stream of settlers abandoned the community for New Orleans and elsewhere over the years.[17]

Until 1786 Terre-aux-Boeufs was composed almost entirely of Spaniards. In that year approximately seventy-five Acadians, many of them passengers on the ships *Amistad* and *Carolina*, settled on the Mississippi's left bank below New Orleans. They were among nearly 1,600 Acadians who came from France at Spanish expense. They settled in many places in lower Louisiana, including St. Bernard Parish. In time, marriages between the Acadians and the Spaniards and their descendants became common.[18]

St. Bernard's population grew slowly in the 1780s, to 576 in 1785 and to 661 in 1788. By the mid–1780s, most of the Isleños were self-sufficient and no longer required help. Because of this, Morales believed it time to recover some of the money spent on them. In June, 1787, he informed DeMarigny that he wished to collect seven hundred pesos from the settlers. In his reply of August 17, DeMarigny protested that a few immigrants still required rations. It appears that Morales did not obtain

17. [Morales] to DeMarigny, New Orleans, October 6 and December 1, 1783, New Orleans, July 9 and 18, December 22, 1785, all in AGI, PC, leg. 608A; Antonio Esteves, petition, New Orleans, December 20, 1783, with DeMarigny's marginal notation of December 21 and Navarro's approval, December 23, 1783, AGI, PC, leg. 689.

18. [Morales] to DeMarigny, New Orleans, December 22, 1785, January 2, February 3, March 3, May 1, June 1 and 5, 1786, AGI, PC, leg. 608A.

the seven hundred pesos; moreover, the government soon after canceled the debt completely.[19]

Little is known about St. Bernard in the late 1780s, except for DeMarigny's absence. He departed for France about April, 1788, leaving Sublieutenant Pierre De la Ronde as acting commandant. Near the end of 1790, DeMarigny returned from his original one-year's leave. Although Governor Miró intended to reappoint him to St. Bernard as commandant, DeMarigny's election as *alcalde* of the New Orleans' cabildo for 1791 prevented it. Miró therefore kept De la Ronde as commandant.[20]

Information about St. Bernard in the 1790s is also not extensive. By the beginning of the decade, most of the farmer-immigrants had probably cleared a few arpents of their lands closest to the bayou to plant vegetables; others had turned to fishing or found employment on the plantations of the upper district. About March, 1790, the settlers requested Governor Miró to survey their lands. The lack of proper boundaries, they complained, resulted in quarrels. Isleños who signed the memorial included Ramón Palacios, Antonio Bienes, and Joseph Solís. Miró acted promptly and soon informed Commandant De la Ronde that provincial surveyor Charles Trudeau would carry out the surveys.[21]

Uniformity in the land grants of Terre-aux-Boeufs did not exist. When the Isleños started to buy and sell their tracts about 1788, formerly accepted boundaries were forgotten. Sizes of several tracts from 1792 illustrate their varying dimensions. Francisco Colonia and Sebastián Ramírez claimed lands on both sides of the bayou near the St. Bernard settlement measuring 120 feet (about two-thirds of an arpent) and 40

19. In 1788 white men numbered 343, white women 301, free blacks 8, and slaves 18 ("Resumen general del Padron hecho en la Provincia de la Luisiana . . . ," enclosed in Miró to Cabello, July 15, 1789, AGI, PC, leg. 1425; [Morales] to DeMarigny, New Orleans, June 3, 1787, and DeMarigny to Morales, at his plantation, August 17, 1787, both in AGI, PC, leg. 608A). By the royal order of January 12, 1787, the king dispensed with the repayment of the assistance given to the Canary Islander families, but also ended help as of August, 1787 (Navarro to José de Gálvez, New Orleans, May 4, 1787, and June 7, 1787, AGI, SD, leg. 2611).

20. Miró to José de Gálvez, New Orleans, January 11 and March 24, 1787, and Miró to Sonora, New Orleans, June 12 and August 16, 1787, all in AGI, SD, leg. 2552; Cabello to Antonio Valdés, Havana, April 30, 1790, AGI, SD, leg. 2554; [Miró] to Pierre De la Ronde, New Orleans, December 20, 1790, and January 1, 1791, both in AGI, PC, leg. 121. See also Spanish File No. 56, February 1, 1788, Louisiana Historical Center.

21. De la Ronde to Miró, St. Bernard, March 9, 1790; Ramón Palacios *et al.*, petition, New Orleans, n.d.; [Miró] to De la Ronde, New Orleans, March 14, 1790, all in AGI, PC, leg. 121.

arpents deep. Joseph Gutiérrez also possessed tracts on both sides of the bayou measuring 2 arpents and 20 toises (a toise equals 2.13 English yards). Santiago Molina owned land 2 leagues from the church, located on both sides of the bayou and measuring 3 arpents and 13 toises of front. Joseph Méndez, meanwhile, had 2 arpents, 25 toises, and 3 feet of front, with the usual depth of 40 arpents. The owners cleared very little of the depth of the land in the Spanish period, or even afterwards, since the rear portions usually consisted of marshes, swamps, and almost impenetrable wilderness.[22]

For the first ten years of its existence, St. Bernard did not have a tavern, and the settlers presumably traveled to New Orleans for their alcoholic spirits. In late 1790, the residents, wishing to remedy that deficiency, approached the commandant with their desire for a tavern. De la Ronde soon informed the governor, who agreed on January 20, 1791. Persons wishing to operate the tavern had to bid for the privilege, with the money going into government coffers. On Sunday, January 30, De la Ronde held a meeting in front of the church of the Isleños wanting to bid. This was the usual time and place for post commandants to talk to the inhabitants of their district. María Hernández offered the winning sum of ninety-one pesos and purchased the right to operate the tavern for one year, beginning on March 1. The next year, in another auction, Gaspar Ortiz obtained the right for an undisclosed sum of money. This practice appears to have been used until the end of the Spanish regime.[23]

From at least 1785 on, the provincial budget set aside 360 pesos for a priest at St. Bernard, and about that same time the government assigned a friar there. Probably the shortage of religious personnel prevented a priest from being sent earlier, and New Orleans served St. Bernard. When six friars reached Louisiana in 1785, Mariano de Brunete received the parish of St. Bernard. He stayed until an irregularity involving the marriage of Juan Fontonel and Francisca Barua (their names were Gallicized into Fontenelle and Bouras) occurred, and Brunete was reassigned to St. John the Baptist Parish on April 1, 1787. In his place,

22.   Charles R. Maduell, Jr., "Federal Land Grants in the Territory of Orleans (State of Louisiana) for the Delta Parishes," adapted from *American State Papers, Public Lands*, Vol. II (MS in Howard-Tilton Library, Tulane University); Spanish File No. 2380, November 11, 1788, Louisiana Historical Center.
23.   [Miró] to De la Ronde, New Orleans, January 20, 1791, and De la Ronde to Miró, St. Bernard, January 31, 1791, both in AGI, PC, leg. 122A; De la Ronde to Carondelet, St. Bernard, February 20, 1792, with enclosure [Carondelet] to De la Ronde, New Orleans, March 8, 1792, AGI, PC, leg. 122B.

Intendant Navarro dispatched Friar Agustín Lamar to St. Bernard, where he stayed until December 19, 1793. Father José de Villaprovedo, another Capuchin, took Lamar's place. It was Villaprovedo's last assignment, as he died there on September 19, 1797. Tirso de Peleagonzalo, a third Capuchin, assumed his post. In 1802 Father Estevan de Valoris, prefect of the College of Capuchins in Havana, asked that Father Peleagonzalo be returned to Cuba because he had been elected head of a college. Governor Manuel Juan de Salcedo, however, suspended the request because of the lack of ministers for the Isleño settlements. In 1803 Governor Salcedo described Peleagonzalo as at the "gates of death," suffering from gout and other infirmities. The governor permitted the friar to depart for the milder climate of Cuba, where his life might be prolonged. With his departure, St. Bernard lacked a permanent priest for several years.[24]

Soon after the founding of St. Bernard, Governor Gálvez had set aside land on Terre-aux-Boeufs, two arpents of front and forty arpents deep, for the eventual construction of a church. Not until 1787, however, did work on the building begin by contractor Francisco Delery, whom the government paid in advance. He built everything except the attic (*sobrado*), and then stopped for several years. Not until the parishioners complained in 1791 did the government pressure Delery to finish. Commandant De la Ronde finally reported on September 2 that the church was completed. This structure remained in use until the early 1850s, when a new building replaced it.[25]

In early 1792, Governor Carondelet appointed DeMarigny captain of the four militia companies he established below New Orleans, called the Volunteers of the Mississippi. The area covered the approximate region of present-day St. Bernard and Plaquemines parishes. Each district raised two companies apiece. In proposing officers for the two St. Bernard companies, DeMarigny overlooked the Isleños, although they made up the bulk of the soldiers. He preferred selecting officers from the planter class.

Meanwhile, Lieutenant De La Ronde remained the commandant of St.

24. "Our Lady of Lourdes Catholic Church, Violet, Saint Bernard Parish, Louisiana," New Orleans *Genesis*, V, No. 7 (January, 1966), 42; José de Villaprovedo to Carondelet, New Orleans, June 2, 1794, AGI, PC, leg. 29; Salcedo to the Marqués de Someruelos, Nos. 302 and 351, New Orleans, December 20, 1802, and February 16, 1803, both in AGI, PC, leg. 155B; Baudier, *The Catholic Church in Louisiana*, 197, 204, 235.

25. De la Ronde to Miró, St. Bernard, January 31, June 8, and September 1, 1791, and [Miró] to De la Ronde, New Orleans, February 3 and June 8, 1791, all in AGI, PC, leg. 122A.

Bernard, even after Carondelet appointed him sergeant major of the Royal Legion of the Mississippi at the end of 1796. De la Ronde was the second as well as the last Spanish commandant of St. Bernard. DeMarigny, for his part, became the colonel and commandant of the New Orleans militia in 1799. He died not long after, in May, 1800.[26]

Among the changes that Governor Carondelet initiated in Louisiana, including St. Bernard, was the establishment of syndics. They assisted commandants in managing local government. Carondelet divided St. Bernard into two districts, wherein several Spaniards served in the 1790s. In the first district, Antonio Gonzáles became a syndic, and in the second, the syndics included plantation owner Antonio Méndez (who was not an Isleño) and Antonio Rodríguez.[27]

In the mid-1790s, the governor decreed that slave owners from throughout the province would be assessed six *reales* per slave in order to compensate the masters for the fifty-four bondsmen executed or imprisoned because of the Pointe Coupée conspiracy. The census Carondelet ordered revealed the presence of sixty-one slaves in St. Bernard, with Antonio Méndez, the only Spanish slave master, owning sixteen. The Isleños did not possess slaves according to the census, but it probably was not accurate.[28]

Runaway slaves (*cimarrones*) became a serious problem in the late 1790s, and they disturbed the tranquillity of the St. Bernard district. Not since 1783 and 1784, when the notorious St. Malo band roamed the region, had *cimarrones* been a source of concern. DeMarigny, De la Ronde, and a number of Isleños had then assisted in rounding up the fugitives. Now, however, the runaways had become numerous again. In February, 1799, the plantation owners of the upper district, including Antonio Méndez and Tomás de Villanueva (a Canary Islander), complained to the governor about the theft of goods and animals. The petitioners wanted to destroy the fugitives' settlements on the lakes east of New Orleans. They offered a reward for the runaways: four pesos per slave if apprehended in the city, seven pesos if in the cypress groves, and

26. [Miró] to De la Ronde, New Orleans, December 7, 1791, and De la Ronde to Miró, St. Bernard, December 12, 1791, both in AGI, PC, leg. 122A; [De la Ronde] to Carondelet, St. Bernard, January 18, 1792, and Carondelet to DeMarigny, New Orleans, March 13, 1792, both in AGI, PC, leg. 122B; Luis de Las Casas to Campo de Alange, Havana, March 30, 1792, AGI, SD, leg. 2560.

27. On syndics in St. Bernard, see AGI, PC, leg. 215A. For Antonio Méndez, see Gayarré, *History of Louisiana*, III, 247–49.

28. De la Ronde, list of slave owners of St. Bernard, July 16, 1795, and statement of the St. Bernard slaveholders, July 18, 1795, both in AGI, PC, leg. 211A.

ten pesos if on the lakes and islands. An additional four *reales* would be paid for each league required to return the fugitive to his owner. The *cimarrón* problem was general throughout Louisiana, as inhabitants from Plaquemines to Natchez complained about them. Despite several efforts to arrest the slaves, it does not appear that the government reduced the fugitive infestation.[29]

Almost nothing is known about St. Bernard in the closing days of Spanish rule. With the American take-over, information increased slightly. How the Isleños greeted the news that the United States now owned Louisiana remains unknown. They probably accepted the event calmly and remained on their lands and at their occupations. With a few exceptions, they were generally an indigent, uneducated, reasonably hardworking people. Their farms produced corn, kidney beans, "ordinary beans," fowl, eggs, butter, hogs, and assorted vegetables, while the district's plantations dedicated themselves to export crops of sugarcane, indigo, and cotton. At the time of the transfer, approximately eight hundred persons resided in St. Bernard.[30]

The new authorities of Louisiana did not always look upon the Terre-aux-Boeufs residents favorably. Pierre Clement Laussat, the Frenchman who ruled Louisiana for three weeks in December, 1803, and the American governor who followed him, William C. C. Claiborne, regarded them, and not without some prejudice, as a "priest-ridden" people. Laussat accused the Spanish government of employing a priest at Terre-aux-Boeufs to make this "fine class of small colonists" promise to follow the retreating Spanish flag. Dr. John Watkins, sent out by Governor Claiborne to visit the settlements of lower Louisiana, labeled the inhabitants as humble, poor, indolent, and ignorant, and as people "who idolize their priests, and feel little attachment for any one else." When Claiborne named the planter Antonio Méndez as commandant of St. Bernard, these "humble" Canary Islanders protested the appoint-

29. Antonio Méndez, Tomás de Villanueva *et al.*, petition, New Orleans, February 5, 1799, and [Gayoso] to Joseph Vidal, New Orleans, February 14, 1799, both in AGI, PC, leg. 134A. See also Gilbert C. Din, "*Cimarrones* and the San Malo Band in Spanish Louisiana," *Louisiana History*, XXI (1980), 237–62.

30. William Darby, *The Emigrant's Guide to the Western and Southwestern States and Territories* (New York, 1818), 8; Stoddard, *Sketches*, 161; Lewis William Newton, "The Americanization of French Louisiana: A Study of the Process of Adjustment Between the French and the Anglo-American Population of Louisiana, 1803–1860" (Ph.D. dissertation, University of Chicago, 1929), 150–51; Marietta Marie LeBreton, "A History of the Territory of Orleans, 1803–1812" (Ph.D. dissertation, Louisiana State University, 1969), 16; Robertson (ed.), *Louisiana Under the Rule of Spain, France, and the United States*, I, 97.

ment for unknown reasons. After other residents also objected to Méndez, he withdrew, and the governor chose an acceptable person for the post.[31]

With the religious confusion at the start of the American period, Claiborne stated that the residents of the various districts sought to elect their own priests and that trouble flared up in St. Bernard in 1805. This trouble was part of the larger religious quarrel then going on between Patricio Walsh and Antonio de Sedella, both of whom claimed ecclesiastical jurisdiction over Louisiana's Catholics. One of them appointed a new priest for St. Bernard. When he arrived at his new parish, his predecessor allegedly assaulted him at the church door and threatened to take the matter of who was in charge before the parishioners. The post commandant predicted that with tempers so inflamed, a riot would occur in the church, but that probably did not happen. Unfortunately, little else is known about the incident.[32]

New Orleans received a considerable number of Canary Islanders through the 1780s and 1790s from the settlements, in addition to those who remained in the city after arriving in Louisiana. Possibly as many as four hundred Isleños never settled in the countryside. They constituted a sizable part of the New Orleans Spanish population, and they entered many of the city's occupations. The Spanish-speaking inhabitants of the city numbered second only to the French. The various Hispanic residents tended to blend together over the years, and it was difficult to distinguish the Isleños from the other Spaniards or from the Cubans, Mexicans, and other natives of the diverse regions of the Spanish empire. Despite this obstacle, a small amount of information about the Canary Islanders can be gleaned from church, notarial, and judicial records of New Orleans in the Spanish period. Two wills illustrate the information that the records provide.

On March 20, 1798, Antonio González, a native of La Orotava on the island of Tenerife and then a resident of New Orleans, made out his will

31. Claiborne to Thomas Jefferson, New Orleans, July 5, 1806, in Rowland (ed.), *Letterbooks of W. C. C. Claiborne*, III, 351–52; Robertson (ed.), *Louisiana Under the Rule of Spain, France, and the United States*, II, 41; Claiborne to James Madison, New Orleans, February 13, 1804, in Rowland (ed.), *Letterbooks of W. C. C. Claiborne*, I, 272–73. François-Marie Perrin du Lac, a French traveler in the closing days of Spanish Louisiana who was not friendly to either Spaniards or blacks, wrote almost sneeringly of the Isleños in *Voyage dans les deux Louisianes* (Paris, 1805), 390–91.

32. Robertson (ed.), *Louisiana Under the Rule of Spain, France, and the United States*, II, 283. See also Stanley Faye (ed.), "The Schism of 1805 in New Orleans," *Louisiana Historical Quarterly*, XXII (1934), 98–141.

before notary Carlos Ximénes. His real property consisted of four houses located at the corner of New (Nueva) Street and Customs (Aduana) Street. In addition, he owned two male slaves, Chano and Simón, and two female slaves, Babé, and María Luisa. The free Negress María Luisa Doriocourt, whom he appointed executrix of his estate, had charge of his slaves. He bequeathed to Babé and Chano five hundred pesos for their good services. The remainder of the estate he left to his father, José González de Silba, who lived in the Canary Islands, and in the event of his death, to his brothers, also of the Canaries.[33]

Five years later, Teresa de Flores, a native of Santa Cruz de Tenerife and a resident of New Orleans for many years, made out her last will and testament, on November 25, 1803. She declared that she had no children and that her husband, Felipe Luz of the Canary Islands, had remained in Cuba years before. Doña Teresa presumed him to be deceased although she lacked positive knowledge. She listed as her property a Negress, Barbara, and Barbara's children Josef, a *Negrito*; Pedro Lorenzo, a *mulatico*; and María Dolores, a *Negrita*, all of whom had been born while she owned Barbara. She also owned a *Negrito* named Juan Luis, and she had permitted an acquaintance, Christobal Badia, to take her slave Antonio with him to Spain, as well as a number of her silver plates and utensils. In other property, Señora Flores had a house, which she had purchased from Badia in 1796, furniture, gold and silver jewelry, a silver service, and additional silver plates. She also claimed that Badia owed her two thousand pesos. She had in her possession three of Badia's slaves: Catalina, a *Negrita* who was lame in one arm; Bernardo, a *Negro*; and Agustín, a *mulatico* who was the son of the *mulata* Martina. In her will, Señora Flores manumitted María Francisca, the oldest child of Barbara, for the sum of 125 pesos. Although María Francisca had been born to Barbara while Badia owned the latter, Señora Flores asserted that María Francisca was as much her property as was her mother and did not belong to Badia. Señora Flores also emancipated Barbara, Josef, Pedro Lorenzo, and María Dolores, and all the other children Barbara might have before Señora Flores died. She declared that her slave Juan Luis, who was learning to be a carpenter, could purchase his freedom for three hundred pesos. Señora Flores appointed Barbara as her universal heir although she divided all her property between Barbara and María

33. Notarial Records, Orleans Parish Civil Court Building, New Orleans, Carlos Ximénes, XV (January-December, 1798), 413–415V.

Francisca. Upon Barbara's death, Señora Flores' property descended to María Francisca and María Dolores. As for the other slaves, Barbara could dispose of them as she saw fit.[34]

The wills of Antonio González and Teresa de Flores illustrate that two Canary Islanders in New Orleans had acquired substantial wealth in real estate, slaves, and other property. No doubt still more Isleños in the city had prospered in a similar manner. The New Orleans Canarians generally fared better economically than those who settled down in the agricultural communities, and this helps to explain the small but steady flow of Isleños from Galveztown, Valenzuela, and St. Bernard to New Orleans. Life in the settlements was arduous, and prosperity for diverse reasons was slow in coming. Unfortunately, it is difficult to trace the fate of the Canary Islanders once they reached the melting pot of New Orleans. Only in the communities of St. Bernard and Valenzuela, where the Isleños remained concentrated in substantial numbers, is it possible to trace their development through the nineteenth century.

34. Notarial Records, Carlos Ximénes, XIX (January-November, 1803), 217–223V.

Five

Valenzuela on Bayou Lafourche

The natural beauty and potential of Bayou Lafourche impressed Governor Bernardo de Gálvez when he visited the headwaters in November, 1778. Except for the land at the entrance to the bayou on the Mississippi, an area known as Lafourche des Chetimachas, the lands on its banks were almost completely empty. Bayou Lafourche was a distributary stream of the Mississippi that carried waters in flood season a hundred miles to the Gulf of Mexico. During the rest of the year, the waters of Lafourche, especially near the Mississippi, stayed low. The lands adjacent to the bayou were the highest, gradually declining as they retreated from the stream. The trees, shrubs, and soil gave every indication that the land was eminently suited to agriculture. Governor Gálvez selected the land along Bayou Lafourche as one of the sites for settling the Canary Islanders, and he named it Valenzuela, probably using the family name of the wife of the minister of the Indies, José de Gálvez. Harnessing the floodwaters by building levees on the bayou constituted the major problem for the settlers, and years passed before they succeeded in protecting their lands, clearing their farms, and making the luxuriant delta earth provide them with a living. The upper Bayou Lafourche region became the home of an enduring Canarian community.

Acadian immigrants, who preceded the Isleños, had settled at Lafourche des Chetimachas in 1770, when Governor Alejandro O'Reilly appointed Louis Judice as commandant. Because they were few in number, they located mostly on the Mississippi and not down Bayou Lafourche. In 1772 a church, La Iglesia de la Ascensión de Nuestro Señor

Jesús Christo de la Fourche de los Chetimachas, otherwise known as the Church of the Ascension, began under Father Angel de Revillagodos. Governor Gálvez first notified Judice in September, 1778, that he had tentatively selected that district for settling some of the Canary Islanders. Several months later, on February 6, 1779, he ordered his brother-in-law Antonio de St. Maxent, Judice, and Michel Cantrelle (commandant of Cabahannocer) to mark out a site for the "Villa de Valenzuela" and construct six cabins, each thirty feet long by fifteen wide, at a cost of one hundred pesos apiece.[1]

Gálvez appointed Lieutenant St. Maxent in either late 1778 or early 1779 as commandant of Valenzuela. He arrived on Bayou Lafourche in February, spending nearly three months in preparation for the coming of the Canarians. In May, as the first Isleños arrived, Gálvez issued elaborate instructions for the settlement. The largest families would occupy the first houses to be built, while smaller families would share their lodgings until more houses were constructed. Gálvez authorized St. Maxent to give the families land in proportion to their size, with each receiving twice what it could then cultivate; industrious families, however, could have even more. The poorest colonists were to receive lands adjacent to Valenzuela, while those possessing either slaves or cattle were to be farther removed since they could afford to have a house in Valenzuela and another on their land. Gálvez wanted most of the settlers to live together in a community.[2]

Gálvez further instructed St. Maxent to keep several books for land concessions, funds received from New Orleans, and expenditures made. In a fourth ledger, he would note the size of each family, the ages and sexes of the members, and what the families received in clothing, food, and implements. Each six months he was to send a summary (*relación*) to New Orleans. The families as well were to keep a booklet (*libreta*) enumerating what the government had given them and what they owed.[3]

<hr>

1. Louis Judice, "Etat des habitants du District de . . . la Fourche des Chetimachas . . . ," [Lafourche des Chetimachas], April 23, 1777, Judice to [Bernardo de Gálvez], Lafourche [des Chetimachas], September 4, 1778, both in AGI, PC, leg. 193A; Baudier, *The Catholic Church in Louisiana*, 184, 191. Judice claimed in 1796 that he had still not been paid for constructing six cabins (Judice to Carondelet, Lafourche des Chetimachas, May 9, 1796, AGI, PC, leg. 212).

2. [Gálvez], "Ynstrucción que deberá observar el Subteniente Dn. Antonio Maxent, Comandante de la Nueva Población de Valenzuela . . . ," New Orleans, May 18, 1779, AGI, PC, leg. 192.

3. *Ibid.*

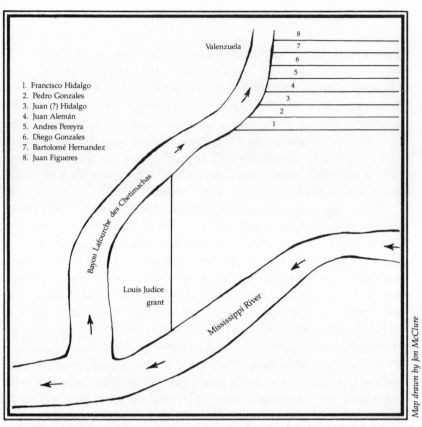

1. Francisco Hidalgo
2. Pedro Gonzales
3. Juan (?) Hidalgo
4. Juan Alemán
5. Andres Pereyra
6. Diego Gonzales
7. Bartolomé Hernandez
8. Juan Figueres

Valenzuela

Bayou Lafourche des Chetimachas

Louis Judice grant

Mississippi River

Map drawn by Jon McClure

Modern representation of 1779 map of the Bayou Lafourche area, showing several land grants to Canary Islanders opposite Valenzuela

Rations for the settlers would last only until their first harvest. They could tell St. Maxent what they preferred to eat, but he had to buy the least expensive items. The governor's father-in-law, Gilberto Antonio de St. Maxent, who was also the commandant's father, would supply the foodstuffs. Anselmo Blanchard received the contract to build the houses and to clear the first lands for planting. Commandant St. Maxent, however, would supervise the hired whites and slaves to verify the accuracy of the accounts Blanchard submitted. In all ways, he was to protect royal interests and property.[4]

Almost immediately after arriving in Valenzuela, St. Maxent had difficulties with Judice, the commandant of neighboring Lafourche des Chetimachas. Through the Spanish era, the two settlements were linked almost inextricably. Judice claimed authority over Valenzuela and so annoyed St. Maxent that the latter asked Gálvez for a clarification of his jurisdiction; was it over the soldiers alone, or did it include the settlers? The governor stated that St. Maxent had military control while Judice retained civil authority in the district; nevertheless, the Valenzuela commandant's duties included settling the Canarians. Probably because Gálvez had not drawn clear lines, Judice continued to make life miserable for St. Maxent. He, in turn, later commented on Judice's jealousy and interference in caring for the settlers; he alleged that Judice stored the settlers' supplies in his house, appropriated the best meats for himself, and in other ways abused his office. The quarrel between the two men came at a bad time, since more urgent military matters beset Gálvez. Until St. Maxent left Valenzuela in 1781, his difficulties with Judice over the question of authority continued.[5]

The first Canary Islanders arrived in Valenzuela in March. After St. Maxent marked out the settlement several miles down Bayou Lafourche on the left bank, he descended to New Orleans to escort them back. When they came, Valenzuela was born amidst dancing and feasting. During the next few months, several more groups of immigrants arrived. By May ten houses had been built, and St. Maxent prepared to plant two hundred arpents of land for a harvest in the fall. Although

4. *Ibid.*
5. Antonio de St. Maxent to the governor, Valenzuela, May 3, June 3, August 20, and October, 1779; [Gálvez] to Judice, New Orleans, May 12, 1779; Judice to the governor, Lafourche des Chetimachas, February 7, June 25, August 16, 20, and 21, 1779; [Gálvez] to [St. Maxent], New Orleans, May 11 and 12, 1779; Judice to the governor, Valenzuela, March 12, 1779, all in AGI, PC, leg. 192.

Valenzuela did not experience the tragedy that struck Galveztown, a number of deaths occurred in the summer of 1779.[6]

While the summer brought hardships and tragedies to the Valenzuela immigrants, it also brought war. Governor Gálvez had been anticipating it and had ordered the men of Bayou Lafourche between ages fourteen and forty-two to form into militia companies. At Valenzuela, St. Maxent drilled his men in the use of weapons by August 1. He appointed Francisco Corbo sublieutenant of the company.[7] The rudimentary preparations had only begun when Gálvez called the men to active duty at the end of the month.

The governor knew of Spain's declaration of war on Britain, and he intended to be first to act. On August 21, he informed Judice of his intention to lead an expedition upriver to conquer the British posts on the Mississippi. The militia units were to be prepared to join him. Gálvez, however, failed to reach Lafourche des Chetimachas at the appointed time, and local commandants spent several anxious days in late August, fearful that the British might attack. The date Gálvez reached Bayou Lafourche is uncertain, but on September 3, he left St. Gabriel, several miles upriver from Lafourche, to seize Fort Bute at British Manchac. After investing Manchac, he attacked in the early hours of September 7, killing one soldier and taking twenty captive. Perhaps the Valenzuela Isleños saw action here and at Baton Rouge, which surrendered on September 21. Only after seizing Fort Bute did Gálvez make public the state of war. On September 8, he ordered Judice to inform the inhabitants of the bayou lands, which Judice did on September 18 at Sunday mass.[8]

---

6. St. Maxent to the governor, Valenzuela, July 9, 1779, AGI, PC, leg. 192; St. Maxent to Morales, Valenzuela, August 1, 1779, AGI, PC, leg. 608B. Morales sent St. Maxent 200 pesos to help the Valenzuela "hospital," with the medicine to be sent shortly ([Morales] to [St. Maxent], New Orleans, August 11, [1779], AGI, PC, leg. 608B; Anselmo Blanchard to the governor, Valenzuela, August 1, 1779, AGI, PC, leg. 192).

7. Blanchard to the governor, Valenzuela, August 1, 1779; Judice to the governor, Lafourche des Chetimachas, July 9, August 26, 1779; St. Maxent to the governor, Valenzuela, August 1, 1779; [Gálvez] to St. Maxent, New Orleans, August 26, 1779; Judice, "Statement of Militia Company," Lafourche des Chetimachas, August 27, 1779, all in AGI, PC, leg. 192.

8. Judice to the governor, Lafourche des Chetimachas, September 4, 19, 1779, AGI, PC, leg. 192; Caughey, *Bernardo de Gálvez in Spanish Louisiana*, 150–51. Antonio de St. Maxent saw action at Manchac and Baton Rouge; see his memoria to the king, New Orleans, July, 1794, attached to Carondelet to Luis de Las Casas, New Orleans, July 15, 1794, AGI, PC, leg. 1443A.

By October, with the war moving on to a new theater of operations, Valenzuela calmed down considerably. St. Maxent devoted himself to record keeping and the dispensation of rations; births, marriages, and deaths kept complicating his bookkeeping. As illness declined, the community finally acquired a physician. After visiting the region, Dr. Juan Vives settled down on Bayou Lafourche, where he spent the rest of his life. The twenty-five-year-old native of Denia, Valencia, in Spain, served the Isleños, the other bayou residents, and the local militia units. The doctor acquired lands above Valenzuela (today the Belle Alliance plantation) and married Marguerite Bujol, the Acadian widow of Joseph Constant, on February 8, 1780. Over the years, Valenzuela commandants employed Vives to take messages to New Orleans and bring supplies back.[9]

St. Maxent's November report emphasized the advancements of his settlers. They produced a small harvest; the construction of houses continued; and they were fencing in the community as well as their farms. The houses were said to be thirty feet by fifteen feet, and to have two doors, three windows, a chimney, and a gallery six feet wide on one side of the house. The same size house was then being built in New Iberia for the Malagueño families. All three soldiers posted at Valenzuela wished to marry Isleño girls. One soldier, Diego Ortiz, married María Antonia Quintana, and they eventually had ten children who lived.[10] Compared to Galveztown and Barataria, Valenzuela had had a good start. The calamities that produced so much hardship elsewhere caused far less suffering there.

Because of better times, the inhabitants had a large celebration on Christmas Eve, 1779. Father Angel of the Ascension church married six couples and baptized two infants; two other weddings were scheduled for the near future. The Valenzuela residents announced that they had

9.   St. Maxent to Morales, No. 4, Valenzuela, November 25, 1779, AGI, PC, leg. 608B; St. Maxent to the governor, Valenzuela, November 26, 1779, AGI, PC, leg. 192; Sidney Marchand, Sr., *An Attempt to Reassemble the Old Settlers in Family Groups* (Baton Rouge, 1965), 100; Catholic Diocese of Baton Rouge, *Catholic Church Records*, 722. Vives' service sheets are in AGI, PC, leg. 161A.

10.   St. Maxent to the governor, Valenzuela, November 1 and 26, 1779, AGI, PC, legs. 193A and 192 respectively; draft; New Orleans, November 15, 1779, AGI, PC, leg. 192. See also St. Maxent to the governor, Valenzuela, October, 1779, AGI, PC, leg. 192. One of the soldiers who wished to marry María Marrero was identified as Diego R, perhaps Romero. See [Gálvez] to St. Maxent, New Orleans, November 30, 1779, AGI, PC, leg. 192. The governor sent patents of sublieutenant for Francisco Corbo and lieutenant for Dr. Vives.

adopted St. Bernard as their patron saint. In January, 1780, St. Maxent brought eighty additional persons to settle there.[11]

Although conditions looked propitious at the start of the year, problems arose in the spring. Indians moved about restlessly, fighting one another and frightening the settlers. St. Maxent wanted to build a small earthen fort as a citadel, although the natives refrained from any overt hostile act. More important was the food shortage as the inhabitants were still far from self-sufficient. St. Maxent searched in the older establishments on the Mississippi for corn, peas, and rice to buy. By June 12, rations cost 14,884 *reales*, but the next month the commandant predicted a good fall harvest. He was wrong, however, and rations continued for many colonists.[12]

Excitement roused lower Louisiana in May, 1781, when the Anglo-American population of Natchez rebelled in a futile effort to support the beleaguered British garrison at Pensacola, which Gálvez was then attacking. Surprised by the rebellion, the Spaniards tried to react quickly. St. Maxent descended to New Orleans to take charge of the New Orleans colored militia, while Judice commanded his own troops as well as the Valenzuela militia. Judice brought them to Baton Rouge to guard against an attack there, but their absence from Valenzuela and Lafourche was short. Upon learning that Pensacola had surrendered in May, the authorities decided to employ peaceful means to reduce the Natchez rebels. Meanwhile, Lafourche des Chetimachas held a celebration to honor Gálvez' victory, and the priest sang a Te Deum at the Ascension church. The militiamen fired a seventeen-gun salute and jubilantly discharged their muskets. In June, Louisiana militia units recovered Natchez without firing a shot.[13]

11. St. Maxent to the governor, Valenzuela, January 4, 1780, AGI, PC, leg. 192; St. Maxent to Morales, Valenzuela, January 4, 1780, AGI, PC, 608B; St. Maxent to Piernas, with Piernas' reply attached, Valenzuela, April 23, 1780, AGI, PC, leg. 193A.

12. St. Maxent to Martín Navarro, Valenzuela, May 1, 1780, AGI, PC, leg. 603B; [Morales] to [St. Maxent], New Orleans, June 28, 1780, and St. Maxent to Morales, Valenzuela, July 2, 1780, both in AGI, PC, leg. 608B; Nicolás López to the [governor], Valenzuela, n.d. but near the end of 1780, AGI, PC, leg. 193A; Judice to the governor, Lafourche des Chetimachas, January 6, 1781, with draft reply of Governor Gálvez to Judice, New Orleans, January 9, 1781, AGI, PC, leg. 194.

13. AGI, PC, leg. 194 contains many letters on the 1781 Natchez uprising and the consequences to the establishments downriver. See in particular [Piernas] to Judice, New Orleans, May 6, 1781; Judice to [Piernas], Lafourche [des Chetimachas], May 11, 1781; [Piernas] to [?], [New Orleans] [May, 1781]; Piernas to López, New Orleans, May 6, 1781; Judice to [Miró], Lafourche des Chetimachas, May 18 and 26, 1781. On published materials, see John Walton Caughey, "The Natchez Rebellion of 1781 and Its Aftermath," *Louisiana Historical Quarterly*, XVI (1933), 57–83.

St. Maxent never returned to Valenzuela, as Governor Gálvez reassigned him to Galveztown to bring it the prosperity that the Lafourche settlement enjoyed. Militia captain Anselmo Blanchard took charge of Valenzuela in August and commanded for the next several years. During this time, the settlers produced a third harvest in the fall, and Brother Casiano de Catanares considered opening a primary school there to educate the children if the government would provide him with a house and small salary. For unknown reasons, the school never opened. That condition did not differ from those at the other rural settlements of Louisiana, where illiteracy and ignorance prevailed. The Isleños had arrived as a largely unlettered population, and the government felt no compulsion to change their status.[14]

In late 1781, sixty-four settlers of approximately two hundred remained on rations. When the government attempted to end them completely, several Isleños protested in New Orleans. Morales, in charge of funding the settlements, asked Commandant Blanchard to identify the neediest families. Blanchard conducted a house-by-house survey of the community, showing that there were more than nine or ten families requiring assistance. Among them was Vicente San Pedro, a Spaniard, who had joined the settlement two years before. When Blanchard sent his report to Morales, Vicente and Gregorio Rodríguez, with their young sister, went to the city to live permanently. Morales approved their relocation and extended rations at Valenzuela until the 1782 harvest. The government also helped in other ways, such as rebuilding Manuel Rodríguez' house after it burned down.[15]

Government help was needed because 1782 brought setbacks. On March 20, a tornado hit Valenzuela, knocking down four houses and strewing debris over a six-arpent area. Miraculously, no one was injured. Morales provided funds to rebuild the houses. That spring, floods

14. Sergeant López was in charge of Valenzuela until Anselmo Blanchard arrived; several of López' letters are in AGI, PC, leg. 608B. Also see Blanchard to Morales, Valenzuela, August 22, 1781, *ibid.* In his memoria of July, 1794, St. Maxent stated that he became a captain on March 1, 1781, and remained as commandant of Valenzuela until July 11, 1781 (memoria attached to Carondelet to Las Casas, New Orleans, July 15, 1794, AGI, PC, leg. 1443A). López to Piernas, Valenzuela, September 20, 1781, AGI, PC, leg. 194; López to Morales, Valenzuela, December 10, 1781, AGI, PC, leg. 608B; [Morales] to Blanchard, New Orleans, October 2, 1781, which is a reply to Blanchard's letter of September 20, 1781, AGI, PC, leg. 608B.
15. Blanchard to Morales, Valenzuela, November 12, 1781 (with Morales' draft reply of November 15 on the margin), November 27, December 15 and 31, 1781; [Morales] to [Blanchard], New Orleans, December 19, 1781, and January 8, 1782, all in AGI, PC, leg. 608B.

harmed the Isleños for the first time since their arrival. The levees the settlers had built on the bayou seem to have held back the high waters until then, when they inundated the lands of Juan José Martínez, destroying his crops. He petitioned Morales for continued rations or to live elsewhere. The official permitted him to leave, and instructed Blanchard to give the Martínez lands to someone who would work them.[16]

Only the Rodríguez children are known to have left Valenzuela prior to 1782, but no doubt others also left. That year an exodus began that continued over the years. Jaime Campana, Juan Martín, and Francisco Machado all asked permission to leave, and they probably did. Although Commandant Blanchard had instructions to give out abandoned lands to others, he did not. Consequently, roads and levees of deserted farms quickly fell into disrepair, resulting in damage and inconvenience to the neighbors. Neglected roads and levees remained a major source of complaint during the Spanish era.[17]

By 1782 the mortality rate for Valenzuela adults had declined, but the hazards of frontier life nevertheless took a heavy toll on children, particularly infants. That year eleven persons died in Valenzuela—eight infants or children below the age of two, two children ages eight and ten, and Domingo Truxillo, who succumbed at forty-eight. Summer remained the deadly season, as eight of the children perished during those months.[18]

When it was expected that Valenzuela would become self-sufficient, misfortune struck again. In early 1783, floods damaged the crops on Bayou Lafourche, and rations continued throughout the year. Residents also claimed that Blanchard was cheating them. Captain Antonio de St. Maxent, who investigated the allegation, learned that since Blanchard received no compensation for collecting the money for rations in New Orleans, he discounted a half peso per person monthly. Governor Miró

16. Blanchard to Morales, Valenzuela, March 21, May 15, August 1, 1782; [Morales] to Blanchard, [New Orleans], March 23, August 20, 1782, all in AGI, PC, leg. 608B. Morales complained in April, 1782, that more people than just the needy were receiving rations in Valenzuela; he sent Captain Antonio de St. Maxent to investigate (Morales to Navarro, New Orleans, April 3, 1782, AGI, PC, leg. 606).
17. Blanchard to Monsieur, Valenzuela, December 27, 1782, AGI, PC, leg. 195; [Morales] to Blanchard, New Orleans, August 10, 1782, and Blanchard to Morales, Valenzuela, September 6, 1782, both in AGI, PC, leg. 608B.
18. Blanchard, "Relación de los . . . que han muerto . . . ," Valenzuela, May 15, 1783, AGI, PC, leg. 196. In the same year, 4 male infants were born.

ordered Blanchard to stop that practice and to give the settlers food, not money.[19]

For several years, Valenzuela Isleños attended church services in neighboring Ascension. Until Father Angel died in December, 1784, he occasionally visited the Isleños in their own settlement for baptisms, marriages, and burials. Perhaps because of the increase in parishioners, in October, 1781, the Isleños proposed a new building measuring 30 feet by 30 feet. The lowest bid they received, however, 1,200 pesos, exceeded their expectations. By negotiating with the contractor, they agreed to make four annual payments of 300 pesos. They met the first installment in 1783 but fell 60 pesos short the next year. An unexpected development in 1782 was Father Angel's departure for Natchez for about a year. Although he asked to remain there, in 1783 he resumed his duties in Ascension.[20]

While Valenzuela lacked a church and resident priest, no shortage of alcoholic spirits existed after 1781. Santiago (Jaime) Campana operated the first tavern for a year. Soon Miguel Homs opened his own establishment. In 1782 Commandant Blanchard allowed Andrés de Vega to take over the concession, but Homs protested successfully to the governor. By December, he was again operating his tavern. Two years later, Governor Miró granted Miguel Suárez, who was physically unfit to perform agricultural work, an exclusive license to run a cabaret in exchange for an eighty-peso yearly fee. Valenzuela residents protested the violation of the 1783 agreement according to which anyone could sell liquor, and they offered to raise the eighty pesos themselves, using the money to benefit the church. After changing his mind several times because of contradictory information, the exasperated Miró finally let both Suárez and Homs operate taverns, with each donating forty pesos to the church building fund.[21]

19. Blanchard to Monsieur, Valenzuela, January 12, March 9, 1783, and Antonio de St. Maxent to Morales, Valenzuela, March [1?], 1783, both in AGI, PC, leg. 608B. The residents, Blanchard claimed, wanted a two-*real* daily ration or twice as much ([Morales] to Blanchard, New Orleans, January 13, 1783, AGI, PC, leg. 608B; [Miró] to Blanchard, New Orleans, June 3, 1783, AGI, PC, leg. 196).

20. Judice to Monsieur, Lafourche [des Chetimachas], October 19, 1781, with petition dated October 1, 1781, and draft [?] to Judice, [New Orleans], October, 1781, both in AGI, PC, leg. 194; Revillagodos to the governor, [Lafourche des Chetimachas?], March 7, 1784, and Piernas to Miró, Natchez, November 3, 1782, February 3, 1783, all in AGI, PC, leg. 9A.

21. Blanchard to Monsieur, Valenzuela, December 27, 1782, AGI, PC, leg. 195; Blanchard to [Morales], Valenzuela, August 13, November 4, 1784, AGI, PC, leg. 608B; López to Miró, Valenzuela, November 21, 1784, and [Miró] to Nicholas Verret, New Orleans, November 28, December 6, 1784, all in AGI, PC, leg. 198B.

When Commandant Blanchard abruptly quit his post in 1784, Sergeant López, the ranking soldier in Valenzuela, wrote an unflattering account of him. Blanchard had cared little for the settlement, performed his duties poorly, and failed to supply rations to the widows and orphans for three months. Twenty-three to twenty-five persons still received aid in mid-1784. The roads and levees had fallen into disrepair because Blanchard had neglected to give abandoned lands to new settlers. López blamed him for the Isleños being burdened with debts. The accuracy of the sergeant's accusations is uncertain because López asked to be appointed commandant of Valenzuela. Governor Miró, however, named Nicholas Verret to the post.[22]

A new census about mid-1784 listed 174 persons in 46 families in Valenzuela. Among them, Isleños numbered 154 individuals in 40 families. The census showed the diminution in the Canarian population. Only the Spaniard Vicente San Pedro owned a slave, while several families reportedly lacked houses. The common farm consisted of 3 arpents of bayou front by 40 deep. The Isleños owned no cattle for beef or for milk, a few had several pigs, and more than half had chickens. Most of the families produced corn, ranging from 30 to 40 barrels. Fewer than 30 persons were on government rations. Of those persons remaining after five years, approximately 80 percent were self-sustaining. Nevertheless, few had prospered, and most lived in poverty. To underscore their wretchedness, in 1785 the entire Isleño community petitioned the government for clothing. The settlers claimed they could not afford to buy even a shirt. While it is not known if they received the clothes they sought, records show that rations continued through the year.[23]

In 1784 Governor Miró restated the boundary line between the Lafourche and Valenzuela districts. The first forty arpents on the bayou from the Mississippi belonged to Lafourche, after which the Valenzuela district began. But Commandant Verret ran into difficulties in measuring the forty arpents because the bayou curved. The problem of the dividing line quieted until late 1789, when the Isleños asked for titles to their land. This raised the question of how far into the interior their lands

22. López to Miró, Valenzuela, October 5, 1784, and Verret to the governor, n.p., September 12 and 24, 1784, all in AGI, PC, leg. 198B; Blanchard to the governor, [Valenzuela], September 10, 1784, and [Miró] to Blanchard, New Orleans, September 21, 1784, both in AGI, PC, leg. 192.
23. Blanchard, census, Valenzuela, 1784, AGI, PC, leg. 192; Verret's service sheet, Lafourche [des Chetimachas], December 31, 1784, AGI, PC, leg. 203.

extended; earlier grants on the Mississippi had given those settlers forty arpents of depth as well. At issue were valuable cypress groves. Miró attempted to compromise by dividing the land between rival claimants in 1790, but the Mississippi residents protested since their grants had been made first. Although they demanded compensation, it is doubtful that the governor acquiesced.[24]

Information on Valenzuela in 1785 and 1786 is not extensive. In this period more than 800 Acadians settled in the vicinity of Valenzuela, on Bayou Lafourche and on the Mississippi, at government expense. The population of Lafourche Interior, as the Valenzuela district was increasingly called, numbered only 352 before their arrival; afterwards, it rose to 1,500 in 1788. While several Acadian families settled among the Canarians, the majority acquired lands below them for several leagues on both sides of the bayou. Their larger numbers in time submerged the Isleños.[25]

In 1787 the Acadians asked for a church, prompting the Canary Islanders to insist that it be built in Valenzuela, where Governor Gálvez had set aside land. If it were not, several Isleños threatened not to contribute toward its construction. Government policy or tradition required the settlers themselves to pay its cost. Commandant Verret, however, preferred a more central location than Valenzuela since farms now stretched for twelve leagues on the bayou. But Governor Miró said he needed royal permission to assign a priest to Lafourche Interior, and Spain failed to answer his request.[26]

Rations, debts, and taverns consumed the time of Commandant Verret in the late 1780s. Although optimistic about a good harvest in 1787, he urged continuing assistance to several settlers. A lack of prosperity had driven others into debt, particularly tavern keeper

24. [Miró] to Verret, New Orleans, December 20, 1784, and Verret to Miró, Valenzuela, January 25, 1785, both in AGI, PC, leg. 198B; Francisco Corbo *et al.*, petition, Valenzuela, March 26, 1785, enclosed in Verret to [Morales], Valenzuela, March 29, 1785, AGI, PC, leg. 608B; Morales to Martin Navarro, New Orleans, February 4 and 12, 1785, AGI, PC, leg. 606.
25. Fernando Solano Costa, "La emigración acadiana a la Luisiana española (1783–1785)," *Cuadernos de historia Jerónimo Zurita* II (1954), 82–125; Oscar William Winzerling, *Acadian Odyssey* (Baton Rouge, 1955). A published census of Bayou Lafourche is in Albert J. Robichaux, Jr. (ed.), *Louisiana Censuses and Militia Lists, 1770–1789*, (Harvey, La., n.d.), 115–46. Valenzuela censuses are in AGI, PC, legs. 202, 213, and 215A.
26. Verret to the governor, Valenzuela, February 25, March 12, 1787; Francisco Corbo, Matías Morrida, and Juan Alemán, petition to the governor, Valenzuela, March 11, 1787; [Miró] to Verret, New Orleans, March 29, 1787, all in AGI, PC, leg. 200.

Homs. After extending 180 pesos of credit to local residents, he could not collect. Homs repeatedly appealed to the governor to help him recover bad debts and to stop the opening of new taverns. Several other people besides Homs also dispensed alcoholic beverages, and all complained about illegal sales. They wanted the property of illegal vendors confiscated and sold to benefit the church. Of the tavern owners, Miró favored Homs, whom he called an honest man, and renewed his license for two years at twenty-five pesos per year.[27]

In 1787 the possibility of a smallpox epidemic alarmed lower Louisiana. Since medical opinion had not fully accepted innoculation as a preventative measure, Governor Miró permitted each person to choose for himself. In November, Commandant Verret took precautions against the dreaded disease. He favored innoculation and railed against the few who refused to immunize themselves. It appears that the threat of an epidemic was only a scare since the smallpox did little harm to Valenzuela.[28]

While Lafourche Interior stayed without a church or priest, Friar Pedro de Zamora, a Capuchin, served Lafourche for two and a half years in the late 1780s. A stern prelate, he complained of the rude conduct of the parishioners and their failure to show respect during mass and other religious ceremonies. On April 6, 1788, he ejected from the church a resident who entered with his hat on, smoking, and talking "as if he were in a public square." Zamora also charged several inhabitants with immoral conduct and demanded that the governor drive the miscreants from the parish. Zamora's allegations must not have been true because Governor Miró removed him instead in early 1789, after the residents lodged numerous grievances against him.[29]

The early 1790s saw the revival of old problems. Homs tried to collect bad debts, and several Isleños owed substantial sums of money. More important, however, the Lafourche Interior inhabitants renewed their

27. Miguel Homs to the governor, New Orleans, June 22, 1786; [Miró] to Verret, New Orleans, June 8, 1786; Verret to the governor, Valenzuela, July 13, 1786, all in AGI, PC, leg. 199.
28. [Miró] to Verret, New Orleans, June 6, October 24, 1787, and Verret to Miró, Valenzuela, November 8 and 22, 1787, all in AGI, PC, leg. 200; [Miró] to Verret, New Orleans, June 5, 1788, AGI, PC, leg. 201; [Miró] to Nicholas Verbois, [New Orleans], July 27, 1787, AGI, PC, leg. 200.
29. Fr. Pedro de Zamora to Miró, Lafourche des Chetimachas, 1788, AGI, PC, leg. 201; see also his earlier letter to the governor, Lafourche [des Chetimachas], April 23, 1786, AGI, PC, leg. 199; Zamora, asiento, AGI, PC, leg. 538B.

effort to obtain a church and priest. They brought the matter to the attention of the new governor, the Barón de Carondelet, in 1792. He responded favorably and said that a priest would be sent out shortly. Meanwhile, they should build him a house in Valenzuela. But Verret still objected to the Valenzuela site for the sake of the settlers at the south end of the district. Moreover, most of the Isleños themselves no longer resided in Valenzuela, as they now lived on their farms. Only seven or eight families continued to live there, Verret claimed.[30]

In March, 1793, Lafourche Interior's first priest arrived, Father Bernardo de Deva, before there was either a house or a church for him. Moreover, the question of where to put the church had not yet been resolved. After Deva and Verret listened to the residents' opinions, they agreed that the center of the parish would be best. Verret and Father Josef Arazena, priest at Lafourche since 1789, also amicably resolved the problem of the dividing line between the two parishes. They placed it on the left bank at Valenzuela's south edge and on the right bank below the land of Andrés de Vega. The line placed twenty-seven or twenty-eight families, most of them Canarian, in Arazena's parish. Although Carondelet approved the boundary on May 19, a number of Isleños appealed unsuccessfully. Ninety of them, led by Francisco López Machado, signed a petition on May 25, insisting that the church be built in Valenzuela. This only delayed construction as Verret again listened to the preferences of the inhabitants. They could only agree that the church building be eighty feet long and thirty-five feet wide, with the presbytery built on the same grand scale.[31]

Before a solution came, Father Arazena of Ascension Parish died of fever on August 25. Governor Carondelet then assigned Deva to serve

30.   [Miró] to Judice, New Orleans, October 1, 1791, AGI, PC, leg. 204; [Carondelet] to Verret, New Orleans, February 16, March 9, 1792, AGI, PC, leg. 206; Verret to Miró, New Orleans, September 29, 1790, Verret to Carondelet, Lafourche Interior, October 30, 1792, and draft [Carondelet] to Verret, October 22, 1792, all in AGI, PC, leg. 216A.

31.   [Carondelet] to Verret, New Orleans, March 14, May 13 and 21, 1793, and Verret to Carondelet, Lafourche Interior, October 30, 1792, April [9?], May 1, 1793, all in AGI, PC, leg. 216A; Josef Arazena, asiento, AGI, PC, leg. 538B; Verret to Carondelet, with Carondelet's marginal notation, Lafourche Interior, May 7, 1793, Thirso Henrique Henríquez to Bernardo de Deva, New Orleans, May 13, 1793, and [Carondelet] to Verret, New Orleans, May 15, 1793, all in AGI, PC, leg. 207B. See also Verret to Carondelet, Lafourche Interior, June 4, July 19, 1793, AGI, PC, leg. 207B; [Carondelet] to Verret, New Orleans, August 28, 1793, and Verret to the governor, Lafourche Interior, September 16, October 6, 1793, all in AGI, PC, leg. 216A. The estimated cost of the large church was between seven and eight thousand pesos.

both parishes temporarily. The friar complained that the two parishes were huge and that he had to travel constantly. Besides that, he lacked adequate housing, horses, and pay. Father Deva pleaded several times to be relieved of the onerous burden thrust on him.[32]

Overall, Valenzuela suffered from fewer natural disasters than the other Isleño settlements. But on the night of August 20, 1794, a hurricane lasting seven to eight hours hit Valenzuela, destroying several houses and leveling fields. Verret predicted mediocre crops that year and suffering for the poor families. He again asked the governor for assistance. But Carondelet was not amenable, replying that each district had the responsibility of caring for its own indigent. The governor's attitude revealed patently that government aid to the Isleños had ended.[33]

In the last decade of Spanish rule, more orders and complaints about roads and levees appeared in the documentation. In 1794 Carondelet instructed Commandant Verret that the inhabitants were to keep the roads and levees in good repair and remove the trees that toppled onto the thoroughfares. Each landowner had responsibility for his own properties; if he failed to keep them in good order, it would be done at his expense, plus a twenty-five peso fine. Carondelet set the months of October and November, after the harvest and when the river was normally low, for work on the levees.[34]

In the 1790s, as the population of the districts increased, the government authorized syndics to assist the local post commandants in government. Pedro Doncel, a former sergeant stationed at Valenzuela and married to an Isleño woman, Juana Ximénez, served as a syndic in the early 1790s; Andrés de Vega, a local leader among the Isleños, served from 1794 on. Verret remarked in 1795 about the difficulty of choosing

32.   Judice to Carondelet, Lafourche des Chetimachas, August 26, September 22, 1793, and Deva to Carondelet, Lafourche Interior, August 30, 1793, all in AGI, PC, leg. 208A; Patricio Walsh to Carondelet, New Orleans, September 3, 1793, AGI, PC, leg. 27A; Deva to Walsh, La Assumpcion de la Fourche de Valenzuela, September 30, December 4, 1793, AGI, PC, leg. 208B; Deva to Carondelet, Lafourche des Chetimachas, May 1, November 12, 1794, AGI, PC, legs. 28 and 30 respectively.

33.   Verret to Carondelet, Lafourche Interior, September 2, 1794, with Carondelet's reply, New Orleans, September 9, 1794, AGI, PC, leg. 209. In a letter to Nicholas Verbois, commandant at Cabahannocer, August 30, 1793, *ibid.*, Carondelet stated emphatically that each district must look after its own poor.

34.   See Carondelet to Verbois, New Orleans, October 10, 1794, AGI, PC, leg. 209, which also applied to Valenzuela.

syndics since most of the people, including the Canarians, were illiterate.[35]

A census of slaves made in August, 1795, in order to collect funds provides another interesting insight into Lafourche Interior. Of the Spaniards, Juan Vives had 21 slaves, José Díaz had 1, and the Acostas owned 5, in a total of 253 slaves. The Acadians owned the rest. The census seems to confirm the destitute condition in which the Isleños arrived. All the owners protested poverty in 1795 and their inability to pay the six *reales* per slave assessment to compensate the Pointe Coupée masters who lost more than fifty slaves. Governor Carondelet rejected their plea and ordered them to pay. He probably correctly surmised that the Bayou Lafourche slaveholders were not as destitute as they affected.[36]

Relief for the overworked priest Bernardo de Deva arrived in 1795. By October 20, the governor assigned Father Francisco Notario, of the Order of Preachers, to Ascension. Three days later, he took charge of the parish, and soon launched a barrage of complaints. He found the presbytery indecent, alleged that the parishioners refused to help him, and reported that unknown persons shot at his pigs. He retaliated by hurling jabs at Commandant Judice, who, Notario claimed, had a bad record of insulting priests: Father Angel de Revillagodos had died of grief brought on by Judice; Friar Pedro de Zamora, now living in Opelousas, had departed rather than submit to mistreatment; and the commandant's unpleasantness toward Father Arazena had produced his death. Judice's other faults included alcoholism, indigence, and poor administration. After repeated pleas to be relieved, Notario was replaced by Father Gregory White in June, 1798.[37]

Meanwhile, Deva returned to his own parish, now named La Assumpción de Nuestra Señora de La Fourche de Chetimachas de Valenzuela. Against the wishes of the Isleños, the church was built

35. On syndics, see Nicholas Verret's note of 1793 in AGI, PC, leg. 207A; Verret to Carondelet, with attachment, Lafourche Interior, June 10, 1795, AGI, PC, leg. 211A; and Verret's proposals for 1797, Lafourche Interior, December 15, 1796, AGI, PC, leg. 203.

36. Verret to Carondelet, Lafourche Interior, August 25, 1795; Judice to the governor, Lafourche des Chetimachas, August 31, 1795; [Carondelet] to Verret, New Orleans, September 5, 1795, all in AGI, PC, leg. 211A.

37. [Carondelet] to Judice, New Orleans, October 20, 1795, and Judice to Carondelet, Lafourche des Chetimachas, October 25, 1795, both in AGI, PC, leg. 211A; [Carondelet] to Judice, New Orleans, December 7, 1796, Francisco Notario, petitions to the governor, Ascension Parish, October 4, November 20, 1796, and an undated letter but probably December, 1796, all in AGI, PC, leg. 212; Francisco Notario, asiento, AGI, PC, leg. 538B.

several miles below Valenzuela, in present-day Plattenville. Here in 1796 Bishop Luis de Peñalver briefly visited the church, which was then little better than a shack. The small edifice remained in use until 1819. Deva served Assumption Parish until the end of the Spanish period.[38]

In September, 1797, Governor Manuel Gayoso removed Judice as commandant of Lafourche des Chetimachas, replacing him with the American Evan Jones. Gayoso also attached the Valenzuela Isleños in spiritual and temporal matters to that district. After taking office, Jones soon clashed with the Canarians. Early in 1798, he exhorted the Lafourche inhabitants to keep the levees in good repair; if they did not, their lands would be forfeited and given to persons who would, or they would be fined the expense of repairing the levees. The Isleños chafed under Jones's high-handed tactics. They charged that he had ordered them to work on royal lands and to pay for repairing the church levees. Jones denied the allegation and suggested that Andrés de Vega be punished for promoting sedition. In July, Vega, Fernando Rodríguez, and Juan Hernández brought more serious charges against Jones. The commandant had ordered Vega to gather a number of men for three or four days to work on the royal levee. They refused because they were then laboring in their own fields. Moreover, the levees Jones wanted repaired were on the Mississippi's left bank (and they lived on the right side), several leagues away. Jones had not offered to pay them, and they knew the government compensated workers for such labor. When Vega so informed Jones, the latter belittled the Canary Islanders and assessed them two *reales* per arpent for the church levee and one *real* per arpent for the levees they refused to repair.[39]

To obtain the truth, Governor Gayoso sent Captain Francisco Rivas to Valenzuela to investigate. On August 23, he met with the Isleños in Vega's house. They told him that they did not wish to work on the Mississippi, where they did not own lands; that their own fields kept them busy; and that Jones's insensitive attitude distressed them. Rivas learned that Vega enjoyed the support of the Spaniards, who feared that

38. Bernardo de Deva, asientos, AGI, PC, leg. 538B; Baudier, *The Catholic Church in Louisiana*, 221, 236, 239.

39. Judice to Gayoso, New Orleans, September 25, 1797, Jones to the governor, Lafourche des Chetimachas, December 28, 1797, [Gayoso] to Jones, New Orleans, December 30, 1797, all in AGI, PC, leg. 213; Jones to the governor, Lafourche des Chetimachas, April 15, 1798, Vega, "Lista de los Avitantes de mi distrito . . . ," Valenzuela, March 4, 1798, petition of Isleños, Valenzuela, March 6, 1798, Andrés de Vega, petition, Valenzuela, July 17, 1798, all in AGI, PC, leg. 215A.

he would be removed as syndic. They petitioned Gayoso to retain Vega and not to appoint a person of a different nation because they did not understand foreign languages.[40]

Before Rivas submitted his report, Jones resigned on September 3, claiming he needed to put his personal affairs in order. Gayoso replaced him with Lieutenant Rafael Croquer, a Spaniard, who took charge before the end of the month. Meanwhile, Valenzuela continued without prosperity, if the settlers could be believed. When Governor Gayoso attempted to collect a money contribution from the Bayou Lafourche residents in May, 1799, to help in the war against Britain, they pleaded that poverty prevented them from making any kind of donation but their lives.[41]

In November, 1799, following Gayoso's death, acting governor Casa Calvo appointed Lieutenant Vicente Fernández Texeiro as commandant of Valenzuela, replacing Verret. Fernández Texeiro's appointment pleased the Canary Islanders since he was a Spaniard. When rumors surfaced that he was being transferred, they petitioned that he remain, praising him for his help to the poor, his zeal for the public welfare, his disinterest, and the love for him by people of various nations. Of those who signed the petition, thirty-two were Spaniards and twenty French. Nevertheless, Casa Calvo sent Fernández Texeiro to Ouachita and temporarily reappointed Auguste Verret.[42]

Nearly a year later, Casa Calvo sent to Valenzuela militia lieutenant Tomás de Villanueva, an Isleño from St. Bernard, who assumed command on July 21, 1801. Villanueva found conditions in the district in a state of neglect. Levees and roads in disrepair and abandoned lands abounded. He gave out vacant farms to new owners and tried to make

40. [Gayoso] to Vega, New Orleans, August 20, 1798, and Jones to the governor, Lafourche des Chetimachas, August 28, 1798, both in AGI, PC, leg. 215A; Rivas to Gayoso, Iberville, September 7, 1798, Domingo Escanio, Juan Alemán, Gaspar Falcón, and Martín de Urso, petition, Valenzuela, August 28, 1798, Vega, petition to the governor, Valenzuela, August 28, 1798, all in AGI, PC, leg. 44.

41. Jones to the governor, Lafourche des Chetimachas, September 3, 1798, [Gayoso] to Jones, New Orleans, September 13, 1798, all in AGI, PC, leg. 215A; Rafael Croquer to Gayoso, Lafourche des Chetimachas, September 28, 1798, AGI, PC, leg. 50; Auguste Verret to Gayoso, [Valenzuela] dans Lafourche, April 8, May 22, 1799, AGI, PC, leg. 216A.

42. [Casa Calvo] to Verret, New Orleans, November 14, 1799, and Verret to Casa Calvo, Lafourche [Interior], December 6, 1799, both in AGI, PC, leg. 216A; Nicolás María Vidal to Casa Calvo, New Orleans, November 9, 1799, June 16, 1800, Vidal to [Juan] Filhiol, New Orleans, June 16, 1800, and Antonio Martínez *et al.*, petition, Valenzuela de Lafourche, June 4, 1800, all in AGI, PC, leg. 71A; Casa Calvo to Vicente Texeiro, June 6 and 10, 1800, and Auguste Verret to Casa Calvo, [Valenzuela] dans Lafourche, July 16, 1800, all in AGI, PC, leg. 217A.

repairs. In agriculture, the residents dedicated themselves almost exclusively to growing cotton as a cash crop, as it was then becoming a major export in Louisiana. Lafourche's soil was eminently suited to cotton, and Villanueva believed that the residents would have a good harvest that year.[43]

Contrary to the repeated protestations of poverty to the government, a number of Bayou Lafourche Isleños appeared to be prospering as the Spanish era ended, and owned more lands, cattle, horses, and even slaves than ever. One such diligent farmer was Miguel Suárez, who, in 1799, proposed to sell his property. Commandant Rafael Croquer presided at an inventory made of Suárez' property, with Estevan Hernández and Fernando Rodríguez acting as witnesses. The appraisal of the property listed a French plow, a 40-foot pirogue, and 8 slaves (3 adults and 5 children); the value of his personal property amounted to 2,953 pesos. Suárez also owned 3 arpents of bayou front 40 arpents deep and a house that measured 28 feet by 13 feet, with a gallery. The land also had a kitchen, a storehouse, a warehouse, a stable, two slave cabins, fences, and a "good" garden with many fruit trees, all valued at a modest 500 pesos.[44]

Among the Ascension Parish records in the last year of Spanish dominion is the marriage contract between José Hernández and Juana Truxillo, made on August 13, 1803. Juana was the daughter of Antonio Truxillo and María Domínguez, and José was the son of José Hernández and Isabel Rodríguez, all of Lafourche, Ascension Parish. The prospective groom owned 3 arpents of front having the ordinary depth, located next to the land of Andrés de Vega (opposite the Valenzuela village), valued at 600 pesos; he also had several head of cattle and horses, worth an additional 114 pesos. Juana's property consisted of a twelve-year-old female slave, estimated at 500 pesos, and a few horses and cattle, appraised at 100 pesos. She was also an heiress of her parents' property. The contract stipulated that if no children were born, each was heir to the

43. Vidal to Casa Calvo, with enclosure [Casa Calvo] to Vidal, New Orleans, May 19, 1801, AGI, PC, leg. 72; [Casa Calvo] to Auguste Verret, New Orleans, June 27, 1801, AGI, PC, leg. 218; Tomás de Villanueva Barroso to Manuel Juan de Salcedo, Valenzuela, August 25, 1801, and Valenzuela dans Lafourche, August 25, 1801, with memorial from the inhabitants of July 31, 1801, all in AGI, PC, leg. 77B; Villanueva to Morales, Valenzuela, August 25, 1801, September 15, 1802, January 2, 1803, all in AGI, PC, leg. 608B.

44. Ascension Parish Courthouse Records, Donaldsonville, Louisiana, "Land, 1799," 107–16.

other; if children were born, they became the heirs. José and Juana married two days later at the Ascension church.[45]

As Spanish sovereignty in Louisiana ended in 1803, conditions became unsettled in Valenzuela. By December several leading Spaniards were making plans for the new era. Father Deva, claiming poor health after twenty-one years of service in Cuba and Louisiana, asked to retire in the province with a monthly pension of twenty pesos. The government granted his request. Almost at the same time, Juan Vives, surgeon to the Isleños for twenty-four and a half years, requested a two-year delay in leaving in order to sell his property, recover debts, and move his family. A royal order of May, 1804, approved his petition. Vives, however, like the majority of the Valenzuela Isleños, never left.[46]

Although Spain surrendered Louisiana on November 30, 1803, for the next seven years Baton Rouge and the western part of West Florida, not more than twenty miles away from Valenzuela, remained in Spanish hands. The nearby presence of Spanish officials and soil probably helped to calm Isleño fears. While a few Valenzuela Spaniards moved to West Florida, most of them accepted American sovereignty. Change came slowly on Bayou Lafourche, and American authorities did not disturb the settlers, allowing them to live quietly on their lands. Perhaps better economic conditions also induced them to remain. Throughout lower Louisiana, several thousand Spaniards—settlers, pensioners, widows, children, and New Orleans residents of many occupations—remained behind when the Spanish flag fluttered away.

45. Ascension Parish Courthouse Records, Donaldsonville, Louisiana, "Marriage Contracts, 1787–1809," 195–98; Catholic Diocese of Baton Rouge, *Catholic Church Records*, II, 380.

46. Salcedo and Casa Calvo to José Antonio Cavallero, New Orleans, January 20, 1804, and Deva, petition, New Orleans, January 18, 1804, both in AGI, SD, leg. 2570; Surveyor Joseph Montegut, Joaquín Ablanedo, and Dom[ingo] Fleitas, affidavit, New Orleans, January 16, 1804, and Deva to Casa Calvo, Lafourche Interior, October 18, 1804, both in AGI, SD, leg. 2570; Juan Vives, petition, New Orleans, December 31, 1803, with approval of Salcedo and Casa Calvo, New Orleans, January 20, 1804, Vives to Casa Calvo, Lafourche Interior, September 21, 1804, all in AGI, PC, leg. 73.

Six

The Beginning
of American Dominion

Writing in his *History of Louisiana*, E. Brunner declared in 1841: "There are scarcely any traces left of [Spain's] dominion of this country. Some Spanish names and a few Spanish families are still to be found in New Orleans; but these are not sufficient to make one suppose that it was ever a Spanish town." Brunner's statement was true only as far as the popular perception of Louisiana in the nineteenth century was concerned. For several reasons, the Canary Islanders became an almost forgotten people. Their numbers became diluted with Louisiana's rapid growth in population. Moreover, the state's Gallic character increased owing in part to the entry of French Creoles from Saint Domingue (Haiti), many of whom were expelled from Cuba in 1809. Furthermore, the French language enjoyed greater popularity with the American take-over, and its use remained strong until the Civil War. Barely one-sixth of the Louisiana population could speak English in 1804. Newspapers, schools, and officials openly employed French. The new currents overwhelmed Louisiana's Hispanic character, which had never been strong. Although travelers occasionally noted the Spaniards in the early nineteenth century, as time passed, their presence on Bayou Lafourche was generally overlooked or, as in St. Bernard, regarded as a curiosity. In many ways, the Isleños seemingly vanished. However, they still constituted a group of people several thousand in number, and in

the parishes of St. Bernard, Ascension, and Assumption, they continued their own way of life.[1]

Perhaps the first American official to visit the Isleño settlements above
New Orleans for Governor Claiborne was Dr. John Watkins. Although
negative about Spanish rule, he commented that the people were docile,
easily governed, and "from habit . . . disposed to respect and obey their
chiefs." He regarded the new, American-appointed commandants of
their settlements as important in beginning the Isleños' cultural transformation. He wrote to Governor Claiborne: "These Commandants must be
just and enlightened men who by degrees will introduce the American
laws and usages, and gradually bring the people acquaint[ance] with
representation and the true . . . principles of the Federal Constitution."[2]
Change, however, came more slowly than Dr. Watkins predicted.

With the American take-over, Spanish officials departed from Louisiana. From Lafourche des Chetimachas, Lieutenant Croquer went up to
Baton Rouge in Spanish West Florida, and Joseph L'Andry, a wealthy
farmer who had already acted as Croquer's substitute in the past,
received the appointment. He enjoyed the title "Juge de Paix," equiva-
lent to "justice of the peace." In the Galveztown district, where Dr.
Watkins observed only twenty-eight families, Lieutenant Tomás Estevan
also left, and Watkins named Alexander Morrie, a Scotsman, as civil
commandant. Watkins described Morrie, a twenty-year resident, as an
able man whose only fault was being a drunkard. At Valenzuela, Isleño
Tomás de Villanueva, who was only a militia officer, remained. In St.
Bernard, De la Ronde contemplated leaving with the Spanish authorities, but he eventually decided to remain in Louisiana, as did the
overwhelming majority of the Spanish civilians.[3]

The end of Spanish rule meant greater mobility for the Isleños since
Spanish policy had tried to keep them on their lands. Although Galveztown soon withered and died, a number of Canarians remained in the

1.   E. Brunner, *History of Louisiana, from Its Discovery and Settlement to the Present Time*
(New York, 1841), 178, 265. See also Joseph T. Hatfield, *William Claiborne: Jeffersonian
Centurion in the American Southwest* (Lafayette, La., 1976), 119; and George Dargo, *Jefferson's
Louisiana: Politics and the Clash of Legal Tradition* (Cambridge, Mass., 1975).

2.   Robertson (ed.), *Louisiana Under the Rule of Spain, France, and the United States*, II,
318–19.

3.   *Ibid.*, 312; [Salcedo] to Someruelos, May 31, 1803, in which is enclosed De la Ronde's
petition, St. Bernard, May 26, 1803, AGI, PC, leg. 155B; William H. Forsyth, "A Memorial to
Col. Pierre Denys de la Ronde," *L'Heritage*, III, No. 9 (January, 1980), 60–64.

district in preference to going to Baton Rouge. They claimed their lands on the Amite from the United States government. The old Galveztown Road, which the Spaniards had opened from the settlement to St. Gabriel on the Mississippi, fell into disuse and, by 1837, was no longer adequate for travel. By then material evidence of the Galveztown settlement had disappeared, and an Isleño descendant, Miguel Gonzales, plowed the site and made it into farmland. Vestiges of the old Spanish fort lasted longer, but they were gone by midcentury. Although the Galveztown cemetery remained in use at least until the 1830s, it, too, eventually vanished. Some of the Isleños who stayed in the district married among themselves, but others intermarried with the Acadians who also lived in the area. Most of the upper Ascension Parish residents preferred life in the countryside to that in the newly formed Galvez village.[4]

In neighboring Baton Rouge and East Baton Rouge Parish lived other Canarians, who through the nineteenth century kept their identity and often the use of the Spanish language. Although submerged by the Americans who flocked into the region, a number of former Galveztown residents lived in Baton Rouge's Spanish Town and elsewhere in the district growing sugarcane and cotton. Little is known about the Isleños of East Baton Rouge Parish, although they often appeared in nineteenth-century censuses. On occasion some of them emerged into the public spotlight, such as D. E. Pintado, who in 1818 was elected treasurer and collector of Baton Rouge. An article in *DeBow's Southern and Western Review* in 1852 commented on the longevity of several Isleños then living in Baton Rouge:

> Madame Acosta, born Truxillo, emigrated to Louisiana in the year 1765 [*sic*], at the age of nine years, and is now ninety-five. She enjoys excellent health, has a mind almost unimpaired, attends church to which she walks a distance of at least half a mile from the residence of her great grandchild, Mrs. Dufrocq, the wife of the mayor of Baton Rouge. Madame Arrayas was

4. Sidney Marchand, Sr., *The Story of Ascension Parish, Louisiana* (Baton Rouge, La., 1931), 43; and his *The Flight of a Century (1800–1900) in Ascension Parish, Louisiana* (Donaldsonville, La., 1936), 107. The voters in Galvez in 1847 numbered 38 (Sidney Marchand, Sr., *Across the Years* [Donaldsonville, La., 1949], 46). See the same author's *House of Marchand* (Donaldsonville, La., 1952), 11. Isleños having claims in Galveztown included Joseph Pereira, Joseph Alamo, Manuel Dias, James Bazilico, Maria Bermudez, Joseph Capitan, Thomas Collado, Maria Del Pino, John Diaz, Maria Dias, John Hernandez, Augustin Lombardo, Mathias Martin, Francis Massias, and Joseph Massias (Charles R. Maduell, Jr., *Federal Land Grants in the Territory of Orleans: The Delta Parishes* [New Orleans, 1975], 228, 246).

among the emigrants from the Canary Islands, who settled in Galveztown in 1774 [*sic*]. Her age is not exactly known, but is supposed to be upwards of ninety; she has but a confused recollection of early events.[5]

Several settlements in St. Bernard Parish probably owed their origins to the Isleños. Perhaps they were the sites where the first Canarian houses were constructed when the settlers arrived in 1779. St. Bernard and Bencheque—the latter community evolved into Reggio—appear to be the oldest Canary Islander establishments in the parish. The village of Violet, situated about two miles above the entrance to Terre-aux-Boeufs, dates from the early nineteenth century. La Chinche, similarly an Isleño settlement, evolved into Hopedale. For these tiny communities, possessing only a handful of houses, perhaps a tavern, and if lucky a store, the word *village* seemed an exaggeration. Despite its proximity to New Orleans, St. Bernard Parish stayed overwhelmingly rural until late in the nineteenth century. Only then did the area nearest to the Orleans Parish line, Arabi, attract growing numbers of people and businesses.[6]

A surge in economic activities in the first years of American rule produced modest development. At the junction of Bayou Lafourche and the Mississippi River, a small settlement had existed for years alongside the Church of the Ascension. In 1806 Donaldsonville was formally founded, and despite its diminutive size through the nineteenth century, it remained the only town of note between New Orleans and Baton Rouge. The name *Lafourche* stayed in use for the settlement until 1822. The town grew slowly and, in 1830, boasted only 492 inhabitants, of whom 261 were white. Over the years, a number of rural Isleños from Bayou Lafourche abandoned the agricultural way of life to live and work in the small delta community.[7]

---

5. J. St. Clair Favrot, "Baton Rouge, the Historic Capital of Louisiana," *Louisiana Historical Quarterly*, XII (1929), 620–21. For a description of Baton Rouge in the early 1820s, see Timothy Flint, *Recollections of the Last Ten Years in the Valley of the Mississippi*, ed. George R. Brooks (Boston, 1826; rpr. Carbondale, Ill., 1968), 215–16; "Statistical Collections of Louisiana: The Parish of Baton Rouge," *DeBow's Southern and Western Review*, XII (enlarged ed., January, 1852), 3rd series 05 II, No. 1, p. 22. In 1810 the Baton Rouge Catholic church was an old frame building that could seat 400. The earliest tombstones in its cemetery date from 1812 and 1816 ("Statistical Collections of Louisiana," 24). See also Frederick Stuart Allen, "A Social and Economic History of Baton Rouge, 1850–1860" (M.A. thesis, Louisiana State University, 1936).

6. Louise Pauline Kaltenbaugh, "A Study of the Place-Names of St. Bernard Parish, Louisiana" (M.A. thesis, Louisiana State University—University of New Orleans, 1970), 44, 61, 77, 86.

7. Marchand, *The Flight of a Century*, 89, and *The Story of Ascension Parish*, 119–20.

The beginning of the steamboat era on the Mississippi helped to spurt the growth and productivity of lower Louisiana. The first steamboat arrived in Donaldsonville in 1812. A few years later, steamboats also appeared on Bayou Lafourche, making the journey all the way up from the Gulf of Mexico to Donaldsonville in high water. At that time, fed by the Mississippi, the bayou would swell to several hundred feet across from one bank to the other. For the rest of the year, with the waters low in the bayou, Donaldsonville could only be reached from the gulf with boats and barges of shallow draught.[8]

Several writers have described life on Bayou Lafourche in the early years of the nineteenth century. William O. Scroggs wrote that the *petits habitants* were "settled thickly along Bayou Lafourche. This district was known as Valenzuela de la Fourche, and in 1803 it contained about 2,800 inhabitants, of whom less than 400 were slaves . . . Bayou Lafourche was lined with farms, only one deep, along its banks for a distance of forty miles." About 1811, after visiting the area, Captain Amos Stoddard wrote: "The settlements on the *La Fourche* extend downwards about forty-five miles, and comprehend upwards of two hundred families, mostly Spaniards, who are by no means in affluent circumstances. They cultivate rice, corn, cotton, and flax, and also afford the New Orleans market considerable quantities of provisions." A modern writer has declared about the small growers of lower Louisiana of that era: "The typical farmer worked hard and long to produce food for his family and a cash crop for export. Since he usually owned very few, if any slaves, he, together with the members of his family, worked the fields, harvested the crops, and brought them to New Orleans for sale. Pirogues, flatboats, bateaux, and barges loaded with cotton, vegetables, tobacco, and corn crowded the city's docks daily."[9]

Like many Americans, Stoddard disliked both the Spaniards and the French. Henry Marie Brackenridge, who visited the bayou about the same time, shared those sentiments. He wrote in a derogatory manner: "The settlers . . . are principally of Spanish origin, and speak little

8. Marchand, *The Flight of a Century*, 32.
9. William O. Scroggs, "Rural Life in the Lower Mississippi Valley About 1803," *Proceedings of the Mississippi Valley Historical Association for the Year 1914–15*, III (1916), 268; Stoddard, *Sketches*, 167; LeBreton, "A History of the Territory of Orleans, 1803–1812," 216–17.

French. They are a poor and miserable population, seem lazy and careless, and are destitute of those little comforts, and that neatness, which are found in the cottage of the poorest French creole."[10]

With the American influx and price rise of Louisiana's agricultural products, land prices soared. The white population in Ascension Parish grew slowly compared to that of the slaves introduced to toil on the newly forming cotton and sugarcane plantations. Whites numbered 1,141 in 1810; 1,725 in 1830; and 3,310 in 1850. By comparison, the number of slaves rose more rapidly, from 1,031 in 1810 to 3,567 in 1830 and 7,266 in 1850. Planters, many of whom were Americans who brought capital and slaves with them, put together large holdings of land by buying out the small farmers. Bayou Lafourche had consisted mainly of small farms until the 1820s.[11]

Some of the small farmers and free Negroes who owned lands on the bayou resisted selling out at even two or three times the value of their property. Many other Isleños, however, did sell out. By 1829 only eleven Canary Islanders possessed lands on the west side of the bayou in Ascension Parish and eight on the east side. Farmers who sold out often moved beyond the lands that fronted the bayou to the ridges of the interior swamps, where they burned off the vegetation and started new farms. In those burned areas, known as brulees, pockets of Isleños attempted to eke out an existence on their small parcels. They lived near the subsistence level, growing vegetables, sometimes cultivating patches of cotton and sugarcane, and raising a few animals and some poultry. To a considerable degree they retained their own culture. Some worked on neighboring plantations. Among the Canarian brulees were Brulee Sacramento, Brulee Maurin (earlier called Brulee Vives), and Brulee Capite. Acadians, too, frequently sold their bayou farms and retreated to the interior ridges. In Ascension and upper Assumption parishes, the Isleños predominated among the brulee dwellers, while in lower As-

10. Henry Marie Brackenridge, *Views of Louisiana, Together with a Journal of a Voyage up the Missouri River, in 1811* (Pittsburgh, 1811; rpr. Chicago, 1962), 173. For an example of Stoddard's racist remarks, see Stoddard, *Sketches*, 328.

11. *Biennial Report of the Secretary of State of the State of Louisiana, 1886–1887* (Baton Rouge, 1888), 84–86; W. W. Pugh, "Bayou Lafourche from 1820 to 1825," *Louisiana Planter and Sugar Manufacturer*, September 29, 1888; Lilian Crété, *Daily Life in Louisiana, 1815–1830* (Baton Rouge, 1981), 277.

sumption and Lafourche parishes, Acadians constituted the bulk of the residents.[12]

American control over Louisiana brought a restructuring of local government. In 1807 Governor Claiborne's administration began to change local government with the creation of nineteen parishes. They included the Canary Islander parishes of St. Bernard, Ascension, and Assumption. The parish judge from the start of American rule exercised great authority, including the right to choose police jurors until 1811, when the jurors became elective. By then the police jury had evolved into the parish's chief administrative body. The office of parish judge, once of paramount importance, lost power as other local offices arose. The Isleños later excelled in the arena of parish politics. In 1810, after a substantial increase in population, part of the territory of Louisiana became a state.[13]

Population growth in Louisiana proceeded quickly in the early nineteenth century. From about 50,000 in 1803, the population rose to 76,500 by 1810 and 153,406 in 1820, while that of New Orleans increased from approximately 10,000 in 1803 to 17,000 in 1806 and 24,000 in 1810. During those years, French Creoles from the Caribbean, together with their slaves, flooded lower Louisiana while Americans settled in the north. The more liberal United States trade policies also brought prosperity for Louisiana's agricultural crops and export commodities, and they probably benefited the majority of the farm Canary Islanders. The prosperity was short-lived, however, as President Jefferson's trade embargo of 1808 soon plunged the territory into depression. Afterwards, the undeclared

12. Sidney Marchand, Sr., *Marchands on the Mississippi and on the St. Lawrence* (Donaldsonville, La., 1968), 48–67, contains figures on the land and the slaves farmers owned in 1807. The farms averaged three arpents of front and were valued at $500. Thomas Albarado, however, had six arpents of front and three slaves; Gaspard Falcon had three arpents of front and four slaves; and Fernando Rodriguez had ten arpents of front and three slaves. See also Frederick Law Olmstead, *A Journey in the Seaboard Slave States in the Years 1853–1854 with Remarks on Their Economy* (2 vols.; New York, 1904), II, 342; Raleigh A. Suarez, "Louisiana's Struggling Majority: The Ante-Bellum Farmer," *McNeese Review*, XIV (1963), 14–31; and his "Rural Life in Louisiana, 1850–1860 (Ph.D. dissertation, Louisiana State University, 1954).

13. Marchand, *The Story of Ascension Parish*, 36; Grace June Savoy, "Louisiana Parishes: Their People and Governments. A Developmental Analysis" (Ph.D. dissertation, Louisiana State University, 1979), 59–60. The Isleños living on the west bank of the Lafourche were Antonio Mendez, Francisco Hernandez, Joseph Hidalgo, Jean Paredes, Joseph Alvares, Joseph Mendes, Antonio Montesino, Diego Gomez, Joseph Corbo, Thomas Albarado, and Christoval Falcon; on the east bank were Andre Vega, Lazard Hernandez, Joseph Cavalier (Caballero?), Manuel Romanos, Diego Suarez, Antonio Perera, Francisque Diez, and Pedro Alleman. The list reveals that Spanish names in 1829 were already in the process of change.

naval war between Britain and the United States also hurt trade. It finally led to President Madison's declaration of war in 1812. The conflict wrote a new chapter in Louisiana's already colorful history.[14]

The War of 1812 affected the Isleños as well as the French inhabitants of Louisiana by raising the question of loyalty. Would these people, different in custom and culture from the majority of the American population, remain loyal and assist in repelling the British? From the start of the war, rumors circulated that Britain intended to invade Louisiana. In 1814 the rumors appeared to have substance, and late in the year preparations for resisting the invasion began. Earlier, when Governor Claiborne had first taken possession of Louisiana for the United States, Creole attendance at militia assemblies had been lethargic; but now, with a threat to Louisiana, Creoles participated in the call-up of military units, and they were well represented in the forces under arms when the British came. Fortunately, the enemy was Britain, which in the past had been the adversary of both Spain and France; and the last time that Louisianians had fought in a war—the American Revolution—both nations had assisted the rebel North American colonials in defeating the British. The Creoles retained vivid memories of their victories at Baton Rouge, Mobile, and Pensacola over the old enemy of thirty years before.

The new conflict involved the Isleños of St. Bernard Parish since the enemy occupied Terre-aux-Boeufs. In December, 1814, the British invasion fleet entered Lake Borgne, defeating several American barges. British troops landed at Fishermen's Village, on Bayou Bienvenu about a mile and a half from Lake Borgne, in easternmost St. Bernard Parish. The village consisted of twelve large cabins made of stakes with thatched palmetto-frond roofs. The enemy soldiers surprised the village and captured the residents and the small military detachment. Of the four persons who escaped, Antonio Rey spent three hazardous days crossing swamps, lagoons, and marshes in order to warn the authorities.

Before he could do so, the British moved up from Fishermen's Village along Bayou Bienvenu toward the Mississippi, using prisoners as guides. They reached the river at Jacques Villere's plantation; Terre-aux-Boeufs, the heart of the Canarian settlement, lay only a few miles to the south. Probably many of the Isleño militiamen were absent, but American general David B. Morgan briefly held Terre-aux-Boeufs with five

14. Edwin Adam Davis, *Louisiana: A Narrative History* (3rd ed.; Baton Rouge, 1971), 173–74.

hundred troops. On the night of December 23, when a clash occurred at Villere's plantation between British and American forces, Morgan's men moved up five miles, perhaps to near the head of the bayou, where they engaged the enemy's rear. Combat broke off before daylight, and a few days later Morgan evacuated his soldiers across the Mississippi to the west bank. Within a day or two, British troops entered Terre-aux-Boeufs and requisitioned thirty or forty Isleño horses. They also seized provisions and slaves. Major Arsene Lacarriere Latour, who fought on the American side, wrote about the enemy: "The British made several excursions into the settlements of Terre-aux-Boeufs. . . . They carried off the cattle of all the plantations, giving to the planters, in payment, one-half or two-thirds of their value, and that seldom in money, but generally in draughts on the commissary general of the army. . . . They also . . . carried off all the Negroes of the plantations they had occupied." St. Bernard planters visited the British at Dauphine Island in order to regain their confiscated slaves; they obtained only one of more than three hundred that the British seized—a loss of $150,000.[15]

Not long after the attack on Terre-aux-Boeufs, General Andrew Jackson thwarted British plans of conquest. On January 8, at Chalmette the main British army attacked Jackson's entrenched positions and suffered a bloody defeat in the so-called Battle of New Orleans. The loss of more than two thousand men killed and wounded made the survivors realize the hopelessness of attempting to seize New Orleans, the mouth of the Mississippi, and lower Louisiana. Also, the British failed to secure the Creoles' support, whom they believed were restless under American rule. The victory emphasized that while the Spaniards and French were different in culture from the Anglo-Americans, they were nevertheless loyal. Powell Casey's *Louisiana in the War of 1812* contains the rosters of the Louisiana troops who fought in the Battle of New Orleans. Numerous Spanish names, many of Isleños from St. Bernard and Bayou Lafourche, attest to their allegiance.[16]

15. Powell A. Casey, *Louisiana in the War of 1812* (Baton Rouge, 1963), 44–53, 88; [Major] Arsene Lacarriere Latour, *Historical Memoir of the War in West Florida and Louisiana in 1814–15* (1816; rpr. Gainesville, Fla., 1964), 82–84, 201–202; *Louisiana Gazette and Mercantile Adventurer* (New Orleans), April 5, 1815. Latour recorded the names of several residents of the "Village of the Spanish Fishermen": Maringuier, Old Luiz, Francisco, Graviella, Hirerling, Antonio el Italiano, and El Campechano (who was probably from Campeche, Mexico).

16. Casey, *Louisiana in the War of 1812*, i–lxxxii. In 1810 St. Bernard Parish had 667 whites, 1,923 slaves, 45 free blacks (*ibid.*, 106). See also Davis, *Louisiana: A Narrative History*, 183–86; Marie Cruzat (Mrs. Edwin X.) de Vergas, *American Forces at Chalmette, Veterans and Descendants of the Battle of New Orleans, 1814–1815* (n.p., 1966).

Upper St. Bernard Parish had long had plantations, but after the war, there was an effort to establish them at Terre-aux-Boeufs. Although wealthy newcomers were trying to put together parcels of ground to form large holdings, the bayou remained predominantly a region of small farmers. St. Bernard consisted of three main divisions: the upper parish, which held plantations; the middle parish, composed chiefly of the small farms of Terre-aux-Boeufs; and the lower parish (Delacroix Island), where a few Canary Islanders lived as fishermen, hunters, and trappers. In the last two regions, the Isleños predominated.[17]

Education, a way for Canarian assimilation into Louisiana's mainstream, started slowly. Before 1830 public schools were virtually nonexistent; the apprenticeship system, however, was an early-nineteenth-century practice for training poor children. A master taught his apprentice his craft, trade, or profession as well as instructed him in reading, writing, and ciphering. One young apprentice of that era was Francisco Joaquin Campo, a five-year-old St. Bernard orphan, who was apprenticed to Pierre Réné de St. Germain of New Orleans for fifteen years and eleven months. The apprenticeship system, however, affected few of the young people of that time.[18]

Before the 1830s, the more wealthy Isleño families provided some education for their children. Plantation owners generally favored tutors or, in St. Bernard Parish, because of its proximity to New Orleans, sent their youngsters to the city for schooling. The majority of the Canarians, nevertheless, needed to wait until the public school era before their children could acquire some learning. The parish elite, mostly members of the planter class, dominated the school boards in the early years and refused to adopt a system that cost the taxpayers money. They also controlled the police jury until the division of the parishes into wards and the election of jury members from the wards. Before long, Isleños ran successfully for both the board of education and the police jury.[19]

The 1830s witnessed a tentative beginning of public education in Louisiana. Eighteen thirty-four records indicate that sixteen students from ages six to fourteen attended a St. Bernard primary school. Three

17. Among the Isleño slaveholders in St. Bernard Parish in 1820 were Elizabeth Alpuente, with 4 slaves; Juan Perez with 7; Manuel Gonzales, with 6; and the non-Canarian planter Antonio Mendez, with 50 (Fourth Census [1820], St. Bernard Parish, in American Census Records, United States Census Office).

18. Marie Louise Renauld, "The History of the Public Schools in St. Bernard Parish to 1877" (M.A. thesis, Tulane University, 1946), 19–20.

19. *Ibid.*, 25.

Isleño families were represented: the Serpas, with four children; the Gutierrez, with four also; and the Solis, with three. The next year enrollment grew. The Isleños were represented by the Marrero family, having six of the twenty-four students; the Alphonse (Alfonso) with four; the Bastian, one; the Solis, four; the Suarez, one; the Armas, one; and the Sanchez, one. Half of the students were girls, ranging in age from seven to fourteen. While most of the pupils were young, Juanillo Alfonso and Antonio Sanchez, who attended school for one month each, were nineteen and twenty-two respectively. In another class in 1835 (or possibly another school), ten more students were enrolled, nearly all coming from the Serpas, Gutierrez, and Solis families.[20]

By 1838 St. Bernard had a regular school building, where 31 children received an education at public expense. Between 1841 and 1845, the parish spent $500 yearly to educate 33 pupils. The free public school system remained modest until 1847, when it expanded rapidly. That year, Louisiana generally adopted a public school system for children ages 6 to 16, with each district having a minimum of 40 students. School boards consisted of 3 members. By 1849 St. Bernard had 2 schools and 249 "educables," of whom 121 attended school. The school year was six and a half months long, and the amount of money spent yearly on education had increased to $1,500.[21]

But students seldom attended school regularly. They often stayed at home to help their parents at harvest time and at other busy times. Parents living far from the schools rarely sent their children. Moreover, many of the parents did not value education since they themselves had never gone to school. As one author wrote, "On the whole, the ordinary folk in Louisiana seem to have looked on education as the profitless pastime of the idle rich." In 1851 only forty-five boys and twenty-nine girls attended school in St. Bernard Parish, a fraction of the total young population.[22]

By that year several Isleño were helping to promote education. Adelaid Estopinal and Andre Morales served on the school board, and Manuel Serpas was the parish school superintendent for education.

20. "Ecole Primaire," School Records for 1834 and 1835, St. Bernard Parish, Louisiana Historical Center, New Orleans.

21. Renauld, "The History of the Public Schools in St. Bernard Parish," 30–31; Thomas H. Harris, "The History of Public Education in Louisiana" (M.A. thesis, Louisiana State University, 1924), 11–12. See also Raleigh A. Suarez, "Chronicle of a Failure: Public Education in Antebellum Louisiana," *Louisiana History*, XII (1971), 109–22.

22. Crété, *Daily Life in Louisiana*, 119.

Classes were taught in French, and Isleños learned that language instead of English. They also learned French in remote areas, often creating the erroneous impression to outsiders that they were Acadian, particularly in Ascension and Assumption parishes. The given names of Isleño children were usually written down in French in school records whether they were originally French in form or not. Spanish surnames suffered as well in St. Bernard Parish and along Bayou Lafourche. The variations in the spelling of Spanish names, and even major alterations, were numerous; for example, *Caballero* became *Chevalier*, *Placencia* turned into *Plaisance*, and *Dominguez*, *Rodriguez*, and *Acosta* were Gallicized into *Domingue*, *Rodrigue*, and *Acoste* or *D'Acoste* respectively.[23]

By 1854 St. Bernard Parish had four schools, each with its own teacher. The one-room schoolhouse seems to have been the typical school, with all grades and students meeting together. The school term had been lengthened—but only temporarily to the relief of the young scholars—to twelve months. One hundred forty-two students attended school; 263 other young people did not. Education emphasized reading, spelling, arithmetic, geography, grammar, and history. Teachers were not highly trained, and indeed, some had no training at all. The low salaries of twenty or twenty-five dollars per month failed to attract better-qualified people to the profession. A report of about 1856 remarked that the teachers were of "ordinary intellectual capacities and mostly deficient in the art of teaching." In 1857, 103 young people attended school while another 310 did not, indicating a drop in enrollment. But in 1859, an incredible 469 children were in school, only 118 staying out. What produced the change in enrollment as well as the increase in parish youngsters is not known.[24]

Education in other parts of Louisiana probably reflected conditions in St. Bernard Parish. On Bayou Lafourche at least one school existed in Assumption Parish prior to 1824. For many years afterwards, improvement was nearly nonexistent. Following the 1847 state law requiring a free public school system, the Assumption authorities rapidly expanded the number of elementary schools. By 1850, 18 schools existed, each with its own teacher, and 693 students were enrolled. Six years later, the parish could boast of 23 schools, only one of them above the primary

23. Renauld, "The History of the Public Schools in St. Bernard Parish," 32–33. See also Newton, "The Americanization of French Louisiana," 15. On the dominance of Cajun culture over other cultures, see Vernon J. Parenton, "The Rural French-Speaking People of Quebec and Louisiana" (Ph.D. dissertation, Harvard University, 1948).

24. Renauld, "The History of the Public Schools in St. Bernard Parish," 36–40.

level, and a school term five months in length. The schools, nevertheless, probably failed to make a significant impact on the parish's educational level, and poorly trained teachers seemed to be the rule. A large proportion of the Isleños living in rural areas probably remained illiterate or acquired only a rudimentary education before the Civil War.[25]

The first half of the nineteenth century witnessed constant change in the priests serving the Canarian parishes. Roger Baudier described the early American era as the dark age of the Catholic church in Louisiana, characterized by parishes without priests, sacraments neglected, church property lost, and morality at a low ebb. In 1805 a French priest, Jean Marie Rochanson, took charge at St. Bernard, where no priest had been since Tirso de Peleagonzalo departed in 1803. After 1809 the church remained vacant, with only occasional visits from the New Orleans clergy. Priests again labored there after the War of 1812, with Father Juan J. Casado employing the Spanish language between 1826 and 1830. In the 1830s, Father Felix Loperanza, Father Jean Martin, Father Jamey, Father Jean Caretta, and Father Savelli served at different times.[26]

On November 26, 1837, Bishop Blanc of New Orleans visited Terre-aux-Boeufs and praised the neatness of the church and the piety of the parishioners. A description of the next year reiterated the care given to the church: "The church, which is eight or nine miles from the river, is a very neat little affair. The exterior is plain, but there are many ornaments and emblematic devices in the interior—among which are twenty-seven paintings and engravings. The building is in a handsome enclosure, planted with trees and grass, fronting on the road; and on the other (the Eastern) side, immediately opposite, is the public cemetery." In 1851 a new church replaced the half-century-old structure. Father Caretta appears to have served the parish for many years, from the 1830s to the 1850s. Father Andre Cauvin replaced him at last in 1859.[27]

On Bayou Lafourche, at the Ascension and Assumption churches, many priests labored in the years before the Civil War. Father John Maguire, who worked at Ascension, left for Spanish Texas in July, 1803. He was replaced by Father Henry Boutin, who drowned in Bayou

25. Norman Edward Carmouche, "The Development of Public Education in Assumption Parish from 1807–1943" (M.A. thesis, Louisiana State University, 1944), 13–16.

26. Baudier, *The Catholic Church in Louisiana*, 249, 252–53, 288.

27. Walter Prichard (ed.), "Some Interesting Glimpses of Louisiana a Century Ago," *Louisiana Historical Quarterly*, XXIV (1941), 48; Baudier, *The Catholic Church in Louisiana*, 350, 586.

Lafourche about March, 1808, and was buried at Valenzuela. Father Charles Lusson ministered to the parishioners for the next four years. Except for occasional visits by Father Bernardo de Deva of Assumption, the Ascension church stayed vacant between 1812 and 1815, and the priests assigned there afterwards never remained long. Through most of the 1830s, the fathers made only short visits to Ascension. The known clerics were Fathers Pichitoli, who served from 1827 to 1829; Brassac, from 1829 to 1835; Boullon, from 1839 to 1849; Gustiniani, from 1849 to 1854; and Calvo, from 1854 to 1858.[28]

At the Assumption church, Father Deva stayed behind after Spain relinquished Louisiana. Although he quit the Capuchin order, he continued to serve the parish whenever needed. He appears to have worked at Assumption continuously between 1808 and 1817, when he retired to his plantation; he had acquired a substantial land grant (the Little Texas plantation and a portion of the Ravenswood plantation formed a part of it) before the end of the Spanish era. In 1817 the Assumption parishioners voted for a new church to replace their twenty-year-old small building. The new edifice was forty feet long and thirty-eight feet wide, with a ceiling sixteen feet from the floor; and the entire building was raised three feet off the ground. In 1818 Deva laid the cornerstone, and the dedication of the new church occurred on December 20, 1819, in the presence of four neighboring priests. The new church was not placed at the same site as the old (in Plattenville today), but two squares (blocks?) below it. Prior to his death at age eighty in 1826, Deva donated one thousand acres for the construction of a seminary. In 1826 a convent school was established in Assumption Parish, which the Religious of the Sacred Heart took over. Through the years, the priests who served at Assumption continued to rotate regularly.[29]

Lengthy descriptions of Isleño life in the antebellum era are few. The New Orleans *Weekly Picayune* of October 22, 1838, contains one of those rare accounts of the Canary Islanders of St. Bernard between statehood and the Civil War. The newspaper editor, having learned of their

28. Baudier, *The Catholic Church in Louisiana*, 319, 353.

29. Elise A. Alleman, "The Legend and History of the Place-Names of Assumption Parish" (M.A. thesis, Louisiana State University, 1936), 81. See also *American State Papers: Public Lands* (Washington, D.C., 1834), II, 509, III, 580. Deva's claim has been described as one square league in size, which made it seven to nine square miles. Deva had petitioned Governor Carondelet for the grant on March 14, 1793 (Baudier, *The Catholic Church in Louisiana*, 267, 285–86, 319).

existence, wanted to sketch their customs before, as he alleged, "the overwhelming tide of improvement, innovation and all kinds of Americanism" obliterated their settlement. The Canarians, he wrote, engaged in farming, hunting, and fishing, and sold their surplus in the New Orleans market. Others worked on the parish plantations. The Isleños had also acquired a reputation for training oxen, and planters from as far away as Attakapas and Opelousas brought their animals to the Isleños for instruction. On the Canary Islanders' fortnight journeys to sell their produce in New Orleans and to buy supplies, the oxen pulled their carts unguided into the city, going directly to their stalls in the market. The trips were a family affair, with wives and children tagging along, all chattering in Spanish, and thus far appearing unchanged from colonial days. After disposing of their produce, the Spanish merchants whom they patronized supplied them with breakfast in exchange for their business. Intrigued by the Isleños, the *Weekly Picayune* editor traveled down to Terre-aux-Boeufs to provide his New Orleans readers, many of whom had no idea that the Canarians resided nearby, with a longer account of this singular people.[30]

Terre-aux-Boeufs extended for twenty miles and was thickly settled with houses; plantations were relatively few in number among the small farms. The ridge that constituted the high ground where the settlement sat was only a mile broad, with a road running along the bayou. Isleño farms grew sweet potatoes, onions, pumpkins, and other vegetables. The editor described their dwellings as "rude," but the people, he stated, possessed a "natural politeness" and an "easy, unaffected address." They respected their elders, and at least one family built homes for the married sons on the parental farm. Their chief enjoyments consisted of visiting and, on Sundays, merrily driving their cabriolets (carts equipped with a bench). The editor ended his essay by stating that the Isleños were a happy although unenlightened people, who cherished social virtues and shared their good fortune with their neighbors.[31]

Although there are no detailed accounts of life along Bayou Lafourche before mid-nineteenth century, several writers mentioned conditions in Ascension and Assumption parishes. William Henry Sparks has left a physical description of the Canarians he observed.

---

30. Prichard (ed.), "Some Interesting Glimpses of Louisiana a Century Ago," 43–48.
31. *Ibid.*

These people are Iberian in race, are small in stature, of dark complexion, with black eyes, and lank black hair; their hands and feet are small, and beautifully formed, and their features regular and handsome; many of their females are extremely beautiful. These attain maturity very early, and are frequently married at thirteen years of age. In more than one instance, I have known a grandmother at thirty. As in all warm countries, this precocious maturity is followed with rapid decay. Here, persons at forty wear the appearance of those in colder climates of sixty years.[32]

The small farmers of Bayou Lafourche were noted for their piety and, perhaps not trusting the local authorities, called upon their priests to be the arbiters in disputes. According to one author, they also had a horror of debts and lawsuits, which might have been responsible for some of them losing their bayou-front lands. Sparks wrote of the Isleño settler as "a diminutive specimen . . . clad in blue cotton made pants and hickory shirt, barefooted, with a palm-leaf hat upon his head, and an old rusty shotgun in his hands." W. W. Pugh described the houses of the Canarians as "small squat dwellings of rustic appearance, with walls made of adobe mixed with Spanish moss, roughly hewed cypress beams, and cypress plank roofs. A covered porch ran along the front of every house." Sparks further wrote, in an unsympathetic tone, that the people lived as if in Eden, with a minimum of clothing and "in a simplicity of primitive ignorance and indolence." They manufactured their own simple, coarse furniture and other household goods, slept on Spanish-moss mattresses, and wore homespun clothing. Their pastimes, Pugh claimed, were gossiping, taking the afternoon siesta, and dancing.[33]

Many writers have commented on the Acadians' passion for dancing, and it was no less a popular form of diversion among the Canary Islanders. They celebrated their arrival in Valenzuela by dancing, and the dance halls of St. Bernard Parish of a later era became legendary. In the years before the Civil War in Ascension and Assumption parishes, the Isleños traveled enthusiastically on foot, by horse, and in pirogue to reach

32. W. H. Sparks, *The Memoirs of Fifty Years* (Philadelphia, 1870), 378. See also Marchand, *An Attempt to Reassemble the Old Settlers*, which was first published serially in New Orleans *Genesis* between 1963 and 1965; and J. Carlyle Sitterson, *Sugar Country: The Cane Industry in the South, 1753–1950* (Lexington, Ky., 1953). For a discussion of the biased attitude of nineteenth-century writers who favored the large planters and wrongly depicted the poor farmers, see Suarez, "Louisiana's Struggling Majority," 14–31.

33. Sparks, *The Memoirs of Fifty Years*, 374. Sparks stated (p. 375) that the Isleños' houses were constructed of clay and moss made into rolls two feet long and five inches thick, which were whitewashed after they had dried. See also Pugh, "Bayou Lafourche from 1820 to 1825."

the Saturday-night dances that went on all year. They were family gatherings, with everyone from infants to grandparents attending. The simplicity of the music, provided mainly by self-taught violinists, did not diminish their enjoyment. Food and alcoholic beverages usually accompanied the merriment.[34]

Life for the Canary Islanders of rural Louisiana revolved around farming that was closely tied to the seasons. The chief crop and staple in their diet from the time of their arrival was Indian corn. The farmers also grew beans, rice, melons, squash, pumpkins, oranges, figs, peaches, and plums for their personal consumption. The Isleño farmers also raised pigs, cattle, and poultry.[35]

Despite the demands of agriculture, the men and boys found time for hunting and fishing. Because much of Louisiana remained undeveloped, game was plentiful throughout the nineteenth century, and hunters never traveled far for deer or even bear; other forms of game and foul similarly abounded. Isleño males loved to fish on the banks of the rivers and bayous and in the Gulf of Mexico. A New England woman left a description of Canarians she saw in 1851: "There is a kind of fish caught here called a cat fish which nobody thinks fitting to eat but the Spaniards [Isleños] over the river, and there they sit with their dogs all day long in the sun, close to the water's edge, fishing and singing at their work. I love dearly to hear them; in the evening they build large fires along the bank for decoys, they look beautifully in the dark." In St. Bernard Parish, the Canarians reached Lake Borgne or the Gulf of Mexico with relative ease. Those on Bayou Lafourche followed that avenue down to the gulf, where they often spent several days fishing. The sea furnished them with enormous quantities of food.[36]

As the antebellum era drew to a close, the United States government took decennial censuses, which provide information about the economic status of the Isleños. The censuses are not without flaws, however; names are frequently misspelled and people omitted. Nevertheless, they do furnish some useful data. According to the 1840 census, the majority

---

34. Sparks, *The Memoirs of Fifty Years*, 377.
35. Marchand, *The Flight of a Century*, 111.
36. Scroggs, "Rural Life in the Lower Mississippi Valley About 1803," 274; Suarez, "Louisiana's Struggling Majority," 27. The quotation is from Augusta to Sarah W. Simpson, February 10, 1851, Louisiana State University Archives.

of the Canarians continued to earn their livelihood from agriculture. They were mainly small farmers, and few of them possessed slaves. Several, however, had emerged from the ranks of subsistence farming to stand out above their fellow Isleños. To provide two examples in Assumption Parish, where many Canary Islanders resided, the widow of Antonio Allman (Aleman) had forty slaves, and Augustin Truxillo owned twenty-eight bondsmen.[37]

La Tourette's Reference Map of the State of Louisiana for 1845 also affords a glimpse at the plantations on the banks of Bayou Lafourche. It lists Manuel Fernandez, Antonio Vela, and two persons surnamed Truxillo as plantation owners. Perhaps one of the Truxillos was Augustus (Augustin) D. Truxillo, who in 1838 served in the Louisiana legislature as a representative. Perhaps, too, he was among the first of the Canarians to be elected to the state legislature (Felix Garcia of the German Coast, who might not have been an Isleño, also served then in the state senate). In the years after 1838, more Isleños would represent their parishes in state government.[38]

The 1850 census included information about the value of property owned by each head of family. In Ascension Parish, the only outstanding Canarian was the planter Mathias Rodriguez, with property worth $50,000. The next richest Isleño was the planter Francis Hidalgo, who owned property valued at only $3,000. Other Isleños were modest farmers with far less property or laborers without any real estate at all. Assumption Parish, where sugarcane cultivation was carried on extensively, had more prosperous Canary Islanders. They were Antonio Diez, whose property was valued at $7,500; Manuel Fernandez, $70,000; Mathias Martinez, $7,000; Desire Plasencia, $10,000; Andre Truxillo, $8,000; the widow of Santiago Truxillo, $8,000; and Antonio Vila (Vela), $96,000. Also residing in Assumption Parish and a Spanish descendant, although not an Isleño, was Hypolite Vives (whose father was Dr. Juan

37. Sixth Census (1840), Ascension and Assumption parishes, in American Census Records, United States Census Office.
38. *La Tourette's Reference Map of the State of Louisiana* . . . (New Orleans, 1845); *Gibson's Guide and Directory of the State of Louisiana, and the Cities of New Orleans and Lafayette* (New Orleans, 1838), 240–41. Other officials mentioned in *Gibson's Guide* (pp. 247 and 249) are Manuel Garcia, sheriff of Jefferson Parish; and O. de Armas, on the New Orleans police jury, who was probably a descendant of Cristobal de Armas, who was a Canarian but not an army recruit of 1778–1783.

Vives, who died in 1822 at the age of sixty-eight), with property valued at $25,000.[39]

An examination of the 1850 census for St. Bernard Parish permits several observations about the Isleños living there. The occupations of farmer and laborer (which was also in agriculture) were the most numerous (held by fifty-seven and nineteen people, respectively) while those of fisherman and hunter were less frequent, held by fifteen and eight people, respectively. Few other occupations existed in the parish, attesting to its underdevelopment. Among the more notable Canary Islander descendants in 1850 were Manuel Serpas, age twenty-eight, parish superintendent of public schools; and Antonio Marrero, age thirty, sheriff. Marrero was also a prosperous plantation owner. Several elderly Isleños, born in the Canary Islands and possibly original immigrants of the 1778–1783 era, still lived in the parish. They were Marie Messa, seventy; Gunonine (?) Oramas, a male, eighty; Mrs. J. Dahlel, eighty; Pedro Herrera, a fisherman, eighty; and, last, the widow of Seege Estopinal, ninety.

The census data do not permit all of the Canarians to be readily identified and the marriage of Isleño women to outsiders, either local people who were not Isleños or foreigners, also prevents their identification. Because of its proximity to New Orleans, by 1850 St. Bernard Parish had received an impressive influx of foreigners, mainly from Europe—Spain, Ireland, France, and Germany. A few of the immigrants had come from other Hispanic countries such as Cuba and Mexico. The Hispanics who settled in the parish tended to gravitate to fishing. When they married, they usually selected their wives from among Canarian girls and women. These Spaniards, Cubans, and Mexicans helped to reinforce the Hispanic character of the parish, particularly in the lower and eastern portions, where the fishing settlements were located and where Isleño culture persisted vigorously. St. Bernard's Canarian population, approximately five hundred in 1850, represented a significant

39. Seventh Census (1850), Ascension and Assumption parishes, in American Census Records, United States Census Office. See also *Cohen's New Orleans Directory for 1855 . . . of the Cotton and Sugar Plantations of Louisiana and Mississippi* (New Orleans, 1855); *Cohen's New Orleans and Southern Directory for 1856 . . .* (New Orleans, 1856); Adolphe Henry and Victor Gerodias, *The Louisiana Coast Directory of the Right and Left Banks of the Mississippi from Its Mouth to Baton Rouge* (New Orleans, 1857). Joseph Valsin Guillotte, in "Masters of the Marsh: An Introduction to the Ethnography of the Isleños of Lower St. Bernard Parish, Louisiana, with an Annotated Bibliography" (report for the Jean Lafitte National Historical Park, n.p., *ca.* 1982), 27, has conclusions somewhat different from my own. His ratio of Isleño "soil" occupations to "collector" occupations is 7 to 24.

percentage of the parish's white population. The number five hundred, however, is a conservative estimate since only those persons who could be identified as Isleño were counted.[40]

The decade of the 1850s appears to have been prosperous for the planter elite of lower Louisiana, which included a handful of Isleños. By 1860 several Canarian planters of Bayou Lafourche had amassed sizable fortunes. In Assumption Parish the heirs of Manuel Fernandez held 134 slaves and property valued at an estimated $105,000. Also, Antonio Vela, whose plantation was tied to a Truxillo, had 99 slaves and property worth $99,000. Numa Vives, not an Isleño but of Hispanic descent, owned 70 slaves and 1,900 acres. He established an Isleño connection by marrying the only daughter of Augustin Truxillo. In St. Bernard Parish, only one Isleño stands out, the planter Antonio Marrero, who possessed property in excess of $100,000. The greater part of that amount stemmed from the value of his 71 slaves. Marrero also owned about 1,500 acres of land.[41]

As the census data reveal, by 1860 several descendants of the original Canarian immigrants to Louisiana, a few in the second and more in the third generation, had prospered abundantly. Despite their success, the majority of the Isleños continued life as common farmers, laborers, and fishermen, as their ancestors before them had. Opportunities for greater numbers of them to achieve economic well-being had not yet come.

For the few fortunate planters, however, 1860 was the final year of prosperity. Beyond the bayous of lower Louisiana, a battle raged over the fate of slavery. The South's planter aristocracy had committed itself to the preservation of that institution when elsewhere in the Western Hemisphere it was ending. In the United States, the 1850s pitted free states against slave states. The members of the southern planter class regarded slavery as necessary for their economic survival and feared that the election of Abraham Lincoln as president endangered their institution. Before the end of 1860, several southern states seceded from the Federal Union. In Louisiana, at a convention in Baton Rouge in

---

40. The 1850 St. Bernard Parish census has been compiled by Priscilla Scott and published in *L'Heritage*, II, No. 7 (June, 1979), through V, No. 18 (March, 1982). Guillotte counted 617 Spanish names (of Isleños and other Hispanics) in a free population of 1,438, or 45 percent of the parish whites.

41. Eighth Census (1860), Ascension and Assumption parishes, in American Census Records, United States Census Office. Joseph Karl Menn, *The Large Slaveholders of Louisiana—1860* (New Orleans, 1964), 341–42; Charles Pierre Roland, *Louisiana Sugar Plantations During the American Civil War* (Leiden, 1957).

January, 1861, the delegates also adopted an ordinance of secession by a vote of 113 to 17. Two months later Louisiana joined the newly formed Confederate States of America. The Federal government, meanwhile, refused to accept the dissolution of the Union. Both sides headed toward war. On April 12, 1861, the first hostile act occurred at Charleston harbor. There Confederate forces under General Pierre Gustave Touton Beauregard, a St. Bernard native undoubtedly known to many Isleños, fired on Fort Sumter, which Federal soldiers held. Those shots marked the commencement of the Civil War.[42]

What the Isleños thought of those events is unknown, but they probably reacted no differently from the rest of Louisiana's whites. Although most of the Canarians were not slaveholders, they would nevertheless serve the southern cause and suffer the consequences of war—death, the loss of property, and the Federal occupation of their parishes. The aftermath of war was no less traumatic. In the postwar era, the poor whites of Louisiana needed to establish a new equilibrium with Louisiana's economy, the growing influences from the outside, and the emancipated blacks. For the Isleños, the Civil War represented a watershed in their residence in Louisiana; it destroyed swiftly and violently the way of life that they had known since their arrival.

42. Davis, *Louisiana: A Narrative History*, 247–48.

Seven

War and Occupation, 1861–1877

The guns of April that signaled the commencement of the Civil War affected all of Louisiana's Isleño community. For nearly four decades, since the British invasion during the War of 1812, the Canarians had enjoyed peace. Now, however, as in 1814 and 1815, the struggle came to the Canary Islanders' very doorstep. Many of the Isleños probably had not thought about war. Most of them, as small farmers, fishermen, hunters, and trappers, had no stake in the preservation of slavery. Nevertheless, like other poor southern whites, they accepted the Negro as socially inferior and little deserving of the freedoms they enjoyed. Perhaps some of the Canarians even agreed on the question of states' rights—that Louisiana could secede from the United States if it so chose. Others perhaps did not share those sentiments but, when confronted with Federal armies invading lower Louisiana, fought for their homes and for their state. Regardless of what thoughts ran through their minds, Louisiana's Isleños participated in the war, and they endured years of Union occupation in the Reconstruction era that followed the conflict.

After Louisiana joined the Confederate States of America on March 21, 1861, it mobilized its manpower for war, as the other southern states were then doing. A frenzy of enthusiasm and optimism gripped most of the state's inhabitants. They believed that victory in the war would come swiftly. Volunteers flooded recruiting stations as nearly 20,000 men enlisted in the first nine months, and by war's end, approximately 56,000 Louisianians had joined the Confederate colors. How enthusiastically the Isleños of the bayous rushed to don uniforms of gray is unclear. In

New Orleans one report stated that Spaniards, who might have included some Canary Islanders, seemed reluctant to commit themselves. Seeing that they were not enlisting, impressment gangs of Irish toughs roamed the city streets, searching for "volunteers" and taunting them with the refrain, "For the love of the Virgin and your own sowl's sake, Fernandey, get up and cum along wid us to fight the Yankees." Reluctance was not characteristic of all of the New Orleans' Spanish population, however. John D. Winters, in *The Civil War in Louisiana*, writes: "As early as April [1861] the Spanish joined the growing list of foreigners who were organizing troops. By fall a company of Cubans joined with the Spaniards and formed the Spanish Legion." By March, 1862, the Spanish Legion consisted of a regiment, and the Spanish Cazadores, another regiment, had in it three Spanish and two Slavonic companies, and one French and one Italian company.[1]

After the eruption of hostilities, the war still seemed remote to Louisiana. Because battles were then being fought in other states, many soldiers of the Pelican State departed to bolster Confederate fighting units. The era of tranquillity, however, did not last long, for in the fall of 1861, the Federal government decided to seize New Orleans and the lower Mississippi Valley. In April, 1862, Flag Officer David G. Farragut led a Union fleet of eighteen ships, six mortar steamers, and nineteen mortar boats up from the mouth of the Mississippi. Forts Jackson and St. Philip below New Orleans momentarily blocked the Union invasion fleet. After six days, Farragut ran the ships past the blazing guns of the river forts to New Orleans. The city was largely bereft of soldiers, and what few remained panicked, running away after seeing the imposing Federal fleet riding high on the river's floodwaters. With resistance useless, they burned military supplies and evacuated the city. Although New Orleans' mayor John T. Monroe stubbornly refused to surrender the city, Major General Benjamin F. Butler, in charge of the Federal soldiers who accompanied Farragut's fleet, ran up the Stars and Stripes and took possession on May 1, 1862. The mutinies and surrender of Forts Jackson and St. Philip made it easier. Soon after taking New Orleans, Farragut ordered his gunboats upriver and captured Baton Rouge.

1. Davis, *Louisiana: A Narrative History*, 247–53. The quotations are in John R. Kemp, *New Orleans: An Illustrated History* (Woodland Hills, Calif., 1981), 97; John D. Winters, *The Civil War in Louisiana* (Baton Rouge, 1963), 73. Gen. Clement A. Evans, *Confederate Military History: A Library of Confederate States History* (12 vols.; Atlanta, 1899), X, 322g, states that the total number of Louisiana men in uniform was 55,820.

Although Union forces had scored a major victory, southern troops still held much of the Mississippi Valley. Farragut's attempt to take Vicksburg in the summer of 1862 faltered. The Confederates then launched a counteroffensive under Major General John C. Breckinridge, who descended from Vicksburg and forced the temporary Federal evacuation of Baton Rouge on August 21. The South controlled much of the rest of the state.[2]

The Mississippi River, however, remained the domain of Farragut's gunboats, and they patrolled the river above New Orleans. Occasionally, Confederate partisans fired on them, as they did in Donaldsonville, seriously annoying Union sailors. Donaldsonville was then a pleasant, tranquil community of approximately two thousand inhabitants, with Creoles making up most of the white population. It contained stores, saloons, two prominent hotels, a brick Catholic church "with two massive but low towers flanking the front," a handsome courthouse, and the "ancient and excellent company" of Cannoneers of Donaldsonville. Because of the shooting by partisans, Farragut ordered his river flotilla to reduce the town to rubble. As Winters tells the story in *The Civil War in Louisiana*:

> A company of Partisan Rangers, "guerrillas" to the Yankees, for several weeks had been firing upon unarmed Union transports as they passed near Donaldsonville. Gunboats were sent to the town, and the citizens were warned that if another shot were fired the navy would bombard the area for six miles below Donaldsonville and nine miles above and would destroy every building on all of the plantations. The citizens appealed to the Partisans, but their appeals were ignored. Finally the transports were given an escort of gunboats, but they were still fired upon, although the shotguns and rifles of the Rangers were generally ineffectual against the gunboats. The irate naval commander, Admiral Farragut, ordered the bombardment of Donaldsonville as soon as it could be evacuated. All the citizens of Donaldsonville and nearby Port Barrow "left their homes and went to the bayou, each house received two or three families from the small abandoned village."[3]

On August 9, Farragut's ships commenced their bombardment at 11:00 A.M. An hour and a half later, a Union detachment of soldiers landed with torches in hand. Winters reports: "The hotels, warehouses, dwell-

2. Joe Gray Taylor, *Louisiana: A Bicentennial History* (New York, 1976), 90–91; Davis, *Louisiana: A Narrative History*, 253–55.
3. Walter Prichard (ed.), "A Tourist's Description of Louisiana in 1860," *Louisiana Historical Quarterly*, XXI (1938), 15–17; Marchand, *The Story of Ascension Parish*, 63–66, and *The Flight of a Century*, 154–55; Winters, *The Civil War in Louisiana*, 152–53.

ings, and some of the most valuable buildings of the town were destroyed. Plantations above and below Donaldsonville were bombarded and set afire. After the boats withdrew, a citizens' committee met and decided to ask Governor [Thomas Overton] Moore to keep the Rangers from firing on Federal boats. Those attacks did no real good and brought only cruel reprisals against the innocents." The New Orleans *Delta* reported on August 12 that "there is nothing left of [Donaldsonville] now but ruins and rubbish."[4]

The calamitous action at Donaldsonville no doubt shocked many of the nearby inhabitants who heard the thunder of the artillery pieces and saw smoke rising above the burning town. They included the Canary Islanders living on Bayou Lafourche and in the neighboring brulees. The Isleños probably did not realize that they and Farragut had much in common, for his father was a native of Palma de Mallorca in the Spanish Balearic Islands, off Spain's east coast. Farragut's father had emigrated to the United States, where he served as an officer in the United States Navy. David Farragut also followed a naval career, rising to become an admiral and a Union war hero.[5]

By the spring of 1862, the Civil War had come to the Isleño parishes of Louisiana. When the Union fleet appeared at the mouth of the Mississippi, Confederate authorities declared martial law below New Orleans, including St. Bernard Parish. All white males above sixteen years were ordered to appear within six days before provost marshals in their districts to register and to take an unconditional oath of allegiance to the Confederacy. Whether all the Isleños living on Delacroix Island and at other extremities of the parish obeyed the order appears doubtful.[6]

To what degree the fighting below New Orleans disturbed the Bayou Terre-aux-Boeufs residents is unknown, but the parish's farms and plantations appear to have been spared the looting and wanton destruction that occurred elsewhere, as on Bayou Lafourche. There the residents experienced the horrors of war. The parishes of Ascension, Assumption, and Lafourche were among the richest in the state in sugar production. Plantations and farms dotted the bayou banks from Donaldsonville to the gulf; the region was ripe for plunder. On October 5, 1862, a Federal

4. Winters, *The Civil War in Louisiana*, 153; Davis, *Louisiana: A Narrative History*, 256.
5. See Loyall Farragut, *The Life of David Glasgow Farragut* (New York, 1882); Alfred T. Mahan, *Admiral Farragut* (New York, 1892); Charles Lee Lewis, *David Glasgow Farragut* (2 vols.; Annapolis, 1941–43).
6. Winters, *The Civil War in Louisiana*, 80, 84, 96.

army of five thousand men under General Godfrey Weitzel moved through the mostly deserted and charred ruins of Donaldsonville, stopping only to destroy what was left of the town. The next day the troops started down Bayou Lafourche, looting and pillaging on both banks. Before long many plantation slaves on the bayou deserted their masters and attached themselves to the Union army. Parties of Union soldiers probably reconnoitered as far as the brulees and seized livestock and poultry from the Isleños living there. At Labadieville, Confederate troops attempted a stand, but Weitzel's men defeated them and pushed down to the Bayou Teche district. By December 17, Federal gunboats steamed past Donaldsonville on the Mississippi and reoccupied Baton Rouge.[7]

Although there were brief periods when Confederate units infiltrated the Bayou Lafourche area, before the end of 1862, the greater part of lower Louisiana, including the Canarian parishes, lay in Union hands. Occasional fire fights then broke out, as did one in 1863 near old Valenzuela (the battle of Cox's Plantation). In other parts of Louisiana, major fighting continued. In 1863 a Federal campaign devastated the Teche country, and by July, with the fall of Vicksburg, the Confederate bastion of Port Hudson also surrendered. With the capitulation of these two river fortresses, the entire Mississippi River came under Federal control, splitting the South in two. In spite of major northern victories in 1863, the Confederacy tenaciously persisted in the war for nearly two additional years. The principal action in Louisiana in 1864 was the Federal campaign on the Red River that saw victories and defeats on both sides. In 1865 the conflict ended, but only after many tragedies and hardships. The Confederate forces in Louisiana west of the Mississippi surrendered on May 26, nearly seven weeks after General Robert E. Lee had given up at the Appomattox Courthouse in Virginia.[8]

The war imposed countless tribulations on Louisiana's noncombatant population. Commerce was often at a standstill and comestibles in short supply. No doubt food scarcities affected rural inhabitants less than city dwellers, but the prices of commodities that the farmer did not grow usually rose to prohibitive heights. Late in the war, butter was $5.00 per

7. Ibid., 157–58; Davis, Louisiana: A Narrative History, 256. See also Morris Raphael, The Battle in the Bayou Country (Detroit, 1975).

8. Davis, Louisiana: A Narrative History, 256–59. See also Edward Cunningham, The Port Hudson Campaign, 1862–1863 (Baton Rouge, 1963); David C. Edmonds, The Guns of Port Hudson: Vol. I: The River Campaign (February–May, 1863) (Lafayette, La., 1983).

pound, eggs $5.00 per dozen, beans $2.50 per quart, and bacon and ham $0.75 per pound. Perhaps a few fortunate Isleños sold their surplus farm produce at advantageous prices, but the war devastated much of rural Louisiana. Those areas hardest hit included the northeast, the Red River Valley south of Natchitoches, the region from Alexandria to Opelousas, and the Teche. Bayou Lafourche was also looted, burned out, and desolated.[9]

Life during the war consisted of poverty, turmoil, and despair, and the era generally imposed new adjustments in conduct and attitude as well. Joe Gray Taylor has written that "the position of the state's whites was immeasurably worsened" by the war and its aftermath. That was especially true for the lower-class whites. Wartime laws in Louisiana discriminated against the poor since plantation owners received an exemption from conscription for each twenty slaves they owned; wealthy men could legally buy a substitute to serve in their place; and Confederate taxes on agricultural produce hit poor farmers more severely than their more wealthy counterparts. More and more of the "struggling majority" of Louisiana's population resented the laws' inequality and saw the conflict as "a rich man's war and a poor man's fight." Desertions from Confederate ranks, consequently, multiplied as the war progressed, and avoidance of conscription became a common practice, particularly among the rural folk who lived near the woods or swamps. Among them the Acadians of southwestern Louisiana resisted Confederate drafts whenever possible. How Louisiana's noncombatant Isleño population fared during the terrible war years is unknown; nor is the fate certain of most of the Canarian soldiers who served the southern cause. But enough information exists about some of the Canary Islanders in uniform to illustrate the experiences common to the soldiers as a whole.[10]

Thanks to *Forgotten Fighters*, by Sidney A. Marchand, Sr., a Donald-sonville historian, knowledge has been preserved about some of the Ascension Parish soldiers. In August and September, 1861, a number of young men of that region enrolled in the Donaldsonville Artillery. At least eighteen Isleños eventually joined. Among the September enlistees were Hypolite Acosta, John Hernandez, Esteve Hidalgo, Silvain Lion (Leon), Francis Montero, François Perrez (Perez), Narcisse

9. Davis, *Louisiana: A Narrative History*, 264.
10. Joe Gray Taylor, *Louisiana: A Bicentennial History*, 95–98; Ethel Taylor, "Discontent in Confederate Louisiana," *Louisiana History*, II (1961), 410–28.

Plasencia, Adam Rodriguez, and John Suarez. Others who later entered included Andre Suarez, Charles Alba, Augustin Alvares (Alvarez), Joseph Prados, and Raphael Suarez. Assisting in the unit's operations were Lieutenants M. Cazares and Antoine Sanchez, Sergeant Mathias Ramirez, and First Sergeant Pierre Ramirez. For several months, the recruits did little more than drill; then came the Union invasion of Louisiana and Farragut's flotilla of gunboats on the Mississippi to Baton Rouge. What became of the Donaldsonville Artillery after the arrival of Federal troops is unclear. On June 27, 1862, in an action that remains obscure, Private John Hernandez was wounded. Major fighting did not occur until August, when the northern boats leveled the town. Shortly afterwards Union forces captured Donaldsonville and, in the fall, launched their foray down the banks of Bayou Lafourche.[11]

With Federal occupation of Donaldsonville, the local soldiers departed from the area and state. Members of the Donaldsonville Artillery are next recorded as being in Virginia later in 1862 and in 1863, in a reorganized unit, suffering wounds or being taken prisoner. John Hernandez endured a second wound at Frazer's Farm, and Andre Suarez and A. Perez were wounded at Fredericksburg. Among those captured were Esteve Hidalgo, Narcisse Plasencia (wounded at Chancellorsville), Joseph Prados, Sergeant Ramirez, Lieutenant Sanchez, Antoine Sobral (possibly not an Isleño), John Suarez, and Joseph Rodriguez. Private Francisco Perrez died in a Richmond hospital on May 4, 1863, from war injuries received in February. As hostilities ended in 1865, the prisoners were paroled. In all, 20 men of the 150-member Donaldsonville Artillery died during the war, 16 in battle.[12]

Physical descriptions preserved by Marchand suggest that the Canary Islanders had changed little from their ancestors who had emigrated to Louisiana eight decades earlier. In height the soldiers ranged from five feet one inch to five feet four inches, and they usually had, although there were exceptions, dark hair and eyes. They were most often in their late teens or early twenties when they enlisted.[13]

The Federal invasion of Louisiana in 1862 sparked a fresh wave of enlistment fever. Ascension Parish Isleños joined the 28th Louisiana Infantry Regiment in April and May. Among them were Antoine Acosta,

11. Sidney Marchand, Sr., *Forgotten Fighters, 1861–1865* (Donaldsonville, La., 1966), *passim*.
12. *Ibid.*
13. *Ibid.*

Augustin Acosta, Rudolph E. Alba, Francis Alleman (Aleman), Henry Centeno, Francis Gonzales, Baltazar Hernandez, Philip Hernandez, Lawrence Lopez, Bernard Martinez, Andre Perera (Pereira), and Edouard Vives, probably a grandson of Dr. Vives. In response to Federal strategy designed to cut the Confederacy in two by seizing all of the Mississippi, the 28th Louisiana Infantry marched off to reenforce Vicksburg, where major Confederate river fortifications existed. (Other Isleños were also at Port Hudson.) What action the regiment saw prior to the spring of 1863 is unknown. At that time, Union General Ulysses S. Grant laid siege to Vicksburg. The Isleños present endured the rigors of the siege along with the other soldiers. In early July, at the same time that Lee's Confederate army lost the Battle of Gettysburg, Vicksburg also capitulated. The Union army paroled the captured soldiers of the 28th Louisiana Infantry on July 4. Many of these men reenlisted before the end of the year.[14]

Other Ascension men served the Confederate cause in the 8th Louisiana Infantry Regiment. Among them, Augustin Corbo died at Fisher's Hill on September 22, 1864. Private Charles L. Gomes (or Gomez) enlisted in 1861 and died at Gettysburg on July 1, 1863, at about twenty-two years of age. Private Eugene Sanchez joined on March 18, 1862, at age twenty-three. Captured and paroled at Gettysburg, he reenlisted in December, 1864. Sanchez died in a Union prison camp after being apprehended a second time. Joseph Garcia and John Gomez were both captured at Fredericksburg. Still other Ascension soldiers included Second Sergeant Jules Lorio and Private Hypolite Vives. They belonged to the 2nd Louisiana Cavalry and were both captured. Privates D. Acosta and A. Vegas (probably Antonio Vega) served in Squires Battalion, while Corporal J. Gomez was in the 22nd Louisiana Infantry Regiment.[15]

Less is known about the soldiers of St. Bernard Parish. Of them Albert Estopinal stands out, largely because of his later political career. Albert was the son of Joseph and Felicia Gonzales Estopinal, who were born in St. Bernard Parish in 1816 and 1821 respectively. Albert's grandfather was a courier in the Battle of New Orleans. His father's second wife, still living in 1892, gave birth to Albert; Victor, a Jefferson Parish planter; Josephine, wife of M. L. Morales; and Olivia, wife of Lovinski Nunez. In the spring of 1862, Albert Estopinal was a student in New Orleans when Farragut's fleet spearheaded the invasion of Louisiana. At seven-

14. *Ibid*. Pp. 85–86 contain the names of the Isleños captured at Vicksburg.
15. *Ibid*.

teen he quit school to enlist in Company G of the St. Bernard Guards in the 28th Louisiana Infantry, which Colonel Allen Thomas was organizing. Perhaps because of his education, Estopinal became the orderly sergeant of his company. In May, 1862, his unit reenforced the Vicksburg garrison and underwent a siege of two months. Estopinal next saw action at the battle of Chickasaw Bayou in December before returning to Vicksburg. He was in Vicksburg when Grant laid siege in May, 1863, but left to escort Union prisoners to a Confederate prison in Richmond before it surrendered. After the men of his unit were paroled at Vicksburg, they and Estopinal joined the 22nd Louisiana Regiment, which consisted of heavy artillery. He served at Mobile as a sergeant in Company B. Following his unit's surrender at Spanish Fort in the spring of 1865, the Federal army paroled Estopinal on May 15, at Meridian, Mississippi. After the war, Estopinal began his phenomenal career in Louisiana politics, rising to become a United States representative. He participated actively in Confederate veteran circles, and the editor of the St. Bernard *Voice* bestowed upon him the honorary title of "General."[16]

Also in St. Bernard Parish, the wealthy planter and sometime sheriff Antonio Marrero took steps to organize a regiment at the start of the war. Briefly the regiment's colonel, Marrero left the unit for unknown reasons and never served. Another Marrero and a cousin of Antonio, Bastian (Sebastian) left St. Bernard Parish to seek employment in Alabama, where his son Louis H. Marrero was born in 1847. At age fifteen, in 1862 Louis enlisted in the Confederate army. He fought in Tennessee and Kentucky, suffered a wound at Murfreesboro, and was captured at Missionary Ridge in 1863. The Union army paroled him in March, 1865. Two years after the war, he and his father returned to St. Bernard Parish, where he married his second cousin Elodie, the daughter of Antonio Marrero.[17]

No doubt many more St. Bernard Isleños served in other units. Some of them were probably in the St. Bernard Mounted Rifles under Captain Jules Delery, which had seventy-eight men in it. In the first year of the war, neighboring New Orleans raised numerous military units in which men with Spanish surnames served. Unfortunately, there is no way of

16. Evans, *Confederate Military History*, X, 406–407; *Biographical and Historical Memoirs of Louisiana* (3 vols.; Chicago, 1892; rpr. Baton Rouge, 1975), I, 403.

17. *Biographical and Historical Memoirs of Louisiana*, II, 238. Louis Marrero's father-in-law was sheriff of St. Bernard Parish for a number of years, a member of the secessionist convention, and a planter until his death in 1878.

distinguishing the Isleños among them. A few of the more outstanding persons with Canarian surnames included Captain R. Beltran, in the Louisiana Legion Brigade; Captain F. Gomez, in the First Company of the Orleans Battalion of Artillery; and Lieutenants A. D. Garcia, P. A. Gomez, and P. Marrero (who probably was a Canarian). Lieutenant Joseph Nunez (who had a common St. Bernard name) served in Company E of the Battalion of Yellow Jackets (10th Louisiana Volunteers).[18]

The Miles Legion had several Isleños, among whom was Lieutenant Rodriguez. A cavalry unit known as the New River Rangers made up a part of the legion and consisted of men from the eastern section of Ascension Parish. It formed in November, 1862, with Captain Joseph Gonzales, who had been born in Galvez on April 13, 1837, and who was the son of Miguel Gonzales, in command. The unit had eighty-eight men in it. In May, 1863, the New River Rangers merged with the Orleans Light Horse and other units to form the 14th Confederate Cavalry Regiment, which participated in the battle of Harrisburg, Mississippi. Soon after, in December, this regiment broke up, and its three Louisiana companies returned home in March, 1864. They were then attached to Ogden's Battalion of the 9th Cavalry Regiment, which never achieved regimental strength. Captain Gonzales surrendered in Alabama at the end of the war after having acquired a distinguished war record. This record served him well in Ascension politics, as he was sheriff in 1866 and often elected to the parish police jury.[19]

Despite gallant Confederate efforts, the military and industrial might of the Union proved insurmountable, and the South lost the war. When the defeated Louisiana soldiers returned home, they found conditions vastly different from those they had known. Gone was the general prewar prosperity. Now, after years of hardship in the army, the veterans encountered more suffering and privation. Louisiana's economy, devastated by the war, improved slowly, and years passed before full recovery came. Meanwhile, many small farmers lost their lands, became sharecroppers, or lived at the subsistence level. Planters, as well, often failed

18. Napier Bartlett, *Military Record of Louisiana, Including Biographical and Historical Papers Relating to the Military Organizations of the State* (New Orleans, 1875; rpr. Baton Rouge, 1964), 248–58.

19. Marchand, *Forgotten Fighters*, 120–21. Gonzales died on November 8, 1915, and was buried in Prairieville. From his marriages to Rosalie Adorea Marchand and Louise Landry, Gonzales had about sixteen children. See *Biographical and Historical Memoirs of Louisiana*, I, 449.

to survive the economic depression of the postwar years and saw their estates change hands. Overall, lower Louisiana continued a trend toward further land concentration and the operation of sugar plantations by corporations possessing more capital than the planters had. The returning veterans also found Federal army rule in the state and, by 1867, Radical Republican government. In the Reconstruction era, which lasted a decade, the Radicals employed freedmen's votes and corruption to dominate state government. Those turbulent years continued to disrupt the lives of Louisiana's people.[20]

The Union occupation of St. Bernard Parish in the spring of 1862 confronted the Isleños with a new relationship toward the freedmen. General Butler, the first governor of federally occupied Louisiana, seized abandoned plantations and worked them with runaway slaves. By October loyal planters of St. Bernard agreed to pay able-bodied freedmen wages of ten dollars per month. By early the next year, the former slaves were also working for wages on Bayou Lafourche, which by then had come under Federal control. When the war ended in 1865, the freedmen continued to be important for their labor, and as in the past, whites made efforts to dominate them. Economically, there was little to distinguish many poor whites from the freedmen, and white supremacy became the instrument to keep them subordinate. Carpetbaggers and scalawags, on the other hand, used black votes during Reconstruction to keep themselves in power. Occasionally, they even tried to protect and improve the lot of the former slaves.[21]

The economic loss Louisiana whites suffered owing to the war no doubt helped to worsen race relations. Evidence of the deteriorated position of the Canary Islanders in property was the United States government's direct tax on real estate in 1865. The tax was relatively light, only .156 percent of the assessed evaluation, and amounted to $15.60 per $10,000 of assessed property. The depressed prices on real estate made the tax lighter, although landowners often found ready money difficult to come by. In Ascension Parish, the only two Canarians standing out in property were Francis Allemand (Aleman), who received a tax bill of $10.36, and Manuel Rodriguez, who was to pay $14.23. Most of the 37 Isleño names listed in Ascension owed between $1.00 and $3.00, while

20. Taylor, *Louisiana: A Bicentennial History*, 115–17. For a fuller account of Reconstruction, see Joe Gray Taylor, *Louisiana Reconstructed, 1863–1877* (Baton Rouge, 1974); Peyton McCrary, *Abraham Lincoln and Reconstruction: The Louisiana Experiment* (Princeton, 1978); C. Peter Ripley, *Slaves and Freedmen in Civil War Louisiana* (Baton Rouge, 1976).

21. McCrary, *Abraham Lincoln and Reconstruction*, 93.

still others paid less than $1.00. At the bottom of the tax bills were Meguel (Miguel) Gonzales, with $0.10, and Mathias Acosta with $0.19. In neighboring Assumption Parish, where a number of prosperous Isleños had lived before the war, 39 Canary Islanders had tax bills ranging between $3.00 and $5.00. Several others owed larger sums, including Florentine Rodriguez, with $12.72; Jean Gonzales Sons, with $11.61; Balthazar Alleman, with $15.90; and P. H. Truillo (Truxillo) and Company, with $11.13. The impressive fortunes owned by prewar Isleños on Bayou Lafourche were now no more.[22]

The 1865 tax roll also revealed more than 40 Canarian names in East Baton Rouge Parish, most of them Gusman (Guzman), Hernandez, Lopez, Martinez, Rodriguez, Sanches (Sanchez), and Tilano. The Isleños' taxes ranged from less than $1.00 to $5.00. However, James Gusman was assessed $9.45, and the business or plantation of Martinez and Landry had a tax of $15.75. In Lafourche Parish, where Isleños also resided, the names of Sanchez, Vega, Barrios, Allemand (Aleman), Rodriguez, Albares (Alvarez), and Gonzales stand out. None of these Canarians owned large amounts of real estate, and their tax bills ranged from $0.32 to about $5.00.[23]

The tax roll listed more Spanish names for St. Bernard Parish than for any other parish. The roll, however, does not distinguish between Isleños and other Hispanics; only familiarity with Canarian surnames provides a clue as to which were Isleños. Approximately 60 Hispanics received tax assessments in St. Bernard (and there were probably others who did not). Antonio Marrero still possessed more real estate than any other Isleño. His tax bill of $48.60 represented property slightly in excess of $30,000. Other Canarians having large amounts of real property, as noted through their taxes, were the Widow R. Acosta, with $11.34, and the heirs of Solis, with $9.72. Most of the other Canary Islanders had assessments below $3.00 and many owed amounts below $1.00. In neighboring Plaquemines Parish, where a few Isleños had drifted over the years, the tax record listed 15 Hispanic names. The most common Canarian names were Solis, Barrios, and Perez. All four Perezes listed—Joseph, Octave, Joseph M., and Johnson—had assessments of only

---

22. *Citizens of Louisiana from Whom U.S. Direct Tax Was Collected in 1865* (Baton Rouge, 1892), 3–10.
    23. *Ibid.*, 60–65.

$0.49. Other Hispanics from New Orleans also resided in Plaque-mines.[24]

The Civil War also served to exacerbate race relations. Isleño treatment of blacks in the postwar era in no way differed from the treatment other whites gave the blacks. Yet Isleños had not always been intolerant. In the eighteenth century, when the Canary Islanders first arrived in Louisi-ana, they did not suffer from racial prejudice, and they appear to have gotten along well with slaves and freedmen. The wills of two Canary Islanders living in New Orleans cited earlier attest to this. Legal documents of the colonial era as well reveal the kindnesses shown by Isleños to blacks. Also, along Bayou Lafourche, Canary Islanders sold small parcels of land to free blacks who settled in their midst; those tiny black communities have survived to the present. But over the course of several decades, the Isleños became imbued with the same attitude toward blacks as their Anglo-Saxon and Gallic neighbors had. That attitude worsened in the postwar era, and the Canarians shared in the effort to keep blacks subservient. That effort led to violence.[25]

Violence toward blacks was modest until 1866, when thirty-four freedmen and three white Unionists died in a New Orleans riot. The riot outraged northerners and resulted in help for the former bondsmen, including the right to vote and the first military reconstruction act in 1867. Louisiana whites despised the laws and military occupation, and looked forward to a Democratic victory in the presidential election in November, 1868, as the means of ridding themselves of Yankee domi-nance. To win the election, they attempted to frighten blacks from going to the polls or into voting the Democratic ticket. Organizations such as the Ku Klux Klan, Knights of the White Camellia, and the Spanish-supported Infantes de [Horatio] Seymour, named for the Democratic presidential hopeful, became active. Violence increased as the election neared. In Bossier Parish, local authorities reported that about forty Negroes lost their lives, while Republicans asserted that the dead were really three times as many. In St. Landry Parish another thirty or forty blacks died; the Radicals claimed that more than two hundred were actually killed. Throughout Louisiana, smaller numbers of Negroes

24. *Ibid.*, 281–83, 296–300.
25. Taylor, *Louisiana: A Bicentennial History*, 120–22. On worsening race relations, see Ripley, *Slaves and Freedmen in Civil War Louisiana*, 90–101; and Henry C. Dethloff and Robert R. Jones, "Race Relations in Louisiana, 1877–1898," *Louisiana History*, XIV (1968), 301–23. On black settlements on Bayou Lafourche, see Alleman, "The Legend and History of the Place-Names of Assumption Parish," and Taylor, *Louisiana Reconstructed*, 168–69.

perished in minor outbreaks. Against those events came the St. Bernard riot in October.[26]

Distressing economic conditions in the parish undoubtedly contributed to the riot. Several plantations were abandoned, and others lay idle. "Colonel" Antonio Marrero left his lands fallow but rented out his buildings as lodgings to the freedmen. Radicals also operated several plantations, having either purchased or rented them from the owners. Poor whites particularly suffered from hard times, with fewer employment opportunities, wages and prices depressed, and competition from blacks. Prior to the riot, the parish's Spaniards (mainly Isleños), French, and Sicilians were described as being rabidly against blacks. Because of the forthcoming election, Democrats held meetings, rallies, and parades. The proximity to New Orleans also frequently involved parish residents in events in the adjoining city. The Spanish club Infantes de Seymour had members in both St. Bernard and New Orleans. Besides being hostile toward blacks, Democrats hurled threats at the local St. Bernard Republicans, particularly at the planter Thomas Ong, General A. L. Lee, who also operated a plantation, and Mike Curtis of the Metropolitan police force, an instrument of the Republicans. All of this served as background to the St. Bernard riot that began on Sunday, October 25.[27]

On Sunday morning, the parish's Democratic clubs—the Constitution Club, the Bumble Bee Club, and the Infantes de Seymour, the latter with representatives from New Orleans—began assembling near the parish courthouse for a procession to the church on Bayou Terre-aux-Boeufs, where the priest would consecrate the Bumble Bee flag. The blessing of the flag, however, appears not to have occurred. Tempers were already hot because the day before, trouble had almost erupted when ten or fifteen Spaniards (most of them Isleños), Sicilians, and others had surrounded the house of Curtis, hurling insults at him and perhaps even threatening to kill him. Now on Sunday, probably in the afternoon, as the Democrats marched back from the church along the bayou road,

26.   See Chapter Four and Archives of the Spanish Government of West Florida, 18 vols., 19th Judicial District Court, Baton Rouge, WPA translation. See also Melinda Meek Hennessy, "Race and Violence in Reconstruction New Orleans: The 1868 Riot," *Louisiana History*, XX (1979), 77–91.

27.   The most descriptive account of the St. Bernard riot is J. M. Lee, 1st Lieut., 39th U.S. Infantry, report to Brev. Major B. T. Hutchins, A.A. Inspector General (New Orleans, Louisiana, November 27, 1868), Louisiana Historical Center, New Orleans. Newspaper accounts of the riot were usually biased and inaccurate; see, for example, New Orleans *Times*, October 24, 26, 27, 28, and 29, 1868.

the whites encountered several freedmen, whom they tried to force to shout "Hurrah for Seymour." The blacks refused, and members of both sides drew guns—including Eugene Lock, a freedman. In the altercation, the whites shot Lock to death and wounded two other blacks. That event sparked the St. Bernard riot, as moderation vanished and lawlessness took charge.[28]

Word of the shooting alarmed everyone in the parish, particularly the freedwomen, who feared a massacre. Many of them gathered up their children, food, and clothing, and fled into the cane fields. Meanwhile Ong, a leading parish Republican, learned about the killings at his plantation, located four miles above the courthouse. He dispatched Curtis with a note to the parish sheriff, Antonio Chailaire, to form a posse and to preserve order. Curtis rode out at twilight to Terre-aux-Boeufs. Near the courthouse, armed whites stopped him and asked that he identify himself. Curtis first hesitated and then admitted who he was. The whites thereupon pulled out weapons, killing Curtis as he tried to flee. A freedman who witnessed the shooting was found dead the next day. Ong received word of Curtis' fate within a few hours. Anticipating further trouble, he sent an elderly black, James King, by a circuitous route to Dr. Thornton's place above his own. Thornton appears to have been the parish magistrate, and he, in turn, sent King on to the Jackson Barracks to summon soldiers to St. Bernard as quickly as possible. Although King ran into a group of New Orleans Infantes de Seymour returning home, they dismissed him as "an old fool nigger." He passed them late Sunday night or in the early hours of Monday morning.[29]

After the killing of Curtis, blacks assembled on the road in front of Ong's plantation on Sunday night. Democratic supporters earlier had threatened Ong's life, and the blacks, some of them armed, had arrived to guard him. The planter tried to calm them and even insisted that they return home; he felt that their presence would only contribute to new outbreaks. The freedmen refused, saying excitedly in broken English and Creole French that they would protect him against the assassins coming to murder him. At about 10:00 P.M., since the whites had failed to appear, the blacks started down the road, returning to Marrero's plantation, about a mile away, where they lived. As they passed the store and home of Pablo San Feliu, trouble erupted. San Feliu, a baker, was a

28. J. M. Lee, report, 4–6.
29. *Ibid.*, 7–8.

Spaniard whose wife seems to have been an Isleña. Although militantly against blacks, in the past he had sold whiskey to the freedmen, and some of them wanted it now. Probably when the blacks insisted too menacingly, San Feliu fired his shotgun repeatedly, killing one black and wounding several more. They, in turn, stormed the house, killed San Feliu, and set the building ablaze, though they did not harm San Feliu's wife and family, who fled to New Orleans. San Feliu's body and that of the dead black, Thomas Morgan, burned in the conflagration. Possibly the blacks also set fire to the house of Manuel Serpas, adjacent to San Feliu's, before they broke up.[30]

On Monday, October 26, disorders, killings, and looting erupted almost everywhere in the parish, with all the victims now being black. Many whites, however, fearing more black violence, filled the road to New Orleans. At Bencheque, on Terre-aux-Boeufs, Spaniards and Sicilians gathered, threatening to fall on the Ong and General Lee plantations.

In the upper parish, the location of most of the plantations and blacks, the freedmen spoke of blocking the road and stopping whites from passing through. Dr. M. L. Lee, General Lee's father, tried to counsel them against it. At about 11:00 A.M. Monday, while he pleaded with them, forty to fifty armed and mounted whites appeared on the road. Dr. Lee went out to speak with them only to be taken prisoner, along with several freedmen; the others vanished into the cane fields after the whites fired several shots in their direction. One of the captured blacks served as Dr. Lee's translator since he could not understand the captors' mixture of Spanish and French. The Spaniards conducted Dr. Lee down the road to Florey's (Manuel Flores') coffeehouse. After dark, several of the black prisoners were shot to death. One black youth of about twenty was only wounded and escaped into the brush, where he remained for the next three days. He later testified that at about 10:00 P.M., the St. Bernard Parish sheriff, Mr. Chailaire, and several other whites arrived from Terre-aux-Boeufs and released Dr. Lee. They gave him safe conduct to Ong's plantation, where United States soldiers stood guard.[31]

Lieutenant J. M. Lee, who investigated the riot for the Federal authorities, later described the events of Monday and Tuesday: "During the entire days of Monday and Tuesday—the 26th and 27th, Oct., parties of

30. *Ibid.*, 10–16; New Orleans *Times*, Oct. 27, 1868.
31. J. M. Lee, report, 17–18.

armed white men, some pretending to be sheriffs Posse, roamed over many plantations of the Parish, shooting and knocking down, and otherwise maltreating freedpeople, driving them pell-mell from their cabins, seizing guns, pistols, knives, —destroying Registration Papers, and stealing bed clothes, wearing apparel, pen knives, soap, candles, etc., in short taking everything they could appropriate to their own use."[32]

Among the events on Monday, whites wounded a freedwoman at the Davis or Millauden plantation and plundered the cabins there. That same morning a party of white men, alleging to be a posse of deputy sheriffs, tried to arrest Ong. The planter and several of his friends, presumably armed, refused to leave the safety of the Ong house. A standoff continued until Major Bates and a company of United States troopers arrived from the Jackson Barracks and prevented further trouble. Elsewhere, on Monday evening, another party of whites rode out to the Dar Quanto plantation, where they killed a freedman and wounded several more.[33]

After Monday, the disorders continued but with less severity. On Tuesday the authorities found the body of a black man on the Marrero plantation. A few days later, on November 1, Eugene Joseph, a black, was shot in the lung at Bencheque, then arrested. The local whites threw him on a cart and transported him to the courthouse. There Radicals obtained his release. Later in November, another freedman died violently in St. Bernard Parish. When election day arrived, blacks stayed away from the polls; the white effort to intimidate the freedmen into not voting had proved successful.

But the spirit of the riot lingered on. Between October 26 and November 6, armed groups of whites, headed by "deputy sheriffs," under the alleged authority of Judge Philip Toca, moved through the parish, arresting and beating freedmen and freedwomen. They charged the blacks with committing crimes at San Feliu's house. Toca, Republicans claimed, lacked the authority to make arrests or to deputize whites; the only legitimate magistrate in the parish, they contended, was Judge Thornton. Nevertheless, Toca's men arrested sixty-four freedmen, accusing them of killing San Feliu and burning his house. They brought the prisoners to the New Orleans parish jail to await trial. Some days later, however, Judge Abel in New Orleans ordered the blacks freed because of

32. *Ibid.*, 20.
33. *Ibid.*, 19–20.

their illegal arrest and insufficient evidence. Their release did not deter Toca back in St. Bernard Parish, for he rearrested Andy May, whom the Isleños accused of being the leader in the death of San Feliu, and several others. This time Toca put May in the St. Bernard Parish jail. However, Brevet Major General Edward Hatch ordered the parish authorities to release the prisoners and not to rearrest any freedmen then at work on the plantations.[34]

After the freedmen's release, affairs in the parish quieted down. In the riot two whites (Curtis and San Feliu) and nine freedmen had lost their lives, and sixteen additional blacks, two of them women, had been wounded. No whites were ever arrested or had charges filed against them. The local Democratic authorities had firm control of the parish in that respect, and only the presence of a company of United States soldiers preserved order. Race relations in the parish had sunk to an all-time low, where they remained for years to come. At a later time, when dates had become fuzzy in the minds of most people, whites erected a tombstone over Pablo San Feliu's grave in the St. Bernard cemetery. The inscription on it reads:

> Pablo San Feliu
> Assassinated by Slaves
> Incited by Carpetbag Rule
> Died Oct. 1869[35]

The tombstone remains as a grim reminder of the St. Bernard riot. The purpose of the riot was to intimidate blacks and to achieve a Democratic victory in the 1868 election. Although St. Bernard Parish and Louisiana voted solidly for Seymour, the Republican candidate, General Ulysses S. Grant, won the presidential election; and Reconstruction continued for the next nine years. Military rule gave the upper hand to the Republicans, who, in turn, sought to protect the freedmen. But the soldiers had limitations in their ability to protect. Once Reconstruction ended in 1877, the position of blacks in Louisiana steadily deteriorated.

---

34. *Ibid.*, 21–22; New Orleans *Times*, December 3, 1868.
35. Author's visit to the St. Bernard cemetery, June, 1982. See also Calvin A. Claudel, "Tombs of Historic Interest in the Saint Bernard Cemetery," *Louisiana Historical Quarterly*, XXIV (1941), 354–59.

Eight

The Bourbon Age in Louisiana

From the end of Reconstruction to the eve of World War I, change came slowly to the Isleño communities, as it did to Louisiana as a whole. The state's population, particularly the lower classes, continued to suffer from economic privation and from social and cultural stagnation. The poor in particular among the rural people suffered from hookworm, pellagra, rickets, and scurvy in addition to other diseases that resulted from inadequate diets and appalling sanitation. This era, nevertheless, introduced innovations that affected the lives of the Canary Islanders. Improvements in transportation and communications placed greater reliance upon railroads, better roads, and motor vehicles (automobiles and trucks), which were slowly replacing horses. Newspapers, usually weeklies, appeared in towns, and entertainment advanced with the arrival of silent motion pictures.

Among the more assimilated and urban Isleño families, greater awareness arose after Reconstruction that education could provide the means to improve their lives. Earlier, social and economic aspirations revolved mainly around joining the dominant planter class. Now, goals were oriented toward the middle class, and entry could be achieved through education to become lawyers, doctors, teachers, professionals of other kinds, white-collar workers, and businessmen. Assimilation into the mainstream of Louisiana life, nevertheless, affected only a minority of the Canarians. Many more continued to live as their ancestors, and they regarded education as subversive to their traditional values. Changes in this era occurred mainly in the cities and towns, and overall, the Canary Islanders of Louisiana remained a rural folk.

The ending of Reconstruction failed to bring betterment for most Isleños. Political conditions in large measure determined life in Louisiana, and elite rule dominated the state. In 1877 a coalition of large planters and New Orleans politicians, the Ring, took charge of the state. The members employed corrupt practices, such as the convict-lease system, the Louisiana lottery, and electoral fraud more blatant than during Union occupation, to retain their hold on government. New Orleans excelled in dishonesty with the stuffing of ballot boxes, voting under the names of deceased people, the intimidation of opponents, and the filing of false returns. The Ring represented self-made men, who sometimes sympathized with working-class people; the latter, in return, showed their gratitude by voting the Democratic ticket. Despite reformers wanting to improve government morality, they ignored the plight of the common people, who, not surprisingly, failed to support them.[1]

Distressing economic conditions and rampant racism characterized Louisiana in the late nineteenth century. Depressed agricultural prices and land values continued after Reconstruction. Dishonest methods in sugar and cotton marketing defrauded yeoman farmers of the rewards of their labor. Many small farmers failed and became sharecroppers. Government expenditures declined, and white illiteracy actually rose between 1880 and 1890. Bourbon politicians waved the "bloody shirt" of Reconstruction and exploited the race issue to rally support from lower-class whites. They threatened poor whites that failure to vote for Democratic (Bourbon) candidates would return blacks to power. Racism proved more powerful than economics in keeping the Bourbons in office. When the lower classes turned to populism in the early 1890s in response to intolerable economic conditions and forged an alliance with the Republicans, the Bourbons resorted to fraudulent vote counts to win the 1896 election. Frightened, the Bourbons destroyed the voting power of both poor whites and blacks. The 1898 state constitution imposed restrictions on suffrage, barring illiterates and most itinerant sharecroppers from voting, decreeing a poll tax, and mandating grandfather clauses. Between 1897 and 1904, the number of black voters dropped from 130,000 to 1,342, and white voters declined from 164,000 to 92,000.

---

1. Taylor, *Louisiana: A Bicentennial History*, 132–37; Bennett H. Wall (ed.), *Louisiana: A History* (Arlington Heights, Ill., 1984), 263.

Other eligible voters no longer bothered to cast ballots. The Bourbon political maneuver had saved the day against lower-class discontent.[2]

The start of the twentieth century saw new economic and political entities in the state. Among them were the Choctaw Club that replaced the Ring in New Orleans, natural gas and petroleum companies, lumber mill owners, and salt and sulphur interests. Their grip on state government obtained the passage of favorable legislation. They evaded taxation and regulation and controlled labor through exploitative wages, yellow-dog contracts, lockouts, and strike breakers. While Louisiana's power elites ruled the state, they made social mobility difficult but not impossible. Greater economic activity, coupled with a gradually improving educational system in the early twentieth century, allowed determined youth to rise.[3]

Nevertheless, improvement came slowly for most Isleños. Descriptions of St. Bernard Parish and the Bayou Lafourche region before the twentieth century reveal that conditions had changed only slightly since Reconstruction. One such description of Louisiana's rural life in 1880s stated: "As before the war, [the rural population] . . . tilled their small acres, tended livestock, or engaged in fishing or trapping. Some raised sugarcane on little plots and sold the stalks to the planter-refiners. Outsiders who passed through the region in the 1880s were astounded by [the] continuing lack of contact with, and indifference to, the rest of humanity."[4]

In an article on St. Bernard Parish dated about 1880, Albert Estopinal, Sr., wrote that local crops grown on the twenty large plantations consisted of sugarcane, corn, rice, and some cotton. He added, "The largest portion of that part of the parish lying on the Terre-aux-Boeufs and [Bayou] La Loutre is cut up into small farms, where vegetables are raised." Small farmers shipped vegetables to the New Orleans market in large quantities (probably in the same way that Isleños had sent them forty years earlier). Estopinal blamed poor communications for the agricultural nature of the parish, its small population, and its lack of development. The steamboats *Daisy* and *Martha* came down the Missis-

2. William Ivy Hair, *Bourbonism and Agrarian Protest: Louisiana Politics, 1877–1900* (Baton Rouge, 1969); Taylor, *Louisiana: A Bicentennial History,* 140–43. See also Roger W. Shugg, *Origins of Class Struggle in Louisiana* (Baton Rouge, 1939).

3. Taylor, *Louisiana: A Bicentennial History,* 145–47.

4. Hair, *Bourbonism and Agrarian Protest,* 39–40; Charles Dudley Warner, "The Acadian Land," *Harper's,* LXXIV (February, 1887), 354.

sippi from New Orleans and stopped at the solitary road into the interior. Stagecoaches, however, penetrated the parish for only ten miles, the distance that gravel had recently been strewn on the road. Beyond that, the road was impassable in the rainy season. Most of the parish inhabitants earned their livelihood from truck farming, fishing, hunting, trapping, and growing fruit, especially oranges. Similar to those in other areas of the state, St. Bernard Parish schools suffered from neglect.[5]

The lower reaches of the parish, Delacroix Island, contained the Isleños who had undergone the least amount of change. In March, 1882, the first parish newspaper, the St. Bernard *Weekly Eagle*, ran a description of Delacroix Island. Dr. Arthur Joseph Padron, who had a Canarian surname but was from New Orleans, established the weekly, preferring to publish than to practice medicine. The lengthy account, written by "Happy Jack," told of a visit to Phillip Guttierrez' place on Delacroix Island. Happy Jack traveled by foot, canal boat, and sailing vessel to reach "Pescadoresville." The settlement consisted of palmetto huts, which dotted the western bank of Bayou Terre-aux-Boeufs for more than a mile. Happy Jack wrote, "The inhabitants of this place are principally those hard working men, but inadequately rewarded, who travel daily from this point to the city to supply the markets with fish, crabs, shrimps, and game, from which source they derive their existence." He called them hospitable, industrious, and "mostly inflexible emulators of total abstinence." The residents, principally Canarians, were proud of their heritage. Their living, however, was a "hand to mouth affair" because the often impassable roads prevented them from selling their produce in New Orleans. Happy Jack advised his readers that his party could never have reached the island by land, and encouraged the parish police jury to enforce the laws for better roads.[6]

Nearly a decade later, Alcée Fortier, a Louisiana historian, made two visits to St. Bernard Parish. In June, 1891, he traveled on the New Orleans and Shell Beach Railroad to St. Bernard Parish and by carriage to Bayou Terre-aux-Boeufs, the land of *les Islingues*, as he claimed the Isleños were known. Fortier wrote about them: "A number of these

5. William H. Harris (ed.), *Louisiana Products, Resources and Attractions, with a Sketch of the Parishes: A Hand Book of Reliable Information Concerning the State* (New Orleans, 1881), 200–201.
6. St. Bernard *Weekly Eagle*, March 16, 1882. Another newspaper published in the 1880s, St. Bernard *Progress*, suspended publication in December, 1889 (St. Bernard *Voice*, January 17, 1931).

people are men of education and of some wealth; the senator from St. Bernard parish is an Estopinal and the sheriff is a Nunez. The great majority, however, as with the descendants of the Acadians, are poor and ignorant. They cultivate their little patch of ground and raise vegetables, chiefly potatoes and onions. They are also great hunters. They all speak Spanish, but a few speak the creole patois and the younger ones speak English." During his visit to Terre-aux-Boeufs, Fortier met an ancient woman who complained that the land was "better for oxen than for Christians." She lamented that the children preferred to speak English rather than Spanish.[7]

In late November, 1891, Fortier returned for a second visit to the Isleños, this time venturing to "la isla" (Delacroix Island) on horseback in company of Ben Olivier. As they rode through Terre-aux-Boeufs toward the gulf, they noticed the strip of high land growing narrower and then changing to the trembling prairie. They passed a number of small farms whose owners all spoke Spanish. Beyond, they encountered a dense wood of large oak trees, whose limbs had been shorn from their gigantic trunks by powerful gulf storms.

Their destination, the Isleño settlement on "la isla," preserved a way of life that had persisted for a century. Fortier described what he saw.

> The dwellings are on both sides of the bayou and are mostly palmetto huts. As it was a cold day nearly all the men had gone hunting and fishing, and the women were indoors; a few children, however, dark-haired and brown, were running about in the cold wind, bare-headed and bare-footed . . . . The Spaniards on l'Ile live entirely by hunting and fishing. The women fish in the bayou in front of their huts, but the men go to the gulf for fishing and to the lakes for hunting. They bring back immense quantities of fish and ducks, which are sent to the Olivier railroad station, ten or twelve miles distant, in small carts drawn by oxen, yoked Spanish fashion, by the horns.[8]

Olivier brought Fortier to the hut of Pepe Martin, who gave his guests coffee and biscuits. While Olivier spoke with "Mr. Pepe," "Mrs. Pepe" listened without uttering a word. A two-year-old boy crouched in a corner and stared at them in fear, Fortier claimed. The historian believed that he was with "the children of nature, where man is supreme and woman is nothing but an obedient being." Of the four hundred island

---

7. Alcée Fortier, *Louisiana Studies: Literature, Customs and Dialects, History and Education* (New Orleans, 1894), 199–202.
8. *Ibid.*, 204–207.

residents, he asserted, not one could read. Despite their poverty, they appeared perfectly contented. He remarked about the people: "The Isleños are a pure race; they have a perfect horror of the negro and marry among themselves. Both boys and girls marry from the age of fifteen . . . and there are many children in each family." Before his guests departed, Pepe sang a *décima* for them about his life and needs. One line stated, "I don't want more than beans, coffee, and bread."[9]

On the journey to New Orleans, Fortier contrasted his own life in the city—that of a civilized man who enjoyed luxuries—with the Isleños' simple existence and ambitions. Fortier failed to realize that the Delacroix Island inhabitants clung to their way of life because they knew no other. Their isolation in the lower parish preserved the manner in which they had adapted to their environment.[10] But in other parts of St. Bernard, the Canary Islander descendants were changing, some of them rapidly.

Life in lower Louisiana, especially in the marsh parishes, was never easy. Storms, cold waves with occasional snowfalls, drought, floods, insects, and blight hurt the St. Bernard Parish farmers and fishermen. Little is known how much the Isleños suffered from hurricanes in the Spanish era or from those of 1812, 1831, 1856, and 1860. More is known about adversities as record keeping improved in the late nineteenth century. The winters of 1880 and 1881 proved disastrous to the citrus orchards of lower Louisiana. Orange orchards, once common, declined in number. (Citrus canker all but destroyed the orchards about 1930.) Minor hurricanes occurred in 1887 and 1892, inflicting minimal damage. In 1892 a crevasse in the Mississippi's bank produced a flood along the Terre-aux-Boeufs farming district that resulted in heavy losses.[11]

The hurricanes of 1893, 1901, and 1909 are better known. The most serious hit from September 30 to October 2, 1893; it was centered at Cheniere Caminada west of New Orleans and caused about five hundred deaths. The storm lashed the lower reaches of St. Bernard Parish, and water stood two or three feet deep in stricken areas. The storm produced no reported loss of life, but flimsy palmetto dwellings,

9. *Ibid.*, 206–209.
10. *Ibid.*, 210.
11. St. Bernard *Voice*, September 3, 1892, March 20, 1909; David M. Ludlum, *Early American Hurricanes, 1492–1870* (Boston, 1963), 75. From 1711 to 1938, thirty-five major hurricanes hit Louisiana. See Ivan Ray Tannehill, *Hurricanes: Their Nature and History* (Princeton, 1938).

personal property, and other Isleño belongings suffered. On August 14 and 15, 1901, another hurricane hit the parish, and as the St. Bernard *Voice* reported: "Down in Terre-aux-Boeufs the ravages of the wind and rainstorm were horrible to contemplate. Bayou Terre-aux-Boeufs had no respect for its banks and charged over them like a gallant soldier charges across a cane field with the enemy in close pursuit; every thing in the path of the roaring waters was swept away and few of its inhabitants were left to tell the tale." Shell Beach, a summer resort on the edge of Lake Borgne for New Orleans people, also sustained considerable damage to its buildings and boats. In addition, the cane, rice, and other crops suffered, yet despite the damage, only one person died. In September, 1909, another tropical disturbance slammed into the parish, the worst one in years, with winds gauged at seventy-five miles per hour. It inflicted damage on roofs, fences, trees, and crops. The waters rose at Shell Beach, Yscloskey, Bencheque, and Delacroix Island, forcing the residents at the fringes of the parish to flee to higher ground, and in that panic two babies drowned. The storm also injured the road to Delacroix Island, which suffered in every inundation that occurred.[12]

Improvements in St. Bernard Parish's educational system came gradually at the end of the nineteenth century. For many years, the parish spent five hundred dollars yearly on education. The upper parish had the schools, leaving Delacroix Island and other remote areas largely without access to learning. The St. Bernard *Voice* editor, on March 31, 1894, deplored the indifferent attitude of many local inhabitants toward education, particularly the farmers. They forced their children to work at home in order to save money and permitted them only a rudimentary education. In 1894, however, the parish established a school for the first time on Delacroix Island. It seems to have opened and closed several times over the years, usually owing to storms destroying the building. In January, 1902, the school board discussed reopening it, paying its teacher the meager salary of $12.50 a month.[13]

Despite imperfections, the St. Bernard school system produced reasonably well-educated eighth-grade graduates. Parents who could afford to sent their children out of the parish to further their education.

12. St. Bernard *Voice*, November 11, 1893, August 24, 1901, September 25, 1909. See also Gordon E. Dunn and Banner I. Miller, *Atlantic Hurricanes* (Baton Rouge, 1960), 302–303.
13. St. Bernard *Voice*, March 31, 1894, January 25, 1902; Renauld, "The History of the Public Schools in St. Bernard Parish," 46–56.

Occasionally, the police jury assisted outstanding students with scholarships, or institutions such as Louisiana State University and Tulane University provided the parish with a scholarship. Among the girl graduates, several attended the two-year teacher-training program at the State Normal School at Natchitoches. Most of them returned home to work. By 1902 the St. Bernard teachers included Azema Estopinal, Ermina Messa, and Rosa Nunez; Mr. A. Gonzales resigned that same year. Among the other teachers of the era were Valerie Morales and Joseph Nunez. While the parish gradually increased its number of schools, student attendance progressed even more slowly. By early 1906, only 328 white and 46 black students attended classes (St. Bernard Parish's population in 1910 consisted of 3,343 whites and 1,933 blacks). In 1907 six white and two black schools existed in the parish.[14]

In June, 1912, for the first time, five eighth-grade graduates from the St. Bernard Consolidated School received diplomas that entitled them to enter high school in New Orleans without examination. Four of the five graduates that year were Isleños: Louisa Guerra (class valedictorian), Rita Morales, Elvira Torres, and Ben Messa. Elvira received a scholarship to the State Normal School, and Ben won a scholarship to Louisiana State University. Louisa obtained a scholarship to Reaser Business College of New Orleans, where her sister Irene also went on a scholarship the following year.[15]

There was a constant need for teachers since most, especially the Isleños, were single women who gave up working as soon as they married. State Normal School graduates usually found employment in the parish, often becoming principals immediately. For example, in June, 1913, Helwige Serpas, a St. Bernard native, was hired as a principal upon completing her studies. She stayed only two years before accepting a teaching position at Raceland, which afforded her greater opportunities. Although parish schools were far from the best, education had improved since post-Civil War days and helped to prepare the youth for employment.[16]

The 1900 United States census confirms that most Isleños in St. Bernard Parish continued in their traditional occupations, with farmers and farm laborers predominating and fishermen found in fewer num-

---

14. St. Bernard *Voice*, September 30, 1902, November 4, 1905, December 21 and 28, 1907.
15. *Ibid.*, June 22, July 20, 1912, October 4, 1913.
16. *Ibid.*, June 7, November 22, 1913, July 31, 1915.

bers and residing mostly in the lower parish. The majority of the illiterates and non-English speakers lived in the wards along Terre-aux-Boeufs and on Delacroix Island. A number of foreigners from Spain also resided there, several of them married to Hispanic women born in Louisiana.[17]

Improved roads and new modes of transportation in this era helped many people, especially the urban dwellers. To keep the roads from turning into muddy quagmires whenever it rained, the police jury began laying shells on them. In 1896 the *Voice* boasted that good roads extended to Delacroix Island and enabled the residents to sell their catch in the New Orleans market, "transporting it themselves in their conveyances, which, though bearing the stamp of home made, are built to withstand the jolts and wear and tear." After the turn of the twentieth century, the picturesque carts and wagons yielded to motorcars and trucks. The new vehicles traveled faster than the horse-drawn conveyances but injured the shell roads because of their "high rate of speed." Despite the abuse, in April, 1910, the police jury raised the parish speed limit from fifteen to twenty-five miles per hour. Distances and isolation began to vanish as the motor age dawned. By then a number of St. Bernard residents had purchased vehicles, including Isleño professionals, authorities, businessmen, and farmers.[18]

Economic activity in St. Bernard Parish accelerated as the twentieth century opened. The ten miles of parish riverfront were well suited to industry. Stocklanding (Arabi) had long had a slaughterhouse, cattle pens, warehouses, and docks for ships. Later, the Standard Oil Company built large storage tanks in Chalmette for petroleum, which was refined in Baton Rouge. In 1909 the American Sugar Refining Company established a refinery in the parish and employed hundreds of workers. That same year, the St. Bernard *Voice* announced the construction of a cypress mill in Friscoville, which would hire three hundred laborers. Soon the Lopez-Greiner Company opened a cannery on the Plaquemines side of Delacroix Island to process oysters, shrimp, and fruit, and another plant went up in the parish to substitute palmetto for moss in mattresses, saddles, and cushions. Finally, the *Voice* informed its readers on September 5, 1914, of the building of a modern automobile plant in Arabi, which would hire hundreds of workers. Most of the labor

17. Twelfth Census (1900), Ascension, Assumption, and St. Bernard parishes, in American Census Records, United States Census Office.
18. St. Bernard *Voice*, September 19, 1896, May 22, 1909, April 9, 1910.

for the new industries came from New Orleans and outside the parish. The majority of the Isleños continued in the occupations that they knew best.[19]

In the farming areas of St. Bernard Parish, change also came slowly. Many "scientific" farmers adhered to development and believed that a labor shortage existed. To remedy that deficiency, the state advertised the virtues of Louisiana's benign climate and fertile soil, and sponsored immigration leagues to introduce European workers. As a result, four families from Malaga, Spain, came to work on the Poydras plantation in 1907 (with many more settling elsewhere in the state), and later Greeks, Macedonians, and Austrians joined them.[20]

After the turn of the century, gas and oil exploration went on in the parish, and the *Voice* confidently predicted a major strike for years. Although that did not occur, the once nearly valueless marshlands took on new importance. In the nineteenth century, few people had seemed interested in them, and the lands had sometimes been sold for taxes. Trappers and hunters had roamed unimpeded over the marshes, taking what they wanted. That changed after 1900 as marshlands again passed into private hands. Large blocks, often thousands of acres, sold first for 12.5 cents and later for 25 cents an acre. For example, in 1902 Fernando Estopinal and associates bought 45,000 acres of marshland, with an option for 10,000 more, paying only 12.5 cents per acre for marshlands and $3.50 for timberlands (the chenier, or oak, was especially valued).[21] As private owners took over the marshlands, the principal losers were the part-time trappers and hunters, who were mostly poor fishermen and farmers.

The 1908–1909 season, which was good, produced furs and skins valued at $61,287. The trappers caught 125,000 muskrats, 10,000 minks, 14,000 raccoons, 300 opossums, 200 otters, and 52 deer. In addition, hunters took 41,000 ducks, 6,000 poules d'eau, 550 snipe, and 250 doves. The catch was enormous but could not be repeated endlessly. Consequently, bad years followed good years, and the state legislature regulated trapping and hunting closely. It shortened the 1912–1913 season and required trappers and hunters to pay a $10.00 license fee. This

19. *Ibid.*, May 22, July 12, August 28, 1909, November 4, 1911, September 5, 1914.
20. *Ibid.*, February 16, March 16, November 9, 1907.
21. Many issues of the St. Bernard *Voice* mention the sale of marshlands and the possibility of a major natural gas or oil strike. On Fernando Estopinal, see the November 29, 1902, issue.

provoked a minor rebellion in the parish and resulted in the creation of the St. Bernard Hunters and Trappers' Association to represent the people's interests. The season opened with prices at $12.00 to $15.00 for otters, $4.50 for minks, $1.50 for raccoons, $0.20 for muskrats, and $0.10 for opossums. But prices fluctuated widely, and wholesale buyers reaped much of the profit. In good years the trappers made money, but in bad years they often suffered a loss.[22]

In the post-Reconstruction era, a few Isleños entered the professions, including the prestigious occupations of medicine and law. By 1903, Dr. Joseph A. Estopinal (son of Albert, Sr.) practiced medicine in St. Bernard Parish, and Dr. Joseph M. Suarez plied his profession in New Orleans. Another Estopinal son, Rene, received a degree in dentistry in 1908 and, after his father became a United States congressman that year, replaced him on the police jury from the fourth ward. Dr. Adrien Nunez, son of P. V. Nunez, also practiced medicine in the parish by 1911. Dr. Arthur J. Padron, editor of the St. Bernard *Eagle*, obtained a medical degree before 1880. Ill health forced his retirement to New Orleans, where he died in 1902. One of the earliest Canarians known to have obtained a law degree was Albert Estopinal, Jr., who was born in Poydras in the parish on December 1, 1868. After graduating from Louisiana State University, he entered the Tulane law school, finishing in 1890. Two years later, he became district attorney for the twenty-fifth district (St. Bernard and Plaquemines parishes). In 1904 Albert, Jr., was elected judge of the court of appeals, where he served for five years. He would hold several other political offices. Albert's younger brother, Fernando, born in 1870, graduated from law school in 1895. In 1898 he became a state livestock inspector and in 1904 secretary of the Lake Borgne Levee Board.[23]

Another prominent St. Bernard Isleño family was the Nunez. Nemours H. Nunez, son of Sheriff Esteve E. Nunez, served in a variety of offices. Born on March 17, 1873, he graduated from the Tulane high school in 1892 and from the university law school in 1899. He was the secretary of the Lake Borgne Levee Board, a member of the oyster commission, district judge, and later district attorney. His brother Fernand graduated from Tulane's law school in 1906, practiced law in the

22. St. Bernard *Voice*, May 15, 1909, October 26, November 16, 1912, January 31, 1914.
23. *Ibid.*, January 3, April 4, 1903, April 1, 1911; Alcée Fortier, *Louisiana, Comprising Sketches of Parishes, Towns, Events, Institutions, and Persons . . .* (3 vols.; n.p., 1914), 152, 154–55; New Orleans *Item, The Book of Louisiana: A Newspaper Reference Work* (New Orleans, 1916), 56, 79.

parish, and later became justice of the peace from the second ward. He died of pneumonia at age thirty-seven in 1920. Finally, Wallace A. Nunez (son of Lovinski, who held many parish offices himself, and nephew of Sheriff Nunez) graduated from Tulane in 1912 and continued his studies at Harvard University. In 1920 he was elected to the state house of representatives. Most of the Isleño graduates in medicine and law played a vigorous role in St. Bernard politics, which resulted eventually in the creation of factions that sometimes pitted one group of Canarians against another. That happened in 1909, upon the death of Sheriff Nunez.[24]

Esteve E. Nunez served as sheriff perhaps longer than any other St. Bernard resident. A parish native, he was born on July 6, 1844, son of Vincent Nunez. He was educated locally and farmed cotton in his early working years. He then succeeded Albert Estopinal, Sr., as sheriff in 1878, and served in that capacity until his death in 1909. His long tenure as sheriff and service in Louisiana law enforcement organizations earned him a statewide reputation. He was also a member of the powerful New Orleans Choctaw Club. Like many other Isleños, Nunez had a large family—eight children—from his marriages to Pauline Aguillard (Aguilar?) and Acelie Roy.[25]

Upon his father's death, Nemours intended to succeed him. Not long before, he had been elected district attorney, but the office of sheriff was then the most powerful in the parish. Opposition, however, came from another prominent Isleño, Albert Estopinal, Jr. He was then in the prime of life, with nearly twenty years of experience as a lawyer, district attorney, and court of appeals judge. Moreover, his father, Albert, Sr., had forty years of political experience and a statewide reputation, and had become a United States congressman only the year before. Meanwhile, Nemours Nunez had the endorsement of the less prominent St. Bernard Progress League. In the Democratic primary on November 2, 1909, Estopinal garnered 252 votes to Nunez' 148, and in the runoff election two weeks later, Estopinal won all 243 votes cast. He immediately appointed as his chief deputy sheriff William Nunez, the son of Lovinski Nunez (the longtime levee inspector for the Lake Borgne Levee

24. St. Bernard *Voice*, May 12, 1906, June 29, 1912, March 20, 1920; Fortier, *Louisiana*, III, 705–706.
25. St. Bernard *Voice*, September 25, 1909.

Board) and nephew of the late sheriff. Estopinal served as sheriff until another major election unseated him.[26]

From the final two decades of the nineteenth century to the 1920s, Isleños dominated St. Bernard Parish politics almost single-handedly. They made up most of the police jury and parish police officers. They were on the parish school board, the Lake Borgne Levee Board, the Democratic Executive Committee (of which Albert Estopinal, Jr., was the longtime chairman), and the Terre-aux-Boeufs Drainage Board. They also dominated numerous other offices, such as postmaster and justice of the peace, and a variety of appointed positions. Two Isleños served in the state legislature in this era. Albert Estopinal, Sr., was in the senate for five terms, from 1880 to 1900. His nephew, Adam Estopinal, was elected for one term each to the house of representatives in 1904 and to the senate in 1908.[27]

Life on Bayou Lafourche differed after Reconstruction in that Isleño-owned large plantations mostly disappeared. Although the trend in land concentration continued, small farmers remained, sometimes even on the bayou. A description of about 1880 stated: "The plantations along [Bayou Lafourche] are generally laid out in large tracts (though there are many small ones), the front portion being appropriated to cane and corn, and the rear lands to tenants who cultivate rice. In the rear of the plantations, which usually extend to eighty acres, are found dry bayous having high lands on each bank; these ridges are mostly occupied by small proprietors, who cultivate cane, corn, cotton, and rice, and such other crops as contribute to the comfort of their homes and the support of their families." As elsewhere in lower Louisiana, sugarcane dominated in Ascension and Assumption parishes. Even small farmers grew it, along with peas, potatoes, pumpkins, and melons. They raised fig, plum, peach, and orange trees, too. The land in the rear (the brulees) could be purchased at reasonable prices, and the soil equaled that fronting the bayou.[28]

According to William C. Stubbs, writing in the mid-1870s, the brulees were located four to ten miles from Bayou Lafourche. The most notable

26. *Ibid.*, September 25, October 2 and 30, November 6, 20, and 27, 1909.
27. Louisiana Legislative Council, *Membership in the Legislature of Louisiana, 1880–1980* (Baton Rouge, 1979), 130–31.
28. Harris (ed.), *Louisiana Products*, 105, 21.

were Sacramento, Pierpart, Grand Bayou, St. Vincent, Big and Little Texas, and l'Abadie. Their lands, Stubbs claimed, would be even more valuable if they did not suffer from floods caused by ruptures in the Mississippi's levees.[29]

In this era, growing numbers of Canary Islanders migrated to the towns, seeking employment outside of agriculture. Besides Donaldsonville, they moved to tiny urban centers such as Napoleonville in Assumption Parish. Located sixteen miles below Donaldsonville on Bayou Lafourche, Napoleonville was founded in the first half of the nineteenth century. One family long associated with the town was the Pintado; Mrs. J. W. R. Pintado became the first postmaster in Napoleonville. Possibly she was related to E. P. Pintado, who had been postmaster in Paincourtville, another miniscule bayou community, in 1857.[30]

Although western Ascension Parish could boast of a town—Donaldsonville—the eastern section stayed rural through the nineteenth century. Its Isleño population was small and located mainly along Bayou Manchac. Before the Civil War, the New River area had only a few residents, a general store, and two small cotton gins. By the 1870s, the number of its inhabitants had increased, and former captain Joseph Gonzales had emerged as one of the leading Isleño descendants. His son, also named Joseph and the operator of a general store, saw a need for a post office. His lobbying effort successful, the government opened a post office on May 21, 1887, with the name of Gonzales. Several years later, the younger Gonzales and a number of east Ascension residents fought the Louisiana Railway and Navigation Company to prevent it from naming the Gonzales station Edenborn, after the company's owner, William Edenborn. They battled the railroad all the way to the state legislature and won in 1910.

Gonzales resisted the railroad in order to preserve the name of the town he had created. In April, 1906, he subdivided his farm twenty miles southeast of Baton Rouge, calling it the Village of Gonzales. Initially, it enjoyed scant success since lots priced at fifty, seventy-five, and one hundred dollars went begging. But Gonzales labored zealously for the town's development and championed the establishment of

29. William C. Stubbs, *A Hand-Book of Louisiana . . . giving Geographical and Agricultural features . . . together with . . . crops that can be grown* (New Orleans, 1895), 17.

30. Sam F. Gilbert, *History of the Town of Napoleonville* (Napoleonville, La., 1936), 21, 31–32. See also Alleman, "The Legend and History of the Place-Names of Assumption Parish," 9.

schools, churches, roads, and drainage. He incorporated the Village of Gonzales on April 15, 1922, and became its first mayor. He served continuously until 1936, when his son Lester assumed the post. Lester remained mayor until 1948.[31]

In contrast to town life, conditions away from the main roads and streams remained primitive. One Bayou Lafourche family of this time casts light on life at the turn of the century. Joseph Martial Rodriguez, originally from Assumption Parish, moved to the White Castle area of Iberville Parish upon his second marriage, by which he had ten children. There he acquired land, cleared it, farmed, and worked at many different jobs in order to support his large brood. Like many of his time, he did not regard education as important, and all of his children grew to adulthood illiterate. His family intermarried with Acadians, who also inhabited the backwoods, and the French language predominated among his descendants. Some members of his family, believing that they had the wrong spelling of their name, changed *Rodriguez* to *Lodriguez*.

Hattie, the daughter of Ariard Rodriguez, who was related to Joseph, was born on Bayou Lafourche in 1897. She later recalled life in the remote woods of Grand Bayou as she was growing up. Travel was usually in boats, often pulled by mules walking along the banks. Roads and bridges did not then exist. Hattie's isolated community lacked both a priest and a church, and local inhabitants appointed elders to marry, bury, and bless newborn infants until such time as a priest appeared. Life was rustic in the woods. Hattie grew up learning Spanish and French songs and dances; later, she learned English as contact with the outside world increased. But not until she went to the city did she become "civilized," as she laughingly described her transformation from country bumpkin.[32]

In the era after the Civil War, few poor whites attended Assumption Parish public schools, while the wealthy continued to send their children to private institutions. The education system remained inadequate into the twentieth century. As one person described conditions at that time, "Salaries were meager, school houses were poor, living accommodations near the rural schools were abominable, and transportation was limited." A few Isleños are known to have been involved in education in

31. Sidney Marchand, Sr., *The Chief in the Land of the Chetimachas* (Donaldsonville, La., 1959), 185; Clare D'Artois Leeper (comp.), *Louisiana Places: Collection of the Columns from the Baton Rouge "Sunday Advocate," 1960–1974* (Baton Rouge, 1976), 11.
32. Mrs. B. M. Rodriguez, *Our Rodriguez Family* (n.p.; *ca.* 1983), 61, 112.

Assumption Parish. Mrs. A. Acosta was a teacher in 1877, and Simon Truxillo served on the school board before 1900.[33]

The outstanding Canarian educator was Samuel A. Alleman, a native of Brulee Maurin in Assumption Parish. Educated in the local schools, he taught in them without a teaching credential before continuing his studies at the Sacred Heart College in Donaldsonville. He then received the appointment as Assumption Parish's beneficiary student at Louisiana State University. Upon graduation from the university in 1898, he returned to teaching. Alleman soon became the principal of the Napoleonville school and, in 1905, the first professional superintendent of Assumption Parish schools, being only the second person statewide to hold such a post. As parish superintendent, he instituted major reforms, attempted to increase teacher qualifications, improved salaries, and consolidated the one-room, one-teacher schools. He ordered the Valenzuela and Kotzville schools to merge with one in Belle Rose in 1906. He provided a "wagonette" and driver to transport the children to their new school; the wagonette remained in use until the school board phased in "motor driven school transfer" in 1919. Alleman's improvements represented a renaissance in education in Assumption Parish. By 1936 Alleman was the oldest working parish superintendent in the state.[34]

The United States census of 1900 revealed that farmers and farm laborers predominated among the Isleños of the agricultural parishes of Bayou Lafourche. It showed that the oldest, and even many of the younger, residents were both illiterate and ignorant of English. In Ascension Parish, besides doing farm work, Isleños worked as carpenters, woodchoppers, boatmen, and peddlers. Still others were sugar makers, retail merchants, farm managers, foremen, and coopers. A few, such as William Corbo, twenty-one, and Frank Hidalgo, thirty-three, taught school.[35]

Perhaps the largest Isleño communities could be found in Assumption Parish, working mostly in agriculture. Few practiced professions; an exception was Dr. Robert A. Truxillo, age thirty-two, a physician. The United States census indicated that the two oldest Isleños were Balthazar

33. Carmouche, "The Development of Public Education in Assumption Parish," 18–19, 25, 35–61.
34. Alleman, "The Legend and History of the Place-Names of Assumption Parish," 9. This author was the daughter of Superintendent Alleman.
35. Twelfth Census (1900), Ascension Parish.

Alleman, eighty-eight, and Theophile Fernandez, eighty-two. Numa Vives, a descendant of Dr. Juan Vives and married to an Isleña, was still farming at seventy-one, and his son, Numa, Jr., thirty-nine, was a physician.[36]

Young and Co.'s Business and Professional Directory of 1908–Louisiana–1909 also provides information about Isleño professions and other occupations. In addition to a handful in medicine, law, education, and engineering, other Canarians had entered the business world, where they became grocers, merchants, and saloonkeepers. Others, meanwhile, were blacksmiths, carpenters, barbers, jewelers, butchers, and shoemakers.[37]

Isleños in Ascension and Assumption parishes also served in many political offices, but only Joseph Gonzales of Assumption was elected to the state legislature in this era. He served from 1890 to 1912. The others held posts on the police jury and school board, and in parish and city government. Despite their office holding, they did not approach the control that their counterparts enjoyed in St. Bernard Parish.[38]

In Donaldsonville, largely because of his business, "Colonel" Antonio D. Vega stood out. His title of colonel was honorific since he had served in the Civil War as an enlisted man. After the war, he entered the dry-goods business, buying at low prices from manufacturers and passing his savings to his customers. He titled himself "Cheap Tony" and advertised in the Donaldsonville *Chief*. For many years his establishment was one of the prominent businesses in downtown Donaldsonville. Vega also felt a civic responsibility and held numerous local offices. He was a longtime member of Donaldsonville's city council and at different times was president of both the parish school board and the city's board of trade. He was also active in the Blue-Gray veteran organization that sought to establish harmony between former Civil War soldiers. By 1900, at age fifty-three, he was in his second marriage and father of nine children, among whom Sidney, twenty-six, was a dentist, Benjamin, nineteen, was a bookkeeper, and Antonio, Jr., twenty-eight, assisted his father as a salesman.[39]

36. *Ibid.*, Assumption Parish.
37. *Young and Co.'s Business and Professional Directory of 1908–Louisiana–1909* (Atlanta, 1908–1909), *passim*.
38. Louisiana Legislative Council, *Membership in the Legislature of Louisiana, 1880–1980*, 6–7.
39. Henry A. Garon (ed.), *Donaldsonville, Its Businessmen, and Their Commerce at the Turn of the Century* (n.p., 1976), 35–36, 61, 107.

Until Bayou Lafourche was dammed, a toll bridge extended across it at Donaldsonville, built in 1882. Earlier, a ferry connected the town on the left bank to Port Barrow on the right bank. Then the Donaldsonville Bridge Company constructed the toll bridge and sold the right to collect fees to the highest bidder. For a dozen years before 1904, Prosper Bernard Rodriguez usually won, paying up to eight thousand dollars annually for the concession. His ancestors, Christoval and Maria Diaz Rodriguez, had settled in Valenzuela in 1779. Andre Hypolyte Rodriguez, Prosper's father and a onetime bread peddler, was born about 1826; and his mother, Marie Louise Chase, was born eight years later. They resided in Port Barrow, where Andre later operated a store and served as treasurer of Port Barrow during the Civil War. Prosper was born about 1856, married Odalie Mollers in 1876, and ran a dairy in the 1880s. After obtaining the bridge franchise, he and his father operated the concession twenty-four hours a day. As early as the 1870s, however, floods on Bayou Lafourche spurred a campaign to close it off at Donaldsonville. The disastrous 1903 inundation was the last straw, and in 1904, an earthen dam on the Mississippi sealed off the bayou. After losing his business, Prosper entered a partnership with Santiago "Sandy" Truxillo, by 1907, to operate the former Dexter livery stable in Donaldsonville. Five years later, at fifty-six, Rodriguez sold out to his partner and went into semiretirement.[40]

Floods constituted the chief problem for the Isleños living in Ascension and Assumption parishes, although hurricanes periodically caused some harm. In May, 1874, a crevasse in the Mississippi's levee inundated Brulee Sacramento, driving out thirty-three families. The Donaldsonville *Chief* reported: "The inhabitants of this brulee are very poor, scarcely making enough any year to keep themselves in food and clothes, and now their condition is pitiable in the extreme and appeals to the charitable hearts of all the members of this community." The town organized a dramatic reading in order to raise funds to assist hundreds of unfortunate people.[41]

A storm almost as severe as the flood from the 1874 crevasse struck Ascension Parish on March 9, 1878, causing the farmers to lose nearly all

40. *Ibid.*, 147–59. On the damming of Bayou Lafourche, see Roland Boatner Howell, Sr., *Louisiana Sugar Plantations, Mardi Gras and Huey P. Long: Reminiscences of Roland Boatner Howell, Sr.* (Baton Rouge, 1969), 31–33, 42; Marchand, *The Chief in the Land of the Chetimachas*, 79.
41. Donaldsonville *Chief*, May 9 and 23, 1874.

their corn and potatoes. The *Chief* called it "a serious drawback to a class of people who have had more than a fair share of such misfortunes during the late years." Again in the spring of 1882, floods inundated Brulees Sacramento and McCall and other lands. Mathias Rodriguez of Brulee Sacramento, the second-ward police juror, had eighteen inches of water in his yard. The waters remained until July and forced many people to live in palmetto huts. The eastern portion of Ascension Parish also suffered from crevasses and inundations in 1890, 1892, and 1893.[42]

In the twentieth century, conditions improved only slightly. In May, 1912, the Mississippi's high waters broke the right bank and again flooded Brulee Sacramento and other regions. Hurricanes also damaged the Isleño parishes along Bayou Lafourche in 1893 and 1909. The June, 1912, hurricane snapped trees and poles and damaged crops. Floods later in the summer also left stagnant pools of water, where mosquitoes bred and caused malarial fevers.[43]

Modernization progressed slowly in Ascension and Assumption parishes. In 1895, paved roads, electricity, telephones, and picture shows still belonged to the future. Donaldsonville alone had electric lights and telephones by 1900. Communications improved as bridges replaced ferries on Bayou Lafourche after the stream was closed and the levees removed. Railroads also entered the parishes. Motorcars were not numerous in Donaldsonville until after 1910, and the first paved roads in Ascension Parish appeared only in the 1930s. The decline of automobile prices, particularly after Henry Ford initiated mass production, made the vehicles affordable even to less affluent Isleños. In 1914 Ford open-top touring cars sold for $550, while the sportier runabout models cost only $500. A crank and a strong arm were prerequisites for starting the tin lizzies. Classy motorists donned dusters, goggles, and gloves as much for show as for protection against the dust storms generated on the dry, unpaved roads.[44]

Before World War I, a small number of Canary Islander descendants moved away from their traditional parishes. They went chiefly in search of new economic opportunities, often in Louisiana's expanding industries, such as natural gas, petroleum, lumber, and sulphur. Others, meanwhile, sought careers in business and in the professions.

42. *Ibid.*, March 29, 1878, April 1, July 15, 1882, September 7, 1907.
43. *Ibid.*, May 25, June 15, August 17, 1912.
44. Marchand, *Across the Years*, 171–73, and *The Chief in the Land of the Chetimachas*, 12.

Two Isleño descendants who succeeded in new areas before World War I were Louis H. Marrero and Lenesse J. Alleman. In 1881, Louis Marrero moved to Jefferson Parish, where he farmed and entered business. He served on the police jury from 1883 to 1893, and on both the Lafourche Basin Levee Board and the state senate from 1892 to 1896. He was sheriff from 1896 to 1920. He was president of the Bank of Jefferson, and he organized the Marrero Land and Improvement Association in 1905 to promote parish agriculture and industry. With his sons, he laid out the Village of Marrero and incorporated it in 1914. Marrero died in 1921 after a full, active life. Three of his sons also achieved prominence in Jefferson Parish. The two older boys, Leo Antonio and William Felix, both assisted their father in business and parish activities. The youngest, Louis, Jr., graduated from Tulane's law school in 1899, served in the state legislature, and was the Jefferson Parish district attorney from 1908 until his death in 1916. Another Marrero, Frank, brother of Louis, Sr., also rose in prominence. Born in Natchez, Mississippi, in 1855, he studied medicine at Tulane University, graduating by 1885. He settled down in Covington, where he served three terms as mayor.[45]

While the Marreros pursued careers in real estate, business, and parish service, Lenesse J. Alleman chose public education. Born in 1873 in Assumption Parish, the son of Narcisse Alleman, a parish native and Civil War veteran, Lenesse attended schools in St. Mary Parish, where his father entered business. The younger Alleman earned a bachelor's degree at the Christian Brothers' College in Memphis, Tennessee, in 1892. He then taught school for several years before completing a professional course at the State Normal School, which enabled him to become an administrator. From 1901 to 1907, he was superintendent of the Lafayette Parish schools, and from 1907 to 1912, he was the state institute conductor, organizing workshops for teachers without certificates. In 1912 he resumed work as Lafayette Parish superintendent. As an administrator, Alleman did his utmost to improve and modernize Louisiana's educational system.[46]

With the sinking of the battleship *Maine* in Havana harbor in February, 1898, the United States prepared for war against Spain, which came in

45. Henry E. Chambers, *A History of Louisiana, Wilderness—Colony—Province—Territory—State—People* (3 vols.; Chicago, 1925), III, 7–8; *Biographical and Historical Memoirs of Louisiana*, II, 238–39; Jack A. Reynolds, "Louisiana Place-Names of Romance Origin" (Ph.D. dissertation, Louisiana State University, 1942), 335; Fortier, *Louisiana*, III, 781–83.
46. Fortier, *Louisiana*, III, 22–23.

April. District Attorney Albert Estopinal, Jr., and his cousin, Adam Estopinal, considered organizing an infantry company for service. But the raising of military units was no longer done in the manner of the Civil War. Instead, volunteers poured into two United States Army regiments forming at the New Orleans fairgrounds. Enlistees had to be at least 5 feet 4 inches tall and weigh 125 pounds. The army would pay them thirteen dollars a month for their services. Since the training of recruits required several months and the war barely lasted the summer, few of Louisiana's volunteers saw action. The only known casualty was the son of Mrs. J. Numa Augustin, killed in the fighting at El Caney. Some of the soldiers of the 2nd Louisiana and 5th United States Volunteer Infantry Regiments served briefly in Cuba after the war. The Spanish-American War, however, seems not to have disrupted life in the Isleño communities.[47]

In 1911 the outbreak of the Mexican revolution resulted in a call-up of the Louisiana State National Guard, in which a number of Canary Islanders served. Among them were Wilfred Serpas (later a marine in World War I), Onezime Estopinal, and James Messa of St. Bernard Parish, all of whom belonged to the United States Signal Corps. They went to the National Guard encampment at Alexandria.[48] The Mexican emergency was not serious, having far less effect than the Spanish-American War.

47. St. Bernard *Voice*, April 9, 1898, and all the other issues of 1898, April 3, 1920.
48. *Ibid.*, July 22, 1911.

Nine

St. Bernard Canary Islanders from War to War

The twenty-five years after 1914 continued to bring change to the Canary Islander communities and to Louisiana. The major events surrounding World War I, the Roaring Twenties, and the depression all had a profound impact. During this time roads improved, the radio came into use, and silent flickers yielded to talking movies. The twenties also brought prohibition and rum-running, gambling, and the politics of Huey P. Long and Leander Perez. The events of the era sometimes wrenched Isleño men and boys from their communities and scattered them across the nation and part of the world. As the Canarian population increased, the younger generation often had to choose between limited opportunities at home and leaving to search for a better future.

In 1914 Bourbon rule still held sway over state politics, and it lasted until the 1920s. The combination of the New Orleans political machine, powerful and influential business corporations and industries, and government by "gentlemen" came under attack by the fiery Huey P. Long in 1924. His neopopulist program called for better roads and schools, free textbooks, and efficient courts. He denounced the influence of corporations on government, concentrated wealth, and the Ku Klux Klan. As governor, from 1928 to 1930, and as United States Senator, from 1930 to 1935, Long carried out much of his program for Louisiana. It resulted in more paved and gravel roads, two bridges over the Mississippi (at New Orleans and Baton Rouge), free textbooks, a heavier severance tax on natural resources, and a homestead exemption from property taxation. Long poured money into schools and state institutions, but the Kingfish's share-the-wealth program and tight grip on state government brought accusations of demagogue and dictator. After his 1935 assassination, the state embarked on the dizzying "Louisiana hayride," one of the most scandal-ridden eras in modern politics. By 1940 the hayride ended as the United States edged closer to war. The period from the eve of World War I to the eve of World War II carried Louisiana farther away from its past and brought, at the same time, opportunity for the future.[1]

Nature continued to be unkind to man in the delta parishes. On September 29, 1915, another devastating hurricane slammed into St. Bernard Parish, inflicting loss of life, destruction of property, and suffering on many of the poorest people. Although nearly every section of the parish sustained flooding, the lower part was the hardest hit. More than thirty people perished, most of them trappers, hunters, and fishermen. The waters at Shell Beach rose five feet, as the farmers and orange and pecan growers lost their crops. In addition, the St. Bernard Cypress Company, the American Sugar Refining Company, the Slaughter House Company, and numerous other businesses experienced losses. The hurricane also damaged all of the schools, requiring those at Delacroix Island and Bencheque to be rebuilt. During the storm, Robert Serpas sheltered 125 persons. Congressman Estopinal, his son Sheriff Estopinal, and others immediately organized relief parties to help the victims. Henry Morales volunteered his house as a center to receive clothing and other items for the needy. Twenty-three Isleños served on the parish relief committee. Before returning home, the refugees collected clothing, utensils, and provisions. Large numbers of fishermen, trappers, hunters, and farmers, descendants of the original immigrants, were probably no better off than their ancestors when they first arrived in the area.[2]

In the 1920s, storms bypassed St. Bernard Parish, but misfortune still plagued the Canarians. On April 27, 1922, a 300-foot bank of the Mississippi, which grew to 1,400 feet, collapsed at Poydras. The waters drowned animals and forced approximately 2,000 persons from their homes. By May 6, all of Terre-aux-Boeufs, except for a few high spots,

---

1. Taylor, *Louisiana: A Bicentennial History*, 145–66; Wall (ed.), *Louisiana: A History*, 273–74, 283–84.
2. St. Bernard *Voice*, October 2, 16, and 23, December 4, 1915, January 21, 1916. See also Isaac Monroe Cline, *Storms, Floods, and Sunshine* (3rd. ed.; New Orleans, 1951).

was inundated. The flood caused an estimated $300,000 in damages, and many victims did not return home for two months.[3]

The 1930s saw several major storms ravage St. Bernard Parish. A tropical disturbance swept through the area on July 11 and 12, 1931, affecting those living closest to the sea. In October, 1937, a violent rainstorm caused $175,000 in damages to the parish. Three years later, another storm, acting at times like a hurricane, dropped an immense quantity of rain. The disturbance of August 5, 1940, flooded many sections of the parish, knocking down trees and drowning animals and poultry. The storms continued to make living near the Gulf Coast hazardous.[4]

Another tragedy for the Isleños was the destruction of the St. Bernard church. In February, 1916, sixty-five years after the church's construction, a fire consumed the building. This left the parish without a church because the 1915 hurricane had destroyed the two chapels at "la isla" and at Borgnesmouth. For several years, no church was constructed. Finally, on August 7, 1924, the parishioners between Poydras and Delacroix Island met to discuss building a new church on the old site. A committee consisting largely of Canary Islanders, with Sheriff Estopinal as chairman and A. C. Gonzales as vice-chairman, undertook to solicit funds. It was mid-1925 before work started on a new $25,000 structure. The new church, which was not as large as its predecessor, was dedicated on April 4, 1926—Easter Sunday.[5]

The outbreak of World War I in 1914 at first seemed not of concern to the St. Bernard Isleños; that attitude changed as young men began to enter military service. One of the first to volunteer was Ferdinand Padron, son of the late editor of the St. Bernard *Eagle*. He enlisted in Canada, alleging to be Canadian; saw fighting in France, including Verdun; and was discharged in 1916 when officials discovered his true identity. When the United States entered the war, among the first Isleños in uniform were the brothers Wilfred and Ralph Serpas, who both joined the marines, Paul Morales, and Alex Nunez. Soon 523 young men registered for the draft in St. Bernard Parish, and many were called. In September, the parish gave a huge send-off to twenty-six inductees,

3. St. Bernard *Voice*, April 29, May 6, 10, and 17, 1922; State of Louisiana, *The Fur Animals of Louisiana*, Department of Conservation, Bulletin 18 (rev.) (New Orleans, 1931), 312.
4. St. Bernard *Voice*, July 14, 1931, October 16, 1937, August 10 and 17, 1940.
5. *Ibid.*, February 19, 1916, August 23, 1924, July 4, 1925, March 13, 1926.

among whom were Anatole Serpas, Tony Leon, Charles Estopinal, James Charles Messa, Joseph Anthony Esteves, Lionel J. Gonzales, Denison Suarez, Ernest Rodriguez, and Joseph Serpas. They received basic training in the army at Fort Pike, Arkansas.[6]

The war affected nearly everyone in St. Bernard. Many persons participated in war-related work on the draft board or in the Red Cross, or just observed days without meat and bread. By January, 1918, the government proclaimed Monday a day without heat as well. St. Bernard residents also oversubscribed in the five national bond drives to raise money for the war effort. During the war, a number of flag-raising ceremonies, patriotic gestures then popular, occurred. Lilian M. Nunez also coauthored a patriotic song. In many ways the parish, including the Isleño population, wholeheartedly embraced the war effort.[7]

In 1918 more young men entered the service. Sidney D. Torres and Fred W. Estopinal transferred from the infantry to the 10th Light Field Artillery Regiment. James Messa became a sergeant in the 144th Field Artillery by August. Later, among the many Isleños in uniform were Manuel Nieves, Malcomb G. Perez, Isidore Martin Serpas, George Estopinal, Paul Fernandez, Albert Molero Ruiz, and Vincent Molero. Soon Nicholas Fernandez, Morris L. Rodriguez, Anthony Sylvester Crespo, Vincent Torres, Lorenzo Morales, and Jerome Gutierrez joined them. James Serpas, meanwhile, followed his two brothers, Wilfred and Ralph, who were now in France, into the marines. Others in uniform in 1918 included Lionel J. Puig, G. P. Serpas, and August Messa. Congressman Estopinal's sons David and Frederick received commissions as lieutenants, and Captain Joseph A. Estopinal served as a medical officer at Camp Beauregard, where he practiced his specialty of nose, ear, and throat treatment. A fourth son, Leonidas, entered the marines. The congressman's grandson, Fernando, Jr., received an appointment to the military academy at West Point.[8]

Only a part of those who entered the service arrived in France or saw action. Nevertheless, St. Bernard Parish had its share of casualties. Joachim Sanchez, Jr., died in France on June 12, 1918, of battle wounds; in April, 1921, his body was buried in New Orleans amidst honors. In

---

6. *Ibid.*, August 12, 1916, April 14 and 21, June 9 and 30, September 22, 1917.
7. *Ibid.*, January 26, February 2 and 9, 1918.
8. Many issues of the St. Bernard *Voice* in 1917 and 1918 are relevant; see in particular July 28, 1917, March 16, May 18, June 22, July 20, August 10 and 31, September 7, November 2, December 14, 1918, January 4, 1919.

March or April, 1918, leatherneck Ralph Serpas was gassed on the battlefield in France and almost died before help arrived. After the war, his career as a pulp chemist was interrupted by bouts of illness; in 1926 he twice almost succumbed. Vincent Molero of Shell Beach perished at twenty-one when his transport, the *Oronto*, collided with another ship and sank.[9]

Two Canarian youths who entered the war as privates gained commissions. Wilfred Serpas won a battlefield commission and citations. He was one of the first in uniform and in France; he possibly held the parish record as well for days at the front. Field Marshal Petain, commander in chief of the French armies in eastern France, personally presented one citation to Serpas, and General John J. Pershing gave him the other. Ben Messa, who dropped out of Louisiana State University to enlist, received an army commission as a lieutenant. In 1919 the St. Bernard police jury restored Messa's scholarship, and he returned to his studies.[10]

On November 11, 1918, news of the Armistice in Europe spread rejoicing through the parish, and a holiday was proclaimed. Editor William Roy of the *Voice* exuberantly called war's end "the greatest event in the world's history." The draft ended, and the military mustered out its men. The parish waited until August 17, 1919, to show its appreciation to the veterans by holding a welcome-home celebration. It took place in the Crescent City Carnival Club hall, presided over by Sheriff Estopinal, with his brother Fernando as the day's orator. Two weeks later, the parish fathers dedicated a commemorative tablet at the courthouse with the names of those who served. The sheriff was the general chairman, Adam Estopinal served as master of ceremonies, and Nemours H. Nunez addressed the participants. In the 1920s, the parish veterans established a chapter of the American Legion.[11]

World War I drew more of the Isleños away from their native parishes and made them feel a part of the nation. It enabled a number of them to travel to other regions of the United States. Some of the Canary Islanders developed a greater appreciation for education, as college graduates usually became officers. After the war, many veterans probably saw

9. *Ibid.*, April 27, June 22, November 9, December 7, 1918, April 9, 1921, January 1, 1927.
10. *Ibid.*, July 19 and 26, August 9, 1919.
11. *Ibid.*, November 16, 1918, August 23, September 6, 1919.

their lives and their future in a different light. The accelerated pace of life in the postwar era brought new developments.

The decade of the 1920s ushered in Prohibition, high fur prices, and Leander Perez. The 1920 election witnessed a new group of Democrats, the New Regulars, rising to challenge the Old Regulars. In St. Bernard Parish for thirty or more years, local officials such as Sheriff Estopinal and District Attorney Nemours Nunez, with ties to the Old Regulars, had run the parish with a minimum of conflict. That changed in the 1920s as the coalition that had long controlled parish politics collapsed.

Leander H. Perez, who claimed more French ancestry than Spanish, led the upheaval of the 1920s. The name *Perez* reportedly originated with a Spanish sea captain from Madrid; but Isleño descent is more likely, and Perez' mother, Gertrude Solis, belonged to a St. Bernard family. In the nineteenth century, a few Isleños from St. Bernard Parish drifted to Plaquemines, and the Perezes appear to have been among them. Leander's father, Roselius, came to own several hundred acres of land on the west side of the Mississippi. He served on the Lafourche Basin Levee Board for thirty-five years and on the police jury for twenty-four years. Leander, born on July 16, 1891, was one of the youngest of thirteen children, attended local grade schools, graduated from New Orleans' Holy Cross College high school, and received a bachelor's degree from Louisiana State University in 1912. After two years of studying law at Tulane, he opened offices in New Orleans and Plaquemines. Perez married Agnes Chalin in 1917, and four children resulted from the union. His two sons, Leander, Jr., and Chalin, both alumni of Tulane's law school, later became partners and followed him in the murky waters of Plaquemines Parish politics.[12]

Leander Perez' entry into politics began on the death of Judge Robert Emmet Hingle of the twenty-ninth judicial district (St. Bernard and Plaquemines) in 1919. Governor Ruffin G. Pleasant gave Perez the temporary appointment as judge until the next election. Perez allied himself with the New Regulars against the Old Regulars who controlled the district. Despite considerable opposition, Perez ran for the judgeship in 1920 against Nemours Nunez, who for twelve years had been district attorney. Perez' cohort, Philip R. Livaudais, simultaneously sought the district-attorney post Nunez vacated. In a hotly contested

12. The most complete study on Leander Perez is Glen Jeansonne, *Leander Perez, Boss of the Delta* (Baton Rouge, 1977). The obituary of Roselius E. Perez is in St. Bernard *Voice*, November 4, 1938.

election with several sets of conflicting returns, Perez won by three votes and Livaudais by sixty. The New Regulars, however, lost all the lesser seats in the two parishes.

Once in power, Perez used his office to favor allies and to harass his political foes. In rewarding friends, Perez acted no differently from past office holders, but his tactics to punish rivals, even bending the law, reached new limits. He found an ally in Dr. L. A. Meraux, a popular local country doctor, who engaged in banking and real estate and dabbled in politics. Meraux had an Isleño as a partner in his real estate business, A. Sidney Nunez, a Tulane graduate who had worked for the Southern Railway for twenty-four years. The Meraux-Nunez business was established in 1925, was incorporated in 1926 at $300,000, and progressed steadily despite the depression in the 1930s. In politics Meraux challenged Albert Estopinal, Jr.'s hold on the office of sheriff and trounced him decisively. The new sheriff ruled as the arbiter of St. Bernard politics until his death in 1938.[13]

Perez' fight against foes and his favoritism to friends are seen in the 1923 "rum murders" of two St. Bernard deputy sheriffs. Glen Jeansonne has described the conditions that prevailed in the 1920s.

> During Prohibition the lower delta served as a haven for bootleggers and moonshiners. Easily accessible to Cuba, Central America, and the West Indies, the delta offered a climate suitable for year-round operations, as well as innumerable water inlets that made close surveillance impossible. "Mother" ships, loaded with booze, anchored offshore in international waters and fishing boats relayed the cargo through the narrow inlets to a secret rendezvous in the swamps. Freight trucks, oil trucks, or passenger cars then completed the run to New Orleans. Sometimes the liquor was disguised as molasses, canned vegetables, or fruit juices. At least once a funeral coach was packed with illegal whiskey rather than a corpse.[14]

Isleños increased their contact with Cuba during Prohibition, and many of them enjoyed their visits and opportunities to use Spanish. St. Bernard people often cooperated in the delivery of Cuban contraband. Parish authorities generally ignored enforcement of the Volstead Act since they were sometimes involved. More reprehensible than the bootleggers, however, were hijackers, who tried to steal the illegal liquor.

13. Jeansonne, *Leander Perez*, 15–18; St. Bernard *Voice*, June 6, December 19, 1925, August 21, 1926, January 14, 1928, and many issues in the 1930s. Harnette T. Kane, who romanticizes the Isleños in his *Bayous of Louisiana* (New York, 1943), 112–13, mentions their contacts with Cuba before the 1920s.
14. Jeansonne, *Leander Perez*, 18–20, 22.

In the early morning hours of April 17, 1923, deputy sheriffs stood guard checking vehicles for liquor at the Violet bridge. As they stopped a truck, a Ford touring car approached and opened fire, killing deputies Joseph Estopinal and August Esteves. The parish exploded in anger and talked of lynching jailed suspects. Among the suspects not in jail was J. Claude Meraux, brother of Dr. Meraux. Evidence indicated that the younger Meraux, former football player, wartime flier, and attorney, had abetted in the flight of one of the alleged murderers. Meraux was indicted as an accessory after the fact. He disappeared two days later, returning in July and being freed immediately on bond. Charges against him were eventually dropped. In the legal proceedings over the "rum murders," Perez showed how calculating he could be. As district judge, he scheduled seven murder trials for the same day and twenty-seven other cases for trial in one week. He did not allow District Attorney Livaudais sufficient time to prepare cases for trial and further hassled Livaudais by indicting him for alleged brutality in obtaining confessions from three suspected killers. Perez' behavior drove Livaudais to break with the judge and join the Old Regulars. Gus Tomes ("Dutch" Garner), the only person convicted of the murders, received a life sentence, but Governor Huey Long pardoned him in 1930. The "rum murders" showed that Perez protected his friends, employed devious legal maneuvers, and thirsted for far-reaching power.[15]

The Old Regulars fought back and tried to impeach Perez. Seven members of the Estopinal family joined in signing a petition against him. The 1924 charge against Perez read that he was "unfit to exercise and discharge with an open and unprejudiced mind the high duties and functions of the office." The proceedings, tried before the Louisiana Supreme Court, revealed a "graft-ridden atmosphere" in the delta parishes. But the prosecution dropped all charges on June 4, and Perez soon consolidated his hold on Plaquemines and St. Bernard parishes.[16]

Later in 1924 Perez was elected district attorney for the two parishes. He recognized that as district attorney he could investigate and prosecute only the cases he chose and that it depended on his discretion to use or withhold incriminating evidence. He was also the legal adviser to grand juries, police juries, and parish boards. In this office, he had considerable power and, allied with the sheriff and district judge, was invincible. In the same election, Dr. Meraux ousted Estopinal from the

15. *Ibid.*, 22–25; St. Bernard *Voice*, October 11, 1930.
16. Jeansonne, *Leander Perez*, 25–29.

office of sheriff, and J. Claude Meraux captured the district judgeship. In addition, the New Regulars won four of the seven St. Bernard police jury seats, which gave them the majority needed to expel office holders who were patrons of the Old Regulars. The 1924 election had far-reaching significance, for it not only gave the New Regulars firm control of St. Bernard but split the Isleños into two opposing camps. Politics divided even families, and employment often hinged on which faction an individual belonged to.[17]

In the mid-1920s, District Attorney Perez (who continued to be called Judge) sought to profit from the fur-trapping bonanza then going on in the delta parishes. Fur prices in the early 1920s climbed to unprecedented heights as fur coats enjoyed widespread popularity. If mink and otter coats were too expensive for housewives and office girls, they bought coats of muskrat, dyed to resemble more costly furs. The popularity of furs meant large incomes for the trappers of Louisiana's marshlands; the state led the nation in the harvest of furs, even outproducing Alaska three to one. In December, 1921, muskrat pelts, which once sold for ten and fifteen cents, rose to fifty cents, and four years later to a dollar. The fur boom enabled experienced trappers to make several hundred dollars in a week, more money than they otherwise earned in a year.

The marshlands of St. Bernard Parish, and to a limited extent neighboring Plaquemines, were the domain of the Isleños. Poor, ignorant, Spanish-speaking, and often victims of nature, many of them in the past had eked out a precarious living from fishing, hunting, logging, farming, and trapping. For decades they had trekked across the wetlands doing as they willed. The region was hazardous and uninviting. Gulf storms inundated the marshes, which were mostly only inches above sea level. Southerly winds also caused the coastal lowlands to flood. Without landmarks on the marshes, inexperienced people easily lost their sense of direction. Even walking on the trembling prairie posed risks. In the trapping season, marsh dwellers lived in shacks, ate canned food, suffered from cold winter weather, and endured solitude. Only people hardened to outdoor rigors could survive. The rise in fur prices, however, brought outsiders into the marshes to exploit both the muskrats and the Isleños.[18]

17. *Ibid.*, 29–30.
18. *Ibid.*, 32–33.

Before the 1920s, the leasing of marshlands that the trappers had earlier worked free of charge started. The trappers poorly understood why and sometimes banded together in the St. Bernard Hunters and Trappers' Association to protect their interests. In doing so, they deferred to Canarians who were more educated and more assimilated in American culture. Good-naturedly and naïvely, they tended to trust their betters. And into this world of marshlands, muskrats, Isleños, and trust entered Leander Perez to manipulate and use the trappers to his advantage.

In November, 1924, Perez called together the trappers, mainly Canary Islanders, to discuss how they could protect themselves by collectively leasing muskrat lands. Each trapper would pay $50 for a share in the St. Bernard Trappers' Association and for an additional $50 would acquire trapping rights on lands the association leased. Although the association had a president and a board of directors, Perez as secretary conducted business, handled funds, and kept the poorly recorded minutes. The directors deferred decision making since several of them were illiterate, one spoke only Spanish, and none understood the workings of a corporation. They trusted in Perez to protect them. Acting in their behalf, the Judge subleased land from his cousin, John H. Perez, who had leased 100,000 acres rich in muskrats (the Phillips tract) for $3,000 annually. The association's cost for the trapping rights was $6,500 for the 1925–1926 season and $8,000 for the following year. And the two cousins soon devised a scheme by which they could bilk even larger profits from the trappers. In addition, the association's treasurer, Leon Meraux (the sheriff's first cousin), lent large sums of the group's money to himself and to the Judge, who invested it in the sheriff's real estate ventures.[19]

In March, 1926, the directors and trappers, believing that they were exchanging a one-year lease, approved the transfer of the Phillips land to J. Walker Michel under conditions not favorable to themselves. In the final agreement, Michel obligated those who wanted muskrat land to work on his terms only; each trapper had to be personally acceptable to him, and he could lease the land to nonassociation members. Moreover, trappers needed to pay $150—not $50—in order to trap. Shocked by the turn of events, disgruntled Isleños approached Manuel Molero for help.

19. *Ibid.*, 34–38. Casimire Acosta became president and Charles Rodriguez vice-president when the St. Bernard Trappers' Association formed (St. Bernard *Voice*, December 6, 1924).

Molero, a well-to-do Delacroix merchant, epitomized the American success story. Born in St. Bernard Parish on February 17, 1886, the son of Valentin and Manuela Nunez Molero, he went to work as a boy. After being a salesman, farmer, grocer, and merchant, he entered the fur business about 1915 and soon prospered. In 1926 he began acquiring several hundred thousand acres of marshlands, most of which he later leased to oil companies for exploration. The discovery of natural resources on them made Molero the wealthiest Isleño in St. Bernard and probably in Louisiana. When the fur trappers sought his assistance against the machinations of the wily Judge Perez, Molero contacted his attorney, Oliver S. Livaudais, who investigated the Michel lease.

Livaudais' examination disclosed Perez' chicanery. The attorney suspected that Michel was the front man for the Perez cousins. He calculated that the Michel lease, at triple the cost to the trappers, would net enormous profits. For the 8-year agreement, Michel paid John Perez (who had obtained it for $3,000 yearly) $70,000. If 500 trappers each paid $150, Michel would clear $5,000 the first year and $75,000 each of the remaining 7 years. If the St. Bernard trappers refused to pay $150, Michel could lease the lands to outsiders. Furthermore, Michel could raise the fees any time he wanted.[20]

The revelation of the Michel contract split the St. Bernard Trappers' Association into two feuding factions, with a majority following Manuel Molero. The opposing trappers filed lawsuits in the Orleans Parish civil district court against the Michel lease. Perez fought for the lease's validity and used personal connections and intimidation to force the association's board of directors to support him. At the same time, the Judge had his St. Bernard cronies harass the opposition with arrests and lawsuits. Although Judge Mark M. Boatner ruled against the Michel lease in the Orleans district court, the Louisiana Supreme Court later overturned his decision on a technicality.[21]

Meanwhile, it was not clear who would trap the marshlands in the 1926–1927 season. John Perez exercised an option in his lease and bought the Phillips land, removing it from the St. Bernard Trappers' Association. The infuriated trappers reached for their guns; they would not surrender without a fight. Since most Isleños refused to pay triple the rate, Leander Perez recruited trappers from Cameron Parish and Texas.

20. Jeansonne, *Leander Perez*, 38–41; James M. Thompson, *Louisiana Today* (n.p., 1939), 288.

21. Jeansonne, *Leander Perez*, 41–51, 53.

He also hired guards to keep the Isleños from poaching in the marsh-lands. And to make even more money, the Louisiana Muskrat Ranch, Incorporated, a Perez enterprise, proposed to change trapping methods. Instead of allowing the men to work independently, the company would force them to stay at the camps all season and evenly split their catches. The company would charge them a dollar per day for board and fine them five dollars for each day of work missed. This innovation alienated the Plaquemines trappers, who joined their St. Bernard counterparts. It created an uglier mood in the marshes and increased the possibility of disorder.[22]

Shortly before the trapping season opened, four hundred irate Isleños met on Delacroix Island to discuss the course of action to take. The meeting was interrupted by a group of hot-headed and intoxicated Perez gunmen, some of them from Texas, who decided to make "Spanish soup" out of the trappers. On Tuesday morning, November 16, a commandeered oyster lugger, the *Dolores*, loaded with two machine guns and armed men, approached the Delacroix settlement. The trappers were ready, and they riddled the *Dolores* with bullet holes, killed Samuel Gowland (a former Arabi justice of the peace impeached for hijacking liquor in 1923), and captured every man on board. The Delacroix violence panicked the outside trappers, many of whom fled. Even Judge Perez scurried across the Mississippi in a rowboat. The Isleños of Delacroix Island declared that they would submit to state authority, but not to "Meraux's law." The sheriff wanted to arrest the four hundred trappers, but he feared setting foot on the island. His appeal for state assistance brought a visit from Governor Oramel H. Simpson on Wednesday. The governor, an Old Regular, observed that the Isleños had gone home, the barricades were down, and tranquillity again prevailed. He did nothing to help. On this occasion, the Perez-Meraux machine lost, inasmuch as no arrests or indictments occurred.[23]

To make the Judge's defeat worse, John Perez sold the Phillips land at a loss to Manuel Molero, whose Delacroix Corporation became a major power in the muskrat industry. Another upshot of the "war of the Tejanos," as many of the Canary Islanders referred to the battle, was the impeachment trial of District Judge J. Claude Meraux, which made public widespread corruption in St. Bernard and Sheriff Meraux's disin-

---

22. *Ibid.*, 51–54.
23. *Ibid.*, 53–59. The St. Bernard *Voice* reported on November 20, 1926, a "miniature war" on Delacroix Island.

clination to eradicate it. And while Perez failed to make money from the trappers, the discovery of natural gas and petroleum in Plaquemines Parish in 1928 more than amply compensated him.[24]

The trappers' victory in the "war of the Tejanos," however, proved ephemeral. The 1926–1927 muskrat season produced good results; then misfortune engulfed them. The spring of 1927 witnessed the worst flooding in decades in Arkansas, Mississippi, and Louisiana, and the swollen Mississippi River threatened to inundate New Orleans. The river's surface rose twenty feet over the city's level. City fathers pleaded to dynamite the levee below New Orleans in order to relieve pressure on the city. In early May, engineers blasted the levee at Caenarvon, between Poydras and Braithwaite, and the river waters poured into St. Bernard and eastern Plaquemines parishes. New Orleans authorities assured the flooded-out residents that they would be compensated for losses. But the victims, many of whom were Isleños, received no or only partial payment. Trappers and fishermen, too, received nothing for the loss of their income.[25]

Soon the fur fad ended, the depression came, and share trapping grew in importance, all of which hurt the trappers. Prices fell from a high in the 1927–1928 season of $1.42 per muskrat pelt to $0.19 in the 1932–1933 season; it recovered to $0.45 by 1939. The movement to lease marshlands jointly lasted only a year. Individuals often failed to obtain lands, and many of them found work with the fur companies, particularly the Delacroix Corporation. In the 1930s, Manuel Molero's reputation tarnished when a number of Isleños accused him of not helping them, importing outside trappers, and instituting a system of shares. Share trappers kept only 50 to 65 percent of their catch, while the landowners received the rest.[26]

Through the 1930s, passions stayed inflamed in the marshlands, and occasional flare-ups of violence occurred. Trappers divided into factions, and belonging to the right political group became a necessity for

24. Jeansonne, *Leander Perez*, 59–61.

25. Kane, *The Bayous of Louisiana*, 114–15. On the 1927 flood, see Pete Daniel, *Deep'n as It Comes: The 1927 Mississippi River Flood* (New York, 1977), 7–9, 50–51; Cline, *Storms, Floods, and Sunshine*, 197–218; and Stanley Clisby Arthur, *Louisiana Tours: A Guide to the Places of Historic and General Interest* (New Orleans, 1950), 83–84.

26. Kane, *The Bayous of Louisiana*, 114–15; Edward J. Kammer, *A Socio-Economic Survey of the Marshdwellers of Four Southeastern Louisiana Parishes* (Washington, D.C., 1941), 101, 108, 110. Editor Roy of the St. Bernard *Voice* (December 3, 1927) estimated that each trapper should have made from $3,000 to $8,000 in the 1927–1928 season; instead he earned virtually nothing since the muskrats had been wiped out.

leasing land or finding employment. Many Isleño trappers persisted in believing that the marshlands were free—that they required neither the owner's permission nor a state license in order to trap. That belief led to poaching and trespassing, and resulted in disorder. The high prices of the 1920s never returned. In the mid-1930s, the federal government tried to assist the trappers by loaning them money for subsistence and land rental, and even to purchase marshlands. Beginning in 1937, the Farm Security Administration lent $479,472.70 to 185 trappers to buy 23,409 acres.[27]

Isleños other than trappers also suffered in the depression of the 1930s. Conditions were already serious in the late 1920s, as the Ford assembly plant in Arabi shut down only one month after the October, 1929, stock market crash. In January, 1930, the Sinclair Oil Company closed its refinery at Meraux. In the spring of 1932, St. Bernard teachers received a pay cut when parish officials lacked funds to meet expenditures, and in the following January, the police jury slashed the salaries of all employees. The lower standard of living seems to have affected the children. In May, 1933, the St. Bernard *Voice* reported malnutrition among many parish youngsters. Children often stayed home from school because their parents could not provide them with decent clothing or lunches. Efforts to combat the depression began in 1933.[28]

Franklin Delano Roosevelt took office in March, 1933, committed to reverse the economic direction of the nation. Among the new programs affecting St. Bernard Parish was the sending of milk, eggs, and vegetables for school lunches, which was an incentive for parents to send their children to school. To help farmers meet mortgage payments, the Federal Land Bank of New Orleans and the Federal Farm Loan Commission provided loans; Richard Estopinal became the agent to help farmers with their applications. By November, 1933, the Home Owners' Loan Corporation was assisting families in meeting payments on their houses. Other Roosevelt New Deal agencies included the National Recovery Administration and the Public Works Administration. The president's measures helped to restore optimism as well as promote modernization. The government extended electrification to rural areas in the parish, making possible electric lights, radios, appliances, and other conve-

27. Kammer, *A Socio-Economic Survey*, 92–96, 103; Stanley Clisby Arthur, *The Fur Animals of Louisiana* (New Orleans, 1931).
28. St. Bernard *Voice*, November 23, 1929, January 4, 1930, April 23, 1932, January 7, May 20 and 27, 1933.

niences to Isleños who had never enjoyed these "luxuries." The Works Project Administration helped the Canarians on Bayou Terre-aux-Boeufs by deepening and widening the bayou in 1937. Another project supplied piped water to at least 2,500 residents on the bayou, which improved their drinking water. A third project, a pumping station, brought water from the Mississippi through a canal to the head of the bayou and kept a current running in it, ending the stagnant waters that bred mosquitoes. The projects also provided employment and helped families ride out hard times. The New Deal programs, however, did not resolve all problems.[29]

Wages had dropped in many businesses because of the depression, but a few employers seized the hard times to purposely lower wages — such as the Dunbar-Dukate Shrimp Packing Plant in Violet, in 1939. Workers charged that management wanted to break up their union, and they walked out. They also wanted a wage increase and picketed the plant. The company kept operating with scab laborers, many of them provided by the Delacroix Corporation. District Attorney Leander Perez, who preferred docile labor, threatened to suspend parish relief for any striker who did not return to work. In addition, the Chain Gang, strikebreakers from New Orleans, appeared on the scene and made violence more likely.

The violence came on August 23. Three men in the hire of Molero, probably Adam Melerine, Peter Guerra, and Sylvero Molero, started firing into a crowd of pickets. The Chain Gang quickly responded. In the fracas, Angela (or Angelina) Treadaway, a fifty-two-year-old picket, was seriously wounded. A Chain Gang automobile rushed her to Charity Hospital in New Orleans, where she died three days later. An investigation of the shooting failed to establish exactly what had happened since many different versions emerged. Adam Melerine, twice indicted for murdering deputy sheriffs, was a prime suspect. Despite his unsavory character, he enjoyed Manuel Molero's confidence. District Attorney Perez, for his part, had helped Melerine to obtain a gun permit and even appointed him special investigator. Perez' inquiry into the shooting, not surprisingly, discovered nothing, and the grand jury similarly failed to issue indictments. Perez' power, however, had begun waning in St. Bernard Parish after the death of Sheriff Meraux in 1938.[30]

29. *Ibid.*, May 20, June 24, and numerous other issues in 1933, January 23, 1937, February 19, 1938.

30. Jeansonne, *Leander Perez*, 88–90; Kammer, *A Socio-Economic Survey*, 154–57.

Meraux's passing brought his chief deputy sheriff of fourteen years, Celestine "Dutch" Rowley, to replace him. Within a year, both Rowley and the dead sheriff's brother, Judge Meraux, broke with the Perez machine. The Judge, nonetheless, could still count on support, such as that of Thomas W. Serpas, longtime president of the police jury and later head of the local Democratic party. In the 1940 elections, Perez sought to eject the renegades from office. In choosing opposition candidates, he selected Manuel Molero, his rival in the trappers' war, to run for sheriff against Rowley. Perez also cracked down on parish gambling, which he had allowed to flourish when the sheriff was on his side. By 1940, however, the Perez machine no longer dominated the parish, owing largely to the influx of outsiders who were not tied to a faction. In the election, Rowley soundly defeated Molero, and most of the Perez candidates similarly lost. Moreover, the Judge's rivals tried to impeach him in 1941. Although Perez saved his office, the trial revealed St. Bernard corruption under the district attorney's auspices. But Perez savored one triumph when his rival Judge Meraux was impeached in 1942 for running a divorce mill.[31]

Perhaps if Louisiana had had a better educational system, the Canary Islanders might have been assimilated earlier. Louisiana traditionally lagged behind other states in education and had the largest number of illiterates in the nation over ten years of age in 1920 (nearly 300,000). Teachers' salaries in St. Bernard Parish were low and unattractive to able people. In the fall of 1915, the parish paid its white teachers an average of sixty-three dollars per month. Only 571 students attended school in a parish population of about 5,000; in addition, absenteeism was usually high. To improve instruction, the parish generally hired Isleño graduates from the State Normal School. In 1916 it employed Lilian Nunez and Elvira Torres. Two years later, upon Lilian Nunez' resignation, Pauline Nunez, a recent Natchitoches graduate, replaced her. School-board members for 1918 included G. P. Serpas, Alcide H. Gutierrez, and Alexandre Nunez. The board's clerk, Irene Guerra, was also a teacher in the district.[32]

After World War I, teacher salaries rose to seventy dollars monthly, with one-room teachers who taught all grades earning an extra five

31. Jeansonne, *Leander Perez*, 73, 85–88, 90–97. Thomas W. Serpas, an employee of the American Sugar Company from 1906 on, was president of the police jury beginning in 1928. He was tied to the Rowleys by marriage (St. Bernard *Voice*, December 14, 1928).
32. Wall (ed.), *Louisiana: A History*, 297; St. Bernard *Voice*, May 20, July 25, September 9, December 23, 1916, July 7 and 14, 1917, July 20, August 3, October 5, 1918.

dollars per month. This still failed to retain better teachers. In August, 1919, the school board raised salaries to eighty-five dollars. That same month the police jury voted to give scholarships to Nunez Pilet (whose parents were Albertine Nunez, daughter of Judge Albert Nunez of the parish, and the late judge August P. Pilet) to attend Louisiana State University and to Victoria Torres to enroll in the State Normal School. The parish hired Torres when she completed her studies three years later.[33]

In the lower parish, Canarian children attended schools less regularly than in the upper parish. The 1915 hurricane destroyed the Delacroix school, and the school board set up a temporary structure. Attendance was irregular, and students usually did not continue beyond the elementary level. By January, 1920, Delacroix had a new one-room school, where Ermina Messa taught with a temporary credential. In 1921 the school had 38 students from St. Bernard Parish and 48 from Plaquemines. Because the classroom overflowed, the school board voted in 1923 to build a 2-room schoolhouse. Felix Ruiz successfully bid $6,500 for the contract. Over the years, enrollment increased, and by 1939, the school had 170 students.[34]

The 1920s and 1930s brought major improvements in St. Bernard's educational system. In 1923 the parish added grades nine and ten, and a few years later, it boasted of having a genuine high school. Parents of modest means could now provide their children with a secondary education. By 1925, twenty-one teachers taught in the parish; seventeen of them were two-year college graduates or better. Isleños finishing the public schools, nevertheless, remained few. For example, in 1928 eight Canarians were among the forty-one white elementary school graduates, and there were none among the nine high school graduates.[35]

School enrollment gradually increased. The parish enrolled 1,092 children in 1928, more than 1,500 in 1931, and 2,073 in 1935, of whom 1,577 were white in the last year. Thereafter, enrollment declined for the rest of the decade. In 1939 the schools had only 1,121 whites and 400 blacks. That year the parish employed 42 white teachers, earning an average annual salary of $1,060. The figures seem to suggest that while the parish built schools, many families failed to enroll their children.

33. St. Bernard *Voice*, February 15, July 19, August 2 and 9, 1919, February 7, 1920, July 22, 1922.
34. *Ibid.*, January 24, 1920, June 10, 1922, June 23, 1923, September 9, 1939.
35. *Ibid.*, August 4, September 15, 1923, November 28, 1925, June 9, 1928.

Indeed, as Edward J. Kammer noted in 1941, "The attitude of the [trappers and fishermen of St. Bernard Parish], both young and old, toward education is practicality . . . an elementary education is sufficient for all practical purposes and high school is a luxury."[36]

Governor Long's administration encouraged better schools and reducing illiteracy, and St. Bernard responded enthusiastically. In 1929 it sponsored classes for illiterates three times weekly. The next year the parish planned a new junior high school in Alluvial City, with housing for teachers, at a cost of thirty thousand dollars. In the 1935–1936 school year, the school board provided pencils and tablets to the young scholars for the first time. Among the teachers for the following school year were Rose Emma Cortes, Henrietta Gomez, Augustine Pereira, Honorine Nunez, Bernie Rodriguez, and Lelia Estopinal.[37]

More Isleño girls graduated from high school than boys. In 1936, all four Isleños of the nine-member graduating class were girls. Winifred Gonzales, the class valedictorian, received a scholarship to a state college. The next year, no Canarians graduated, but in 1938, six of the twenty-one graduates were Isleños—Frank Fernandez, Adele Messa, Lois Molero, Alfred Nunez, Stanley Serpas, and Leander Suarez. In 1939, all five Isleños of the graduating class of twenty-eight were girls.[38]

During the years after World War I, a number of Canary Islanders are known to have pursued higher education. In August, 1918, Nemours H. Nunez, Jr., received a bachelor's degree from Tulane. His younger brother, Bruce, graduated from Loyola University's law school in 1923—the youngest member of his class at not quite twenty-one. He returned to St. Bernard Parish to practice. In the 1930s, he became an assistant district attorney and, in 1948, judge of the twenty-ninth judicial district. Frederick N. Estopinal, son of Congressman Estopinal, received a Master of Law degree from Loyola in 1923. Nunez Pilet, who attended Louisiana State University on a police jury scholarship and participated in the Reserve Officer Training Corps (ROTC) program, graduated in 1924. He received a commission in the United States Army and traveled to Texas, Panama, Georgia, California, and New York. Fernando Estopinal, Jr., qualified for a position with the state engineering department.

36. Kammer, *A Socio-Economic Survey*, 70; St. Bernard *Voice*, September 22, 1928, September 21, 1929, September 27, 1930, September 19, 1931, September 9, 1939.
37. St. Bernard *Voice*, March 23, April 20, October 12, 1929, December 6, 1930, September 14, 1935, August 1, 1936.
38. *Ibid.*, June 13, 1936, June 11, 1938, September 30, 1939.

He advanced rapidly and, by 1935, was a senior United States engineer and chief of the engineering division of the second New Orleans engineering district. In the 1930s, Leander Suarez enrolled at Louisiana State University, Alfred Nunez and Adele Messa entered the State Normal School, and Frank Fernandez and Lorraine Perez continued their education at Southwest Louisiana Institute at Lafayette.[39]

East Baton Rouge Parish also produced a noteworthy Isleño in this era—Dewey Sanchez. He was born about 1898 to an old Canarian parish family. His grandfather, Anthony Sanchez of Baton Rouge, served as a captain in the Civil War with General Joseph E. Johnston, and later as a deputy sheriff and an inspector of Baton Rouge markets. Anthony's son Joseph spent his life in the cattle and meat business. Dewey, Joseph's son, graduated from Louisiana State University in 1918 and from law school in 1920. In 1924 he was elected to the state legislature as a representative, and in the 1930s he won the office of East Baton Rouge Parish district attorney.[40]

While some Isleños began their careers in the era between the world wars, others concluded theirs. Most prominent was Albert Estopinal, Sr., who passed away at his home in St. Bernard Parish on April 26, 1919. After his start on the local level as assessor, sheriff, and state senator, Estopinal served as Louisiana's lieutenant governor from 1900 to 1904. He went to Washington, D.C., as a United States congressman in 1908, keeping that office until his death. In addition, Estopinal was president of the St. Bernard police jury for many years and served on numerous local and state boards and committees. After he lay in state in the parish, a special train conveyed his body and mourners to New Orleans, where Governor Pleasant and Mayor Martin Behrman joined the entourage. He was buried at St. Louis Cemetery Number 3.[41]

On January 11, 1932, an Isleño who, like many of his generation, had come from modest origins died after a lingering illness at the age of seventy-two. In his early years, Ambroise C. Gonzales farmed, as most Isleños had in the grim days after the Civil War. He then switched occupations several times before Governor W. W. Heard appointed him parish assessor at the turn of the century. He held that post for more than

39. *Ibid.*, September 20, 1922, June 2 and 9, 1923, August 16, 1930, August 11, 1934, October 12, 1935, September 30, 1939. Nunez Pilet became a captain in 1935. Numerous issues of the St. Bernard *Voice* trace his career.
40. Chambers, *A History of Louisiana*, II, 72.
41. St. Bernard *Voice*, May 3, 1919.

two decades until defeated in the 1924 election that brought Perez and Meraux to power. Gonzales became parish coroner the next year and kept that office until ill health forced his resignation several years later.[42]

Within a span of six years, three sons of the late congressman Estopinal died. On September 28, 1934, Fernando succumbed to a heart attack. The sixty-four-year-old attorney was the first of Congressman Estopinal's nine sons to die. His younger brother David followed him on November 15, 1938, at age forty-eight. As one of the younger sons, David had grown up in Washington, D.C., and had acted as secretary for his father. After the congressman's demise, he had worked on the legal staff of the Veterans' Bureau in Washington, D.C. He was buried in Arlington Cemetery. A third Estopinal son, Dr. Joseph Alcibiade, died of a heart attack on October 9, 1940, at sixty-four. He had worked for the St. Bernard Parish school board before World War I, examining school-children. During his four decades of practicing medicine, he had moved about but always returned to his native parish.[43]

In 1940 Wallace A. Nunez, son of Lovinski and nephew of Sheriff Esteve E. Nunez, died. He succumbed to a long illness on September 23, at the age of forty-nine. Nunez had been a member of the state house of representatives from 1920 to 1924.[44]

42. *Ibid.*, January 16, 1932.
43. *Ibid.*, October 3, 1934, November 19, 1938, September 28, October 12, 1940. Congressman Estopinal's only daughter, Lelia, died in 1912 as a young woman (*Ibid.*, May 3, 1919).
44. *Ibid.*, September 28, 1940.

Ten

Bayou Lafourche
from War to War

Life on Bayou Lafourche before World War I resembled life during the nineteenth century. Passenger and freight-carrying boats and ferries and animal-drawn conveyances yielded slowly to larger numbers of motor vehicles, paved roads, trains, and bridges. Donaldsonville, which before 1914 acquired a movie theater, paved streets, telephones, and electricity, continued to modernize in the following decades. New inventions and trends appeared first in cities and towns; the countryside remained largely mired in the past. Rural housing saw little improvement from the nineteenth century; few houses had electricity or modern plumbing. As late as 1932, less than 2 percent of the rural population enjoyed electricity. Country roads were usually primitive. The Canary Islanders of the brulees, in common with Delacroix inhabitants, continued to cling to a century-old way of life. For them the world beyond the brulees seemed largely alien and remote. Only in the 1930s did new influences creep into their small communities.

Providing one of the few descriptions of the Bayou Lafourche region during this era, a Dallas *Morning News* reporter wrote about his trip from the Gulf of Mexico to Donaldsonville, 125 miles away, in June, 1922. According to him, the area consisted of swamps, marshes, and small farms. Farmers, fishermen, trappers, and hunters lived along the banks of the bayou. Near the gulf, he saw numerous small boats and old stern-wheelers. Farther up the bayou, a luxuriant vegetation flourished; the reporter identified magnolias, wild Cherokee roses, Spanish moss, and wild flowers. Many "colonial" mansions stood along the bayou. He described the people as a "simple-minded, unassuming, hospitable folk." Every Friday, Saturday, and Sunday the bayou residents flocked to dances held at pavilions scattered along the stream. Girls and unmarried young women never appeared in public unless chaperoned. The reporter probably saw Isleños but was unaware of them since he stated that the prevailing language was French, with less than 10 percent of the population speaking English and only when they had to. He made no mention of Spanish and claimed that only within the last decade had the bayou residents started to learn English.[1]

In 1931 the editor of the Donaldsonville *Chief* left an account of several brulees inhabited by Isleños in Ascension Parish.

> Brusly McCall, situated in the rear of Evan Hall (McCall) plantation, is exclusively a farming community. Up to several years ago it was thickly populated with industrious farmers of Spanish extraction. Backwaters from crevasses on the Atchafalaya River, so devastated the country and impoverished its people, until only a small number remain, the greater portion having moved to the front on the Mississippi River and Bayou Lafourche. The brusleys known as Sacramento and Capite are situated nearby. Formerly a school and Catholic chapel were maintained here, but both have been discontinued. A gravel road extending from the river at McCall to the interior was constructed in 1924.[2]

Although the *Chief*'s editor separated Brulees Sacramento and McCall, other writers often regarded them as the same brulee.

Eight years later, the *Farm Credit News* provided an image of the small farms on "the longest street in the world," as Bayou Lafourche was often called. The narrow width of farmland was the reason for there being so many houses on the bayou. Farms stretched back from the bayou for forty to eighty arpents (one and a half to three miles). A concrete road running down the bayou, completed in 1931, connected Donaldsonville with Lockport near the gulf. Sugarcane was the dominant crop along the bayou. The magazine stated, "Nearly all operations, particularly on the very small farms, included cane, corn and at one time or another during the season, onions, shallots, peas, potatoes, rutabagas, cabbages, turnips, okra, and livestock." In addition, nearly all farmers had chickens, hogs, and one to three milch cows. A typical division of a farm with only twenty arpents in cultivation was two arpents for the house, eight arpents in cane, eight arpents in corn and peas, and two arpents in Irish potatoes, onions, and "commercial truck." The magazine also claimed

1. Donaldsonville *Chief*, June 17, 1922.
2. Marchand, *The Story of Ascension Parish*, 116.

that the farmers were mostly self-sufficient and that few of them had debts.[3]

As in the past, the inhabitants of Ascension and Assumption parishes were less bothered by storms than the coastal residents. The hurricane of 1915 that so devastated the gulf was described by the Donaldsonville *Chief* as a tropical storm. Wind velocity in Ascension Parish reached only thirty-five miles per hour. The storm nevertheless dropped four and a half inches of rain, stripped fruit from trees, and blew down some of them. But the majority of the inhabitants experienced no harm.[4]

In the 1920s several other storms struck the area. In September, 1920, a weather disturbance knocked over several brick walls, collapsed the iron and wood superstructure of the Donaldsonville theater, and caused other harm. On August 16, 1926, a tropical storm, the worst in fifty years, moved through the region with winds of sixty to seventy-five miles per hour and deposited more than fourteen inches of rain. In the Donaldsonville area, it blew down power and telephone poles, trees, roofs, chimneys, and fences, and damaged the crops. It sank the ferry *Ruth* and the steamer *Terrebonne*. It also blew in a number of stained-glass windows of the Donaldsonville Catholic church and damaged the building's walls and roof.[5]

Five years later, on July 15, 1931, another tropical storm inflicted similar harm. In the spring of 1934, two storms hit the area—in April and again in June. The second storm was perhaps a hurricane, although wind velocity in Donaldsonville reached only fifty-five miles an hour. The storm caused harm to roofs, trees, and fences. For the remainder of the 1930s, storms did not bother the area, and unlike during the previous era, floods, too, appear to have become a thing of the past. Even the heavy flooding on the Mississippi in 1927 bypassed the Bayou Lafourche district and spared the residents. Work in the 1930s had made the Mississippi's levees sturdier but, in turn, had forced the removal of houses and buildings situated too close to the banks.[6]

Economically, the Ascension and Assumption parishes remained agricultural. Two major currents within the parishes seriously affected the inhabitants. First, land concentration continued. The major crop of sugarcane was grown most efficiently on large holdings and was worked

3. Donaldsonville *Chief*, April 8, 1939.
4. *Ibid.*, August 21, 1915.
5. *Ibid.*, September 25, 1920, August 21, 1926.
6. *Ibid.*, July 18, 1931, June 13, 1936.

increasingly with machinery. Raising sugarcane required large amounts of capital, which medium and small farmers usually lacked. Before 1914 the sugar industry in Louisiana experienced a decline and, in the succeeding years, never fully recovered. American sugar companies often moved to the Caribbean—to Cuba, Puerto Rico, Haiti, and the Dominican Republic—to exploit cheap lands and cheap labor. By 1930 not a single sugar mill was left in Ascension Parish, which once had many. The Caribbean competition produced an abundance of sugar and depressed prices. In addition, fewer workers on Bayou Lafourche were willing to labor on cane plantations since the industry provided only seasonal employment. A few of the more fortunate bayou residents found work as sugar makers in the Caribbean. Among these were Camille S. Hernandez, Tony Rodriguez, Jr., Come Rodriguez, and Charles Vives.[7]

Isleños owned many small farms and even a number of "plantations" (holdings as small as one to two hundred acres) along Bayou Lafourche. Land frequently changed hands, and occasionally estates were sold at public auction because of foreclosure. In July, 1926, the foreclosure of the Cosa Natural plantation in upper Assumption Parish, one mile below Belle Alliance (Valenzuela), occurred. The thousand-acre plantation, operated by Henry R. Aleman, Sidney Aleman, and Gustave Car- mouche, was "overcome by adverse conditions which ha[d] prevailed [the] last few seasons," and was sold to satisfy a $40,000 debt. In the nineteenth century, Balthazar Aleman had owned the plantation and left it to his heirs, including eventually Sidney Aleman, his grandson. Sidney spent almost his entire life on the plantation, working at different jobs. The loss of the estate was a blow and reduced him to operating a store on another plantation. He died eighteen months later at fifty-six from heart trouble and was buried in Plattenville.[8]

Economic conditions in the 1930s remained poor. Elise A. Alleman in mid-decade described how they were in her native Assumption Parish: "Plantation homes lie neglected and abandoned; fields lie uncultivated. One can tell that financial misfortune has not forgotten Assumption Parish that boasted formerly of plantation splendor." No doubt the landless and the jobless had a worse time during the depression, often relying upon relatives and friends to help them survive the tough times.

7. Many issues of the Donaldsonville *Chief*; see in particular, November 24, 1923, August 14, 1926, October 18, 1930, June 18, 1938, October 21, 1939.
8. *Ibid.*, July 27, 1926, December 31, 1927.

In an account of her marriage in the 1930s, Mrs. Beauregard (Inell Reese) Rodriguez recalled:

> [Beauregard] went into the C.C.C. [Civilian Conservation Corps], which gave young men work to help their families during the depression. I graduated from high school and went to Franklinton to work for friends of my parents . . . When we decided to get married in December, Beauregard had to get out of the C.C.C. [as it was] only for single men. He had hitched a lot of rides to be with me and to look for jobs. Then he got a job on the W.P.A., which was established to help families. It paid seven dollars a week. We lived with his parents until we rented a house near his folks for seven dollars a month. That was on Bayou Lafourche between Thibodaux and Raceland. His folks had lived on both sides of the bayou as far up as Labadieville. Many times we would not know what the next meal would be and then someone would share from their garden. It was hard times. [Beauregard] worked with his dad building truck bodies to haul cane. . . . Finally, he got a job driving a truck for a man they built bodies for. We had lived in Thibodaux for a while. We moved to New Orleans. Things began to improve. [Beauregard] worked for the freight lines until he retired. I never worked except at home, or temporary jobs, as was expected of a wife back then.[9]

The second major current in Ascension and Assumption parishes was the growth of population coupled with the lack of opportunity. The Canarian population before the Civil War had grown slowly but steadily. In the last decades of the nineteenth century and early twentieth century, however, it expanded prodigiously. Large families seemed to be even more common than in the past, and the children usually survived to have families of their own. In 1923 Lucien Acosta, Sr., of Donaldsonville boasted that he had approximately 130 nephews and nieces in Lafourche Parish. When Marie Ramirez died in January, 1936, at an advanced age, she and her late husband John had celebrated their golden wedding anniversary twenty-one years before. She left twenty-three grandchildren, thirty great-grandchildren, and nine great-great-grandchildren. Mrs. Evariste Alonzo died in June, 1938, at eighty-two years of age, leaving forty grandchildren and twenty-six great-grandchildren. Upon the passing of Joseph J. Falcon at eighty-eight in February, 1939, a lifelong resident of Brulee McCall, the Donaldsonville *Chief* reported that he had had nine children, sixty-eight grandchildren, seventy great-grandchildren, and two great-great-grandchildren.

9. Alleman, "The Legend and History of the Place-Names of Assumption Parish," III; Rodriguez, *Our Rodriguez Family*, 139.

Although not all Isleños had such large families, their numbers grew rapidly in the first half of the twentieth century.[10]

Despite Louisiana's population as a whole rising between 1920 and 1940 (from 1,800,000 to 2,364,000), Ascension and Assumption parishes lost people from 1920 to 1930. Ascension Parish lost 3,721, and Assumption Parish 1,922 (about one-third of whom were white). From 1930 to 1940, however, the population of Ascension Parish rose from 18,434 to 21,212, and that of Assumption Parish from 15,990 to 18,542. Because the countryside could not provide sufficient employment, many Isleños drifted to the cities, to other states, and to jobs outside of agriculture. At that time, the gas, petroleum, and mineral industries of Louisiana were expanding, and Canary Islanders sought work in them. The Donaldsonville *Chief* reported many local people migrating to New Orleans, Baton Rouge, and other towns in Louisiana as well as to other states. Many of the people also moved down Bayou Lafourche, following a trend that had started in the early nineteenth century. Increasingly, the Canarians entered business, industry, and the professions. Education was usually the key to success, and more Canary Islanders along Bayou Lafourche were becoming educated.[11]

Writing about education on the bayou in 1935, Helen M. Bowie stated: "Previously, it was hardly considered necessary for [farm] children to go to school, chiefly because they were needed to help with the work at home. The town children always went and those near the little country schools but many did not have that advantage." She added that many of the older and poorer people could do little more than sign their names and occasionally read part of the newspaper.[12]

In the 1920s and 1930s, the state spent more money on education than in the past, built better schools, and paid the teachers slightly higher salaries than previously, although inequities persisted. In Ascension Parish in 1927, men received about $1,400 while women averaged $1,000; women then made up 86 percent of the teachers. The school year was 172.4 days long. School consolidation reduced the number of one-room schoolhouses, and the parishes provided transportation to the schools. Although the parishes allegedly paid more attention to truants, in 1930 an estimated 30 percent of those who were educable were not in school.

10. Donaldsonville *Chief*, September 22, 1923, January 11, 1936, June 11, 1938, February 25, 1939.
11. Helen M. Bowie, "Bayou Lafourche" (M.A. thesis, Louisiana State University, 1935), 37; Donaldsonville *Chief*, September 7, 1940.
12. Bowie, "Bayou Lafourche," 35.

Along Bayou Lafourche, the brulee children and others who were not well assimilated either did not go to school at all or frequently played hooky. In the late 1920s, Donaldsonville and Gonzales had the only public high schools in Ascension Parish, and they offered only a general literacy course for many years. Gradually, they added courses in manual training, commercial training, and home economics. In 1935 the Donaldsonville high school offered the general course to boys and a two-year home economics course to girls.[13]

In addition to those who enrolled in the public high school in Donaldsonville, many Isleños attended and graduated from the Catholic high school. It originated as St. Vincent's Institute for girls, established in 1843 by six of the Sisters of Charity, and as St. Joseph's Commercial Institute for boys, founded in 1886 by the Brothers of the Sacred Heart. About the late 1920s, the two institutes were reorganized into a high school. High schools at that time attempted to prepare youth, particularly boys, for employment. But girls as well as boys often continued their education beyond high school.[14]

Among the Bayou Lafourche Canary Islander descendants who entered higher education was Elise Aurela Alleman, the daughter of longtime superintendent of public schools in Assumption Parish, Samuel Alleman. Elise Alleman graduated from the four-year program at the State Normal College in 1926, at nineteen, with the highest honors. In 1922, following graduation from the Napoleonville high school as valedictorian, she had entered the college to study English and Latin as one of the first four-year students. While there, she was an editor of the college biweekly *Current Sauce*, a member of Delta Sigma Epsilon, and a participant in student government. As valedictorian of the four-year graduates, she spoke on the trend of modern American poetry at the commencement exercises. After graduation, she did additional work at Loyola University. She then taught high-school English for several years while working toward a master's degree at Louisiana State University, which she received in 1936.[15]

Other Canarians who attended institutions of higher learning included Jesse J. Sanchez, who in 1918 studied at Mississippi A & M College; Clarence J. Fernandez and Leonce Falcon of Smoke Bend, who

13. Donaldsonville *Chief*, March 30, 1939; Davis, *Louisiana: A Narrative History*, 366.
14. Donaldsonville *Chief*, March 30, 1935.
15. *Ibid.*, April 10, June 5, 1926; Alleman, "The Legend and History of the Place-Names of Assumption Parish," 91.

were at Tulane; and Alvin Corbo, who attended Alabama Polytechnic Institute. In 1922 Sidney Vega, Jr., was a sophomore at Louisiana State University, while Albert Corbo of McCall reenrolled at Chillicothe Business College in Missouri; by 1926 Sidney Vega had transferred to the University of Louisville, Kentucky, as a dental student. The next year Cecil Lois Gonzales entered Dominican College in New Orleans in a four-year program. She graduated in 1931. In 1930 Lucille Truxillo, daughter of Santiago Truxillo, entered a nursing program at Hotel Dieu (a New Orleans hospital); she graduated three years later as a nurse. Claude Fernandez was a student at Louisiana State University. Ethel Acosta attended the State Normal College in 1933. By 1935, eighty-three Ascension youth had graduated from the Natchitoches school, and three were then studying there. In 1936 Paul and Philip Barrios were both students at Louisiana State University.[16]

Although the Isleños were overwhelmingly Catholic, not many of them are known to have entered the Church as priests and nuns. In 1935 the daughter of Mrs. B. Cabaliero (Caballero) took her first vows in the Order of Sisters of Mount Carmel in New Orleans; she was then known as Sister Francis Xavier. Another nun, the daughter of Prosper Rodriguez, Sr., in 1935 was called Sister Angela of the Order of the Sisters of Charity and was living in El Paso, Texas. For years Vernon Pierre Aleman, whose parents, Mr. and Mrs. Henry R. Aleman, lived in Lauderdale, studied for the priesthood at St. Joseph's College near Covington and later at Notre Dame in New Orleans. Finally, he was ordained in the St. Louis Cathedral in New Orleans on June 15, 1935. The next day, Father Aleman celebrated his first mass in Donaldsonville before a large group of Sunday well-wishers. The Donaldsonville *Chief* reported: "A vast multitude of people from this city and from the parishes of St. James and Assumption and many from New Orleans, Plaquemine and other places, including many members of the clergy, packed the spacious Ascension Catholic Church." Among them were another seminarian, Lloy Caballero, and Dr. Ruth G. Aleman and Dr. Slattery Aleman of New Orleans.[17]

Military service helped to break down the isolation of the Canary Islanders on Bayou Lafourche, accelerating a movement that was already

16. Many issues of the Donaldsonville *Chief*; see July 20, August 17, 1918, January 22, December 16, 1922, June 19, 1926, September 17, 1927, August 16, 1930, June 20, 1931, March 4, 1933.

17. *Ibid.*, November 21, 1931, June 1, 15, and 22, August 10, September 7, 1935.

occurring. When the United States entered World War I in April, 1917, Brother Damien, a member of the faculty of Donaldsonville's St. Joseph's Commercial Institute and a Spanish-American War veteran, began drilling volunteers three times weekly. Among them were H. Acosta, L. Falcon, C. Falcon, A. Montero, L. Montero, and A. Rodriguez. In early June, 1,823 men between the ages of twenty-one and thirty-one registered for the draft in Ascension Parish. Other men and women offered to work in the Red Cross; among them were Miss A. Acosta, Mesdames H. Aleman, S. Aleman, L. Acosta, and S. V. Vega, and Messieurs L. L. Fernandez, Bennie Vega, E. P. Ramirez, and J. F. Truxillo. Still others showed their loyalty by beginning "war gardens" and holding flag-raising ceremonies.[18]

Before long, young men from Ascension Parish found themselves in uniform. Among the Isleños known to have entered the service in 1917 were Sidney Acosta, Arthur Montero, and Lester S. Gonzales. Meanwhile, Slattery Aleman and Tilden Fernandez applied for admission to officers' training camps. Another Canarian who soon entered the service and went to France was Dr. Jaffrey Vega. He had been on the medical staff of the National Home for Disabled Volunteer Soldiers in Dayton, Ohio, when the war broke out. By late summer, he was in France in a hospital unit. His brother Claflin J. Vega, who had been living in New York City, entered the army there. A third Vega brother, Eddie, then residing in Dallas, Texas, also entered the service.[19]

The closeness that Canarians felt for their families is illustrated in an incident involving Manuel Ourso of Brulee Sacramento. He had enlisted in the army in the summer of 1917. Stationed in New England and about to go overseas, he learned that his brother Desire was severely sick. He left camp without leave in order to go to his brother's side, and was there when military authorities apprehended him. The army chose not to punish him and only returned him to duty. Before long he was in France as part of the American Expeditionary Force in the 1st New Hampshire Infantry.[20]

In 1918 other Isleños from Ascension in uniform were Lynnwood J. Rodriguez, Mack Acosta, Ernest J. Acosta (who went overseas in July), Damien Peter Falcon, Antoine Sanchez, Carlton Gonzales, and Willie J.

18. *Ibid.*, May 8, June 9 and 23, 1917.
19. *Ibid.*, April 14, July 14, August 11, September 1 and 15, October 27, December 8, 1917.
20. *Ibid.*, April 6, June 8, 1918.

Acosta. Meanwhile, by June, A. C. Alleman was a sergeant in the Base Hospital Detachment at Camp Beauregard. In September, Clarence Fernandez, who had been stationed at Camp Martin, left to go to officer training school.[21]

When the war ended, the men in Europe returned home to be discharged. Among them were Mack Acosta and Delmayne Falcon (who was gassed at the front). Sidney Acosta, who had been in Company B, Machine Gun Battalion 119, 118th Division, and saw action, returned home by May, 1919. Sergeant Ernest J. Acosta also came back from France, after serving in the 38th Division. Unfortunately, only a few of the Canary Islanders from Bayou Lafourche who served in the war are known. Those who joined the American Legion post when it was first established in Donaldsonville included Sidney Acosta, Willie Ourso, and Lawrence Acosta.[22]

Exposure to the outside world undoubtedly motivated several Isleños to remain in uniform or to join the service in the postwar years. Earlier, probably few young men from Ascension Parish considered a career that would take them from home; now, however, some of them developed different attitudes. Among the more adventurous was Alvin J. Albarado of Donaldsonville, who was in the marines in 1922. His brother Edward, following his example, joined the marines that same year. In the 1920s and 1930s, Sergeant Simon F. Falcon, Jr.—whose father, Simon, Sr., was a Donaldsonville iron and sheet boiler maker—was in the army. By 1933 Falcon had completed courses required for promotion to first lieutenant in the reserves; he already held a reserve second lieutenant's commission. In 1919, when Simon first enlisted, he declared—perhaps in the manner of other dissatisfied youth—that he would not "chop" cane any longer. Falcon's statement reflected the lack of opportunity in the traditional Isleño areas. Also in the military in the early 1930s was Ned Sanchez, stationed in Panama in the army; his brother Henry served in the navy for several years before 1933.[23]

In 1935 David Peter Falcon, who was the brother of Simon and who had been in the ROTC while he attended Louisiana State University, earned a commission as an army second lieutenant. In 1932 he had received the [university] president's medal in recognition of his outstanding ability. William David Montero, also of Donaldsonville, who

21. *Ibid.*, March 6, June 22, July 20 and 27, September 14, 1918, December 21, 1935.
22. *Ibid.*, February 22, May 10, June 21, 1919, November 6, 1920, June 25, 1921.
23. *Ibid.*, October 28, 1922, August 30, 1924, March 18, April 15, November 4, 1933.

joined the navy in 1924 and was a first-class seaman, was killed in an automobile accident in Virginia. His father, Auguste Montero, Sr., for many years was a pilot of tugboats on the river.[24]

Also in uniform since 1928 was Ulysses Ourso, son of Mr. and Mrs. Frank Ourso of Brulee Sacramento. In May, 1938, he arrived home on a three-month furlough, from his post in the field artillery at Schofield Barracks, Honolulu. In early 1939, he was transferred to Fort Sill, Oklahoma.[25]

After war broke out in Europe in 1939 and the United States began building up its armed forces, other sons of Simon Falcon, Sr., entered the service. In June, 1940, Andrew joined the marines and went to San Diego, California, for training. The next month, his brother Glynn Peter enlisted in the navy and was sent to San Diego for boot camp. Meanwhile, their brother David, who had spent several years on active duty in the 1930s, was recalled as a first lieutenant. While out of the army, he had taught algebra and helped to coach the football and boxing teams at the Donaldsonville high school. His wife and child accompanied him to Fort Benning, Georgia.[26]

In 1940 the government established the selective service for the second time in twenty-three years and required young men between twenty-one and thirty-six to register. In Ascension Parish 2,637 men registered for the draft in October. Two months later, Harold Joseph Ramirez volunteered to enter the service before being drafted. Parish officials, relatives, and friends gave him and several other men a warm send-off. They went to Camp Beauregard in Alexandria for basic training.[27] In the coming war, many more youth from Ascension and Assumption parishes entered the service and saw more of the nation and the world.

As conditions changed in lower Louisiana in the era between the wars, Canary Islanders who had been prominent for several decades passed from the scene. Among them was Antonio D. Vega, whom the Donaldsonville *Chief* usually called "Colonel." His demise came on February 2, 1917, at the age of seventy, from heart disease. The son of H. J. Vega, he had enlisted in 1864 in the Barnes Battery of Semms' Artillery, Army of the Trans-Mississippi Department. He was captured and paroled in 1865 at Alexandria. After the Civil War, he clerked in a dry

24. *Ibid.*, January 2, 1932, November 2, 1933, June 16, 1934, June 29, 1935.
25. *Ibid.*, May 21, 1938, March 18, 1939.
26. *Ibid.*, June 22, July 20, September 7, 1940.
27. *Ibid.*, October 19, December 14, 1940.

goods store, changed jobs, and rose to become a partner of Henry Loeb. When Loeb died of yellow fever in 1878, Vega took over their business. He enjoyed many years of success in the dry goods business and built the Vega Building in Donaldsonville, which was described as "one of the largest and most modern store buildings in this section of the state." He retired only a few years before his death.

Vega was married twice, first to Armide Dugas, with whom he had seven children (Antonio Vega, Jr., Dr. Sidney Vega, Attorney Benjamin J. Vega, Edward J. Vega of Dallas and later Denver, and three daughters), and then to Eliza Vives of Assumption Parish, with whom he had three additional children (Dr. Jaffrey Vega, who returned to Ohio after the war, Mrs. A. L. Landry of Opelousas, and Claflin Vega of New York).[28]

Ten years later, another well-known Donaldsonville personality died. In February, 1927, Santiago "Sandy" Truxillo, a native of Plattenville in Assumption Parish, passed away at fifty-six, after a lingering illness. For several years he and Prosper Rodriguez, Sr., had operated the Dexter Livery and Sales Stable. He had made numerous trips to buy horses and was well known to the region's planters. After Rodriguez retired, Truxillo had entered the motor vehicle business with the Hudson sons. He had had eleven children, eight from his first marriage to Corinne Arceneaux, and three more from his second marriage.[29]

Perhaps the easier life that Prosper Rodriguez, Sr., enjoyed after retiring prolonged his life. He remained somewhat active as a beekeeper. About 1925, at sixty-nine, he moved to Baton Rouge, where he spent the remaining ten years of his life living with a married daughter.[30]

Captain Auguste Montero, a retired steamboat captain from Donaldsonville, died in 1927. For many years, he had worked the ships and boats of the rivers and bayous of lower Louisiana. He had moved to New Orleans, where he spent his final years as the pilot of the ferry that crossed the Mississippi between Jackson Avenue, in New Orleans, and Gretna. He had seven children and was fifty-four at the time of his demise. Montero's wife, Hyacinth, nee Maria Suarez, lived on until March, 1936. Among her children, Captain Joseph Montero was then the superintendent and engineer of the steam ferry *Bisso* at Donaldsonville.[31]

28. *Ibid.*, February 3, 1917.
29. *Ibid.*, February 19, 1927.
30. *Ibid.*, September 7, 1935.
31. *Ibid.*, September 3, 1927, March 20, 1936.

Another well-known Ascension figure to pass on, in 1940, was Joseph Gonzales, son of Captain Joseph Gonzales of Civil War fame and founder of the Village of Gonzales. Born in St. Amant in 1862, he grew up in eastern Ascension Parish, worked at several jobs, and became postmaster of Gonzales in 1887. He was in the state legislature for four years, on the parish police jury for twelve years, and on numerous local committees and boards. His last office was that of mayor of Gonzales, which he held from 1920 to 1936.[32]

Little is known about how the Isleños weathered the depression of the 1930s. From descriptions of the era, it appears that the large plantations fared poorly. The Isleños who owned small farms perhaps survived by growing vegetables and raising a few animals. New Deal legislation probably helped the inhabitants overcome hard times and even retain their land. Conditions improved slowly through the decade and by 1940 seem to have been much better.

Among trends of this era, the dispersion of the Isleños continued, and even the elderly moved away at times. Often they joined their children living in New Orleans, Baton Rouge, or more distant places. The elderly nevertheless retained a fondness for their native parishes, and when they died in New Orleans or in more remote locations, their bodies were returned to Donaldsonville or its environs for burial. But their children who had moved away, although they made brief visits, generally severed their ties with the traditional Isleño parishes. Moreover, leaving their families usually meant the loss of old customs and ways. And with the passage of time and their parents deceased, the members of the younger generation tended to all but forget the places of their birth. These Canary Islanders, who often left because of limited opportunities at home, fitted in the larger movement of Americans who were becoming increasingly mobile and willing to take jobs and live in places where they had neither roots nor family.

For those who remained, education improved in the 1930s, gradually becoming compulsory and necessary for obtaining decent employment. Its inevitable result was assimilation into the dominant culture. For the most part, the children growing up in Spanish-speaking Canarian families in the 1930s would be the last ones to know the language. And even they belonged to two culture worlds, that of their ancestors and that of the prevailing culture of lower Louisiana.

32. *Ibid.*, February 12, 1938, April 27, 1940.

Eleven

World War II and the Decline of the Isleño Communities

The most disruptive force to affect the Canary Islanders and their way of life in one hundred and sixty years of living in Louisiana was World War II. It brought together trends toward improved communications, better schools, and more opportunities in new occupations, which had been gradually changing the face of rural Louisiana. Most recently, New Deal programs of the 1930s had helped to introduce innovation. The outbreak of war in Europe in 1939 accelerated the pace of economic recovery in the United States, but it also brought about American involvement. It pulled into uniform large numbers of Isleño youth and scattered them more widely than World War I had. Radio, newspapers, and their men abroad all served to increase the Isleños' awareness of the size of the United States and the world.

By the beginning of 1941, St. Bernard Parish's population had grown to 7,280. Its 205 foreigners consisted mainly of Spaniards, Malays, and a few Frenchmen.[1] Fishing and trapping continued in the lower parish, truck farming remained the mainstay of the middle parish (Terre-aux-Boeufs), and industry increasingly appeared in the upper parish—the area that experienced the greatest change.

In early 1941, a St. Bernard *Voice* editorial remarked, "In the past quarter of a century St. Bernard has trudged behind in material development, and the reason for it is . . . [c]omplete dictatorship, with gambling regarded as an asset and a contribution to property." The editorial claimed that corrupt parish politics had frightened off investors and

---

1. St. Bernard *Voice*, January 11, 1941, January 3, 1942.

capital. Despite the newspaper's contention, some investment had occurred. For example, in 1941 a bus line began in the parish for the first time in sixty years. In the past, a horse-drawn carriage had operated between Arabi and St. Bernard village; now a modern bus transported passengers between Arabi and Violet. Conditions in the middle parish had also improved from what they had been recently. "Dilapidated buildings and fences; neglected yards and other eyesores have vanished," boasted the local newspaper, "and in their stead are neat-looking homes and surroundings." Nevertheless, rainstorms still damaged parish roads, particularly the Reggio to Delacroix Island highway, which was subject to tidal overflows.[2]

Upon the outbreak of war on December 7, 1941, there came the rapid mobilization of manpower for military service and a growth in defense industries that provided jobs while creating a parish labor shortage. St. Bernard seasonal workers flocked to shipyards in neighboring New Orleans for full-time employment and higher wages—many of them following the path to New Orleans that the elderly of both St. Bernard and Bayou Lafourche used in order to spend their declining years in more comfortable surroundings. Not all of the Canary Islanders, however, abandoned shrimping and trapping altogether, for they took leaves of absence to return for the seasonal work. Steady employment resulted in Isleño income rising dramatically. The *Voice* editor remarked that this was the first time that all the inhabitants of "these villages" enjoyed so much contentment and prosperity. Truck farmers as well reaped substantial profits from the sale of their produce.[3]

Despite improvements, problems did not vanish. The waters in Bayou Terre-aux-Boeufs had become stagnant and cluttered with vegetation and debris; the pumps that brought Mississippi water into the bayou had broken down and not been repaired. In August, 1943, however, Ernest Guerra, Sr., Joseph Guerra, Sr., Billy Serpas, Ralph Messa, and Joseph Guerra, Jr., fixed the pumps and restored a current to the bayou. The high cost of food also brought complaints despite efforts by the Office of Price Administration to keep the cost from soaring. While shrimpers bellowed about low prices, consumers bewailed the rise of shrimp to twenty-five cents per pound (when it had been a quarter for

2. *Ibid.*, February 22, June 7, October 11, 1941.
3. *Ibid.*, June 19, July 24, 1943.

three pounds) and of oysters to forty cents a dozen (when prewar prices were ten to fifteen cents).[4]

Trapping also recovered with wartime prices for furs and skins. Nonetheless, some trappers grumbled about the low controlled prices and about "market manipulators." In the 1942–1943 season, new faces appeared in the marshes as veteran trappers stayed in the war plants. An estimated six million muskrats were harvested that year, and with some tongue-in-cheek humor, Louisianians urged other people to consume muskrat flesh, marketed as "marsh hare," to help alleviate the wartime meat shortage.[5]

During the war, Delacroix Island finally acquired the new chapel that the inhabitants had wanted for years. On the last day of March, 1943, the archbishop of New Orleans, the Most Reverend Joseph Francis Rumel, came to dedicate it, naming the chapel St. James, for the patron saint of Spain. The name was in recognition that most of the population of "la isla" was Spanish. Five hundred persons, mainly Isleños, attended the dedication. The St. Bernard *Voice* editor acknowledged that Spanish was generally spoken on Delacroix Island, even by the younger members of the population, although they had become "Americanized."[6]

Politics in St. Bernard Parish remained as Machiavellian as ever during the war. A charge of corruption against the Perez faction came in October, 1940. Carmella LeClerc said that she was dismissed as deputy registrar for refusing to destroy a registration book containing the names of seven hundred fictitious voters. She claimed that the Perez gang prevented genuine residents from voting. That soon changed, and by 1942 LeClerc was the new registrar of voters. That June, Sheriff "Dutch" Rowley, in an open letter to the community, proclaimed the rolls of registered voters open to the public. Moreover, any qualified person could register to vote, unlike in the past. St. Bernard voters had then included Mae West, Al Jolson, and Babe Ruth.[7]

In the summer of 1942, the political factions of St. Bernard prepared for another major election, which pitted the forces of Sheriff Rowley against Judge Perez, with the Isleños divided. Perez this time supported Albert Estopinal, Jr., his political foe of the 1920s, for judge of the twenty-

4. *Ibid.*, August 14 and 21, September 25, October 2, 1943.
5. *Ibid.*, December 6, 1941, November 7, 1942, January 2, 1943.
6. *Ibid.*, March 20, April 3, 1943.
7. Jeansonne, *Leander Perez*, 93–94; St. Bernard *Voice*, June 27, 1942.

ninth judicial district. In the September primary, the Perez-Estopinal group won by a large margin, but St. Bernard voted mostly against the Perez candidates. In the November general election, only 744 of 2,800 registered voters bothered to cast ballots.[8]

Partisanship occasionally reached deplorable depths. In 1942 the police jury, loaded with Perez cronies, denied a scholarship to Noemie Josephine Suarez, who graduated first in her class of forty students from Maumus High School. (Helen Suarez received the scholarship instead.) Noemie's irate father, Dennison Suarez, alleged that the members of the police jury denied the scholarship because he did not support them. To vent his anger, Suarez took an advertisement in the *Voice* to denounce the jury's behavior as an outrage and as "playing politics with school children."[9]

Late in 1943 another parish political contest awakened local interest as Sheriff Rowley's term ended. Several opponents announced their intention to run for sheriff; among them, Perez supported Dr. Nicholas P. Trist, while Manuel Molero, Perez' candidate in 1940, ran independently. In the January, 1944, primary, Rowley trounced all five of his rivals. In other races, J. Claude Meraux of the Rowley faction defeated Martin Fernandez for representative in the state legislature, and several other Rowley candidates won seats on the St. Bernard police jury. The next month, Molero sought to soften hard feelings engendered in the heat of the primary, and urged joint efforts by the factions to improve parish roads, potable water, and sewer lines.[10]

Politics in the war years remained as animated as ever. Passions finally subsided in 1948 when Perez reconciled with Sheriff Rowley and J. Claude Meraux. That same year, Judge Albert Estopinal, Jr., concluded his lengthy career in public service, and Assistant District Attorney Bruce Nunez, a Perez supporter, replaced him. Judge Estopinal lived four additional years, dying in January, 1952.[11]

St. Bernard elections were minor affairs compared to the "little war of 1943" in Plaquemines Parish. When Sheriff Louis D. Dauterive died on June 1, 1943, Judge Perez appointed Dr. Ben R. Slater as interim sheriff

8. St. Bernard *Voice*, July 25, September 5 and 12, November 7, 1942.

9. *Ibid.*, September 5, 1942.

10. *Ibid.*, October 9 and 30, December 18, 1943, January 22, February 5, 1944; Jeansonne, *Leander Perez*, 98–99. Adam Estopinal, who had served in the state legislature between 1904 and 1912, withdrew from the state representative race owing to ill health (St. Bernard *Voice*, November 23, 1943).

11. Jeansonne, *Leander Perez*, 99.

until the 1944 election. The appointment clashed, however, with Governor Sam Jones's attempt to improve public morality in Plaquemines. He named Walter Blaize to be sheriff of Plaquemines Parish and then had to use force in order to install him. With the state guard (which replaced the activated National Guard), Jones "invaded" the parish in October. But Perez fought back, filing numerous lawsuits against the harassed Blaize. Moreover, Slater conducted most of Plaquemines Parish business through an underground sheriff's office. Governor Jones's attempt to clean up delta politics faltered, and Perez emerged from yet another political encounter perhaps stronger than ever.[12]

While his foes compared Judge Perez to a delta version of Adolf Hitler, Isleños in uniform fought against Hitler himself. In 1941 draftees and volunteers entered the service as the nation edged closer to war. When hostilities began, civilians joined in the war effort. The parish established a defense council to mobilize the citizenry, gather aluminum, and set up five observation posts to watch for enemy planes. Sheriff Rowley asked for one hundred volunteers to act as "secret service men" to ferret out spies and saboteurs. Anticipating a teacher shortage, the school board accepted married women when spinsters were not available. Before long the parish inhabitants immersed themselves in Red Cross work, blood drives, scrap-metal collection, bond drives, and countless other wartime activities. Isleños participated along with the rest of those in the parish. As air-raid wardens, they were most numerous in Violet, St. Bernard, Toca, and Reggio.[13]

Shortly after the war's start, St. Bernard had a hero. Lieutenant Colonel Nunez C. Pilet, following duty at various posts in the country in the 1930s, went to the Philippine Islands, where he joined General Douglas MacArthur's staff. Immediately after the bombing of Pearl Harbor, the Japanese invaded the Philippines, defeating the undermanned American and Filipino forces. Soon only the island of Corregidor in Manila Bay resisted the invaders. MacArthur fled to Australia by P.T. boat and submarine with a handful of his staff. Pilet's mother in Arabi learned by mid-March, 1942, that her son was safe. Following

---

12. *Ibid.*, 121–41.
13. St. Bernard *Voice*, July 12 and 26, December 13 and 20, 1941, April 4, July 4 and 11, 1942, and many other issues. Among the St. Bernard Isleños believed to be in the service in 1941 were Fred Acosta, August Lawrence Nunez, Peter Morales, Sidney Paul Assevedo, Johnnie Frank Estopinal, Jr., Robert Jules Estopinal, Joseph Perez, Herman Joseph Deogracias, Francis Joseph Estopinal, Martin John Esteves, Abdon Paul Estopinal, Joseph Fred Estopinal, Frank Fernandez, Roger Nunez, Joe Acosta, and Raymond Campo.

secret orders, however, he returned to Corregidor, parachuting in only days before the surrender of American forces. At the end of 1942, St. Bernard learned that he was a prisoner of war, had received a promotion to full colonel, and had been awarded the Distinguished Service Cross. In January, 1943, word arrived that Pilet was a prisoner on Formosa with General Jonathan Wainwright, the last American military commander in the Philippines. The next month, Nunez' wife spoke with him via shortwave radio.[14]

Two Isleños saw action on the Solomon Islands early in the war. "Pat" Pereira, Jr., volunteered for the marines on December 8, 1941. By mid-1942 he was fighting on the Solomons and had suffered a leg wound. In October he enjoyed a furlough at home. Sergeant Joseph F. Gonzales of Arabi, who entered the marines at seventeen, fought on Guadalcanal and in several other major engagements with the First Marine Division.[15]

By January, 1943, 384 St. Bernardians were serving in uniform, and more entered the armed forces in the following months. Many of the recruits were still in their teens, and some were married. Good numbers of Canary Islanders were among them, including Paul Hernandez of Toca. By April he had participated in two major battles on his ship in the Pacific. Meanwhile, Sergeant Harold Serpas fought Germans in North Africa; Josie Menesses and Private First Class Rene Joseph Esteve performed their duties in England; and Corporal Walter Molero was in Iceland. At an early date, Ben Messa, a World War I veteran, returned to uniform as a captain. By September, 1943, he had been promoted to major and was overseas. Thomas R. Nunez was also somewhere overseas in the army. Manuel Perez of Reggio served in the Medical Corps in Egypt; Petty Officer Raymond Menendez of Delacroix Island worked with the Seabees; and marine corporal August Deogracias of Violet and navyman Lawrence Perez of Delacroix Island were both in the Pacific. On November 10, 1943, the St. Bernard *Voice* published the news that Lieutenant Hector A. Alfonso of the parish had died in action. He

---

14. *Ibid.*, December 13, 1941, March 18, November 14, December 5, 1942, January 23, February 27, 1943.

15. *Ibid.*, October 31, December 5, 1942; *L'Heritage*, VI, No. 18 (March, 1982). The Canary Islanders in the service in 1942 included Walter Molero, Edwin Messa, Jr., Lawrence Molero, Wilson Campo, Paul Pereira, Jr., George Joseph Ruiz, Jr., Casimire Perez, Bernard Ernest Assevedo, Walter Esteves, Bernard Nunez, Adam Lawrence Nunez, Renoldy Messa, Anthony Molero, George Marrero, Peter Assevedo, Jr., Adam Joseph Alonso, Douglas Raymond Hernandez, Freddie Nunez, Donald Nunez, Archibald Puig, Clarence J. Dias, Andrew Jackson Serpas, and Richard Campo.

appears to have been the first of several St. Bernard Isleños to perish in the war.[16]

As fighting increased in 1944, so did Canarian participation. Seaman First Class Albert J. Gonzales, Jr., was in four major battles in the Pacific; Private First Class Ernest J. Serpas of Violet served in North Africa; Sergeant Donald E. Puig of St. Bernard suffered a wound in action in the Mediterranean; August Deogracias of Violet was now in India; Jules H. Nunez of Violet, a former trapper and shipyard worker, was in England; Henry Gallardo fought in the Pacific; Sergeant Emile Perez was in the 9th Air Force Service Command in Europe; Private First Class Woodrow F. Lopez of Meraux saw action in the Aleutians, where he spent twenty-seven months with the Engineers; and Sergeant Benjamin Acosta, Jr., of Reggio saw action in the Pacific while his brother Ralph, seaman third class, was in Hawaii.[17]

Major Ben Messa, discharged in late 1944 after spending two years overseas, soon worked to start an American Legion post in St. Bernard. By December the Chaplain-Pereira American Legion Post Number 245 formed with Messa as its commander and Sidney Torres, also a veteran of World War I, as vice commander. Anthony Leon, another First World War veteran, contributed one hundred dollars in order to help the post. The post was named for Chaplain, a World War I casualty, and for "Pat" Pereira, Jr., who had been killed in the South Pacific not long before at age twenty-four. The Chaplain-Pereira post sent packages to convalesc-

16. St. Bernard *Voice*, January 23, September 18, December 4, 11, and 18, November 10, 1943. In 1943, among the Isleños in the armed forces were Tony Fernandez, Alfred C. Fernandez, August Fernandez, Alex Ruiz, Jr., Claude Joseph Serpas, Reo Gonzales, Valery Gonzales, Jr., Merrill Victor Perez, Jr., John Molero, Jr., Eugene Menesses, Charles Joseph Assevedo, Michael Gonzales, Joseph Arthur Sanchez, Earl Smith Acosta, Joseph Assevedo, Samuel Joseph Nunez, John Menesses, Wilson Felix Gutierrez, Lloyd Arthur Estopinal, Ralph Joseph Gutierrez, Edwin Esteves, Irvan Joseph Perez, Eddie Molero, Albert Acosta, Walter Albert Assevedo, Clifton Joseph Perez, Robert Assevedo, Jr., Henry Gonzales, Benjamin Perez, Albert Alcide Estopinal, Felix Morales, August Jerome Serpas, Morris Vincent Morales, Wallace Joseph Nunez, Leon Nunez, Jr., Thaddeus Joseph Pereira, Thomas Adams Serpas, Leonce Joseph Hernandez, Milton Menesses, Peter Ruiz, Nathan Jules Serpas, Joseph Frank Lopez, Torivio Molero, August Davis Gonzales, Sidney Gallardo, Adam Perez, Manuel Wilson Fernandez, George Joseph Perez, Jr., Joseph Bernardino Campo, Wilfred Nunez, Jr., Adam Campo, Paul Hernandez, Frank W. Esteves, Alex L. Ruiz, Jr., and Claude Acosta.

17. *Ibid.*, January 22 and 29, March 11, April 8, September 9, November 4, December 16, 1944. Isleños known to be in the military in 1944 included Donald Estopinal, Wallace Raymond Gonzales, Lester Nunez, Samuel Bernard Nunez, Frank Joseph Campo, August Bonaventure Gonzales, Richard Acosta, Jr., Manuel Perez, Arnold Francis Rodriguez, WAC Eunice A. Morales, Victor Molero, Jr., Alfred J. Perez, John Milton Perez, Wallace A. Morales, Andrew Serpas, August Serpas, Junnie Messa, Joseph Assevedo, and Roy Gonzales.

ing soldiers and assisted World War I widows in obtaining pensions. To raise funds for charitable work, the post held dances, often at Victor Molero's hall in Yscloskey.[18]

In the last year of the war, Lieutenant U. L. Rodriguez became a captain; Colonel Nunez Pilet arrived in Manchuria, still a prisoner of war; Petty Officer First Class Paul F. Reyes of the Coast Guard came home after participating in the invasions of Kiska, Tarawa, Kwajalein, and Leyte; and Stanley Serpas returned to the parish after a twenty-two-month tour in the Caribbean that took him to Trinidad, Puerto Rico, Cuba, and the Virgin Islands. Sidney Paul Assevedo of Shell Beach came home in March after thirty-eight months in the Pacific. On the grimmer side, Casimere Perez of Delacroix Island became a German prisoner of war, Jules Nunez was wounded in action, and Private First Class Walter P. Estopinal died in battle. The son of Mr. and Mrs. Jules Estopinal of Arabi, young Walter Estopinal had been stationed in Panama for two years before going to an active theater of war. Two other casualties were marine private Daniel P. Nunez and army sergeant Archibald A. Puig.[19]

Canary Islanders who served in Europe at the end of the war included Tony Molero and Albert Acosta in England, Walter Molero in France, and Richard Acosta, Jr., in Germany. With the war over in Europe in the spring of 1945, a few St. Bernardians came home on leave. Among them were Alex Ruiz, Jr., of Violet, who served on board the battleship *California*; Freddie Acosta, who spent thirty months in Africa and Europe; and Sergeant Frank Lopez of Delacroix Island.[20]

Other battle casualties late in the war included navyman Lester Messa, who received the Purple Heart. Technician Fifth Grade Roger T. Nunez of Reggio, also wounded in action, arrived at Brooks Army Hospital in San Antonio, Texas, by July to convalesce. He had entered the army in January, 1941, spent seventeen months overseas, and sus-

---

18. *Ibid.*, October 7, November 4, December 2, 1944, January 6, February 10, 1945.

19. *Ibid.*, February 3 and 17, March 3, 10, and 17, 1945; *L'Heritage*, VI, No. 18 (March, 1982). Powell A. Casey, *Try Us: The Story of the Washington Artillery in World War II* (Baton Rouge, 1971), contains a list of Louisiana's World War II casualties. In the army and air force, 3,964 persons died of battle and nonbattle injuries; that number includes 14 listed as missing. Another 2,497 died in the navy, marines, and Coast Guard. For casualties in St. Bernard Parish, see pp. 484, 500, and 501.

20. St. Bernard *Voice*, March 17 and 31, April 14 and 21, 1945. In the last year of the war, Isleños in the service included Harold Leon Acosta, John Martinez, Charles Anthony Leon, Lawrence Guerra, Sam Sanchez, Jr., Richard Gonzales, Clarence Menesses, Bruce Nunez, Jr., Philip Gutierrez, Joseph W. Alfonso, Elmo Vega, Jr., Onezime Pereira, Paul R. Hernandez, Sidney A. Serpas, Jr., Alex Menesses, Jr., Alex L. Ruiz, Joseph R. Acosta, and Ronald Estopinal.

tained an injury in Germany. Of his two brothers, Donald and Jules, also in uniform, Jules was wounded in Europe, where he spent fifteen months, winning a Purple Heart and three battle stars.[21]

Contrary to the riotous celebrating that marked Nazi Germany's surrender elsewhere, St. Bernard Parish observed the occasion soberly. Sheriff Rowley had prudently closed the parish bars and saloons. As the war ended, the exploits of several Isleños came to light. First Sergeant Emile Perez was in Belgium, having spent 23 months overseas thus far. His group had made over 200 missions and 7,500 sorties, and had dropped 11,292 tons of bombs on the enemy. Sidney Gallardo of Delacroix Island, in the 275th Engineer Battalion, helped in the crossing of the Rhine River, for which he received a commendation. The two sons of Judge Perez served as officers in the war. Leander H. Perez, Jr., entered the army as a second lieutenant in June, 1942, arrived in England in January, 1944, and moved to the Continent after the invasion. In September in Belgium, he led several men against a company of German soldiers, killing 1 and capturing 153. He received the Bronze Star for his valor. His brother Chalin received an ROTC commission in the navy as an ensign. Assigned to a destroyer, he participated in five invasions in the Pacific, including those of Leyte and Iwo Jima. By war's end, he was a lieutenant, junior grade.[22]

In August, 1945, as the Japanese surrendered, word arrived in St. Bernard Parish that Colonel Nunez Pilet was freed after three and a half years of captivity. In November he returned to Arabi to visit his mother. Although he spoke before parish groups about his wartime experiences, he never revealed the reason for his return to Corregidor that resulted in his capture.[23]

Many of the forces that affected St. Bernard Parish in the late 1930s and 1940s were also at work in Ascension and Assumption parishes. Ascension's population had risen to 21,215 in 1940, a 15-percent increase since 1930. The bulk of the people lived in the countryside, as Louisiana's population of 2,363,880 in 1940 was 70 percent rural. The number of tenant farmers had declined statewide in the past decade from 107,551 to 89,167, while the number of farm owners had risen from 53,159 to 60,312. No doubt Isleños benefited with others from these changes, but

21. *Ibid.*, March 17, May 5, June 23, July 14, October 27, 1945.
22. *Ibid.*, May 12, May 19, June 9, July 7, 1945.
23. *Ibid.*, September 1, November 17, 1945.

agricultural work for the landless provided little remuneration. In early 1941, sugarcane field workers averaged $0.13 cents an hour for men and $0.09 cents for women. Tractor drivers and teamsters fared little better, averaging $1.20 for a 9-hour day. As recovery from the depression proceeded, many farm workers fled from the countryside for better-paying employment in cities and industry, both in and out of Louisiana. Their flight produced a wartime labor shortage in agriculture.[24]

Beginning in about 1939, economic recovery on Bayou Lafourche could be seen in the need for workers, the sale of merchandise, and the region's general prosperity. Growing military preparedness led to more young men from this area entering the armed services as volunteers and draftees. In the fall of 1940, 2,637 men registered for the draft in Ascension Parish. Among the first to be called in March, 1941, were John Curtis Hernandez, Octave Ourso, and Joseph Gomez. But Ascension and Assumption parishes already had career military men. Among them in 1941 were Lieutenant Abram Diez, brother of Dr. Walter Diez; Arthur Falcon in the navy; Sergeant Harold Ramirez, stationed at Camp Shelby, Mississippi; and Sergeant Ulysses Ourso, who served at Camp Beauregard.[25]

When the war began, Bayou Lafourche civilians threw themselves into the struggle. They organized a civilian defense force and soon launched local bond drives, with Sergeant Ulysses Ourso, of Brulee McCall, coming home to help in an early bond rally. Community leaders encouraged scrap-iron drives, rubber collection, and war or victory gardens. Government agents also encouraged rural inhabitants to grow more of their own food and to supply neighboring communities.[26]

The war aggravated the labor shortage. The draft and war industries took an estimated 30 percent of Louisiana's farm labor. Moreover, 20 percent of the women between twenty and thirty had left the farm for city work since 1939. Some sections of Louisiana lost more than 50 percent of their rural labor. Isleños who departed for higher-paying industrial work included Tony Carbo, Wilbert Sanchez, and Albert Falcon, who became shipyard employees in Oakland, California, in 1942. Because of the critical labor shortage, German war prisoners arrived on Bayou Lafourche in 1943 to help in agriculture, and they made

24. Donaldsonville *Chief*, January 11, May 31, June 14, 1941.
25. *Ibid.*, March 15, May 17, June 14, November 22, 1941; Marchand, *The Chief in the Land of the Chetimachas*, 177.
26. Donaldsonville *Chief*, May 16, 1942, and many other issues of this year.

a significant contribution. Meanwhile, Camille S. Hernandez and C. J. Hernandez spent the cane harvesting season throughout the war in Puerto Rico working as sugar boilers. The wartime labor shortage was nationwide, and advertising for jobs reached down to the Donaldson-ville *Chief*, no doubt helping to induce Canary Islanders and others from Bayou Lafourche to desert their homes for higher-paying employment.[27]

Education, too, took a backseat to the war effort. Many Isleños dropped out of higher education to join the service, including E. J. Ourso of Donaldsonville. A journalism major, he had entered Louisiana State University in 1940. In 1942 and 1943, he was the sports editor of the university's student newspaper the *Reveille*, having acquired experience on the Donaldsonville *Chief* and the Baton Rouge *Morning Advocate*. In his last year at the university, he was senior class president, maintained an "A" average, and received an American Legion award. By the summer of 1943, he was at Alexandria, undergoing army basic training before going to officer candidate school. Pierre Barrios of Donaldsonville, an ROTC graduate, received a commission as a lieutenant in the infantry.[28]

With so many men in uniform and the size of Isleño families, it was rare for a Canary Islander not to have kin in the service. Often, families had several sons in uniform; one of the more prominent families was that of Simon Falcon, Sr. Several of the eight brothers had joined the armed forces long before the war. Clifton, the oldest, had entered the navy in 1919 as a sixteen-year-old and worked his way up to chief petty officer by 1941. Simon, Jr., had enlisted in the army and climbed up the ranks while earning a reserve commission as a first lieutenant. With mobiliza-tion, he became a captain in 1941. David, meanwhile, was recalled in 1940 as an army first Lieutenant. Glynn and Andrew, in the navy and marines respectively, and Clifton were all at Pearl Harbor on December 7, 1941. In 1942 Simon became a major and went to India for nearly three years. David entered the paratroopers after a brief tour in Panama. Clifton rose to warrant officer and later to naval lieutenant.[29]

Besides the Falcon brothers, a large number of Bayou Lafourche Canary Islanders became officers in the war. In 1942 Signa M. (Patsy) Gonzales, from the town of Gonzales, went through officer candidate

27. *Ibid.*, January 18, December 27, 1941, January 2 and 9, August 21, November 6 and 20, 1943, and many other issues.

28. *Ibid.*, July 18, 1942, January 2, June 19, 1943.

29. *Ibid.*, February 22, May 10, July 5, 1941, January 17, September 26, November 7, 1942.

school in the Women's Army Corps. Before the war, she had earned a bachelor's degree, taught school for a few years, then quit to help her father, A. T. Gonzales, proprietor of Donaldsonville's X-Ray Pharmacy. Soon her sister Cecil Lois, a teacher at the Donaldsonville high school, followed her into the Women's Army Corps, also becoming an officer. Dr. Sidney V. Vega, Jr., was drafted into the navy in 1942. He, like his father (a son of Antonio D. Vega), was a Donaldsonville dentist. Given a commission as a lieutenant, Sidney, Jr., went to San Diego for training before being assigned to Hawaii.[30]

Among Bayou Lafourche Isleños overseas early in the war was Vernon Acosta, who arrived in Hawaii before June, 1942. In North Africa about late 1942 was Private First Class Cleveland J. Caballero, who had been employed by the Evan Hall Sugar Cooperative for three years before putting on a uniform. He landed with invasion troops first in Oran, Algeria. After North Africa, he moved on to Italy in 1943 and 1944. Two other men overseas in 1943 were Corporal Ray A. Falcon, in the Pacific, and Sergeant Arthur Caballero, in Alaska.[31]

Several more Isleños were in the Pacific by early 1944. William J. Acosta met his brother Vernon in the southwest Pacific in mid-1944, when their ships came together. William, a pharmacist's mate, later landed with the marines on Peleliu as a hospital corpsman. He worked on the beach under enemy fire in a first-aid station, giving his own blood to help two wounded leathernecks. In 1944 army private first class Simon Alleman saw action in the southwest Pacific. He served on Bougainville and Guadalcanal as a bazooka man in an antitank company, seeing much combat.[32]

On October 19, 1944, Harding J. Alleman was reported missing. Sent overseas in January, 1944, he had served with the 5th Army in Italy, where he distinguished himself for bravery and rose to first sergeant. His valor had earned him medals, the Silver Star, with oak-leaf cluster, the Bronze Star, and the Purple Heart. He had repeatedly exposed himself to enemy fire, and his luck had eventually run out.[33]

A serviceman who dropped out from Louisiana State University because of the war was Lawless C. Falcon, who had finished three years

30. *Ibid.*, October 3, 17, and 31, November 7, December 5, 1942, January 30, May 22, June 19, December 18, 1943.
31. *Ibid.*, June 20, 1942, August 28, September 18, 1943, January 29, March 18, 1944.
32. *Ibid.*, February 26, September 9 and 23, December 16, 1944, February 23, 1945.
33. *Ibid.*, July 15, November 18, 1944.

of college. Rather than enter active military duty immediately, he attended Southwestern Louisiana Institute in Lafayette as a "V-12" student, which permitted him to finish school while undergoing marine training. Afterwards, he attended marine officer candidate school at Camp Lejeune, North Carolina.[34]

Two Isleños who sustained injuries in 1944 were Private George Martinez and Joseph J. "Bronco" Acosta. Martinez was wounded in Europe on November 29, after being overseas only a few weeks. Late in the year, navyman Acosta suffered an injury in the South Pacific. The navy rushed him to a hospital in San Leandro, California, before transferring him to a New Orleans facility.[35]

Mr. and Mrs. Sidney F. Gonzales had three sons in the service. Elmer entered the navy on September 17, 1940, and was at Pearl Harbor on December 7, 1941. By February, 1945, he had participated in eight campaigns, including those at the Aleutians, Saipan, Tarawa, New Guinea, Midway, and the Philippines. Meanwhile, Sidney entered the army in May, 1940, rose to first sergeant, and returned home in early 1945, after eighteen months in Greenland. Their younger brother, Edwin, joined the Coast Guard in May, 1942, and attended radio school in California in 1945.[36]

In late 1944 and early 1945, several Canary Islanders, having had their share of overseas duty, returned to the States for new assignments. Among them was Private First Class Roland Sanchez, who had spent twenty-eight months abroad. Staff Sergeant Alvin Truxillo, son of "Sandy" Truxillo, came home from the Pacific in January, 1945, for reassignment. Navyman Lloyd G. Acosta also returned home in 1945. In March the Donaldsonville *Chief* named him "sailor of the week." Acosta had entered the navy on October 12, 1941. After he spent a year in New Orleans, the navy put him on a tanker supplying oil to other ships in the Pacific. His vessel made numerous supply runs between islands seized from the Japanese. In 1945, during the liberation of the Philippines, the enemy attacked his ship for many days at a time, finally sinking it. Acosta, twenty-two, spent nearly an hour in the water before being rescued. He soon returned home.[37]

The Ourso family of McCall, near Donaldsonville, had four sons in

---

34. *Ibid.*, October 7, 1944.
35. *Ibid.*, January 12 and 26, February 9, 1945.
36. *Ibid.*, February 9, 1945.
37. *Ibid.*, December 23, 1944, February 2 and 16, May 18, 1945.

the service. (The name *Brulee Sacramento* was rarely used now, as *McCall* had replaced it.) In the spring of 1945, Claude, the oldest at thirty-six, was an army private. Since 1941 he had served as a medical corpsman in Hawaii, New Guinea, and the Philippines. Edmond, twenty-nine, entered the ground service of the Army Air Corps in February, 1942. He was on Saipan first, then Guam, caring for B-29 bombers. Gordon, an Army Air Corps corporal, attended school to become an aerial engineer, but punctured eardrums later grounded him. In 1945 he worked on a military installation near Lake Charles. Floyd, eighteen in 1945, had only recently enlisted in the army and was training in Arkansas.[38]

The Caballero family of Smoke Bend also had four sons in uniform. In April, 1945, William was an infantry private in Germany. He had dropped out of Tulane when the draft called. Oneal, twenty-eight years old, volunteered for the army in July, 1942, went to the Pacific the next year, and fought in three major campaigns. In 1945 he was on New Caledonia. Arthur, thirty-two, an army sergeant, entered the service in 1942. He fought the Japanese on Kiska in the Aleutians and stayed on the islands afterwards. The oldest son, Cleveland J., thirty-five, served from 1943 on in North Africa, Sicily, and France in the 36th General Hospital Unit of the army. He earned seven ribbons and four battle stars.[39]

Canary Islanders known to be overseas in 1945 included Lawrence J. Falcon, who entered the navy in October, 1943, and went to the Pacific in June, 1944. Vincent Ruiz was a private in an armored infantry battalion in the 1st Army in Germany. By May, 1945, he had served for twenty-six months, four of them overseas. Private First Class Simon Alleman was then in the Philippines, after duty in Bougainville, Leyte, Cebu, and the Negritos. He was among the first American soldiers to land in Japan; his unit, the 164th Infantry Regiment, disembarked only days after the surrender. Private First Class Gus Falcon, overseas for a year, was with the army in Europe in the 238th Engineers Battalion, in northeast France.[40]

Two brothers from McCall, Petty Officer First Class Roland A. Gomez and Petty Officer Second Class Emanuel J. Gomez, met in the Pacific. By mid-1945, Roland was a veteran of five and a half years in the regular

38. *Ibid.*, February 2, March 30, 1945.
39. *Ibid.*, April 20, 1945.
40. *Ibid.*, December 16, 1944, May 25, June 29, July 13, October 26, 1945.

navy, and Emanuel had served three and a half years, of which twenty months were spent overseas.[41]

Keith Falcon, who had spent three years at Louisiana State University preparing to enter medical school, went into the army instead. In the Pacific, he served in Hollandia, Leyte, Mindoro, and Mindinao with the 21st Infantry Regiment. Twin brothers Warren and Ward Ramirez, whose family had moved from Donaldsonville to Baton Rouge, entered the navy in July, 1942. They served together on the battleship *West Virginia* beginning in the fall of 1943 and went through the invasions of Luzon, Mindoro, Leyte, Okinawa, and Iwo Jima. They were also in the battle of Surugao Straits, and their ship participated in the surrender ceremonies in Yokohama Bay in September, 1945.[42]

The family with more sons in uniform than any other Louisiana family—seven—received special recognition in 1945. New Orleans radio station WWL acknowledged Mrs. Simon Falcon, Sr., (who was an Alleman) as "mother of Louisiana" on Mother's Day that year. Almost all of her sons had come through the war without injury. Clifton, then forty-three, with twenty-five years of naval duty, was a naval lieutenant on the staff of Admiral King in Washington, D.C. Simon, Jr., with twenty-three years in the army, was a major stationed in New Orleans. David, thirty-two, also an army major, served in the war in Panama, Australia, and New Guinea. Glynn, thirty, after his ship, the USS *Northhampton*, was sunk in the Pacific, attended submarine school and was reassigned to the Washington, D.C., area. Warren, twenty-six, an Army Air Corps first lieutenant, flew thirty missions as a copilot over Europe, earning the Air Medal with four oak-leaf clusters and the Distinguished Flying Cross. Back home in late 1944, he was reassigned to Victorville Air Base in California. Stewart enlisted in the army in July, 1943, and probably saw more action than his brothers. He fought in Italy, France, Belgium, and Germany, and participated in the airborne invasion of southern France in 1944. He won the Purple Heart, the Combat Infantryman's Badge, several ribbons with four battle stars, and an invasion arrowhead. Andrew, twenty-one, volunteered for the marines in June, 1940, upon finishing high school. A veteran of Pearl Harbor, he served in both

41. *Ibid.*, July 27, 1945.
42. *Ibid.*, August 10, October 19, 1945.

Europe and the Pacific. By February, 1945, he was in a marine detachment in New Orleans.[43]

A number of Isleños from the Bayou Lafourche area were casualties during World War II. The first Canarian known to have died in action was Private First Class Ulysses Hidalgo. Word arrived at home in October, 1943, that he had been killed in North Africa at twenty-five. He had had two years of army service. His parents, Mr. and Mrs. Olibert Hidalgo, were from Assumption Parish. Near the end of the war, two more Canary Islanders were listed dead. In June, 1945, the army revised its earlier report that Private First Class Wilfred Morales had been wounded in Germany to state that he was killed. Before entering the army, Morales had worked in New Orleans shipyards. He had been in the army for four years and overseas since mid-1944. Also in 1945, marine lieutenant Lawless Falcon was killed in action in Okinawa—his first taste of combat. He was about twenty-three years of age. Another war casualty, from East Baton Rouge Parish, was Sergeant Amor Ramirez. He died from a nonbattle injury. Many more Canary Islanders sustained wounds during the war, and others, too numerous to mention, both served and fought in uniform.[44]

Even before the war ended, St. Bernard Parish and the Bayou Lafourche region, along with the rest of Louisiana and the nation, were making the transition to peacetime. By the spring of 1945, the first soldiers came home to stay, schools prepared for the enrollment of the veterans, and local authorities made plans for the postwar era. With Japan's surrender, war plants closed in Louisiana, and many St. Bernard Canarians returned to their former occupations. Shrimping, in particular, attracted them. Louisiana's educational institutions acquired new importance with the ending of the war; they had the task of helping veterans adjust to civilian life and acquire skills for decent employment. Many of the former servicemen from rural areas, having traveled to distant parts of the world, now rejected the drudgery and isolation of farm life. In 1944 only 16 percent of Louisiana's farms had electricity. The Donaldsonville *Chief* editor, aware of the mood of the returning veterans, wrote in August, 1945, that they looked to "city wages," not those of the countryside, and that they were thinking of education.[45]

43. *Ibid.*, February 16, May 11, June 29, 1945.
44. *Ibid.*, October 16, 1943, May 25, June 22, 1945; Casey, *Try Us*, 468, 473.
45. Donaldsonville *Chief*, May 18, August 31, 1945.

The integrity of the Isleño communities suffered during the war. The mainstream of Louisiana life penetrated them more than ever, further breaking down their isolation. The physical distances between the communities and Louisiana's cities and towns had never been great, and the proximity was now more apparent than ever. If the Canary Islander communities somehow retained some of their identity in 1945, the postwar era soon hastened their demise. Isolation was a trait of the past. Moreover, the youth looked forward to assimilation in Louisiana society and in the nation as a whole through education, jobs, and intermarriage. Most did not see themselves as a people apart. By 1945, only a minority of the Canary Islanders could trace their ancestry to the original immigrants through both their parents. Because of intermarriage, the vast majority of descendants with Isleño names were mixed with other people, which greatly accelerated their assimilation.

Twelve

The Canary Islanders
Since World War II

"Like most of the world, Louisiana has seen more change since the beginning of World War II than ever before in history." So writes historian Joe Gray Taylor, and no one acquainted with the Pelican State can doubt the accuracy of that statement. Increased urbanization, mechanization of agriculture, clearing of additional woodlands and swamps for crops, expansion in the natural gas and petroleum industries, and further change in the social order (racial integration) are only some of the manifestations of change since 1945. The new conditions prompted Willie Alfonso of Delacroix Island some years ago to lament the passing of an age with his *décima*, "Ya la Isla no es la Isla como era de primero" — "The Island is no longer the island as it was in the beginning."[1]

Just as the Isleños have continued to increase in numbers, so has Louisiana's population as a whole grown over the last four decades. It has zoomed from 2.3 million in 1940 to 2.7 million in 1950 to 3.75 million in 1975 and to almost 4.4 million in 1982. In 1920 only a third of Louisiana's inhabitants were urban; by 1970 the reverse situation existed, as only a third were rural. The farm population has dropped to less than 5 percent of the state's total. Meanwhile, metropolitan New Orleans has continued to grow, reaching 1.25 million people in 1980 and spilling into neighboring parishes, including St. Bernard. Arabi and Chalmette have become urban areas and bedroom communities for New Orleans; by 1980 they gave St. Bernard most of its population of 64,000.

---

1. Taylor, *Louisiana: A Bicentennial History*, 167, 171–76. Willie Alfonso's *décima* is in Raymond R. MacCurdy, "Los Isleños de la Luisiana. Supervivencia de la lengua y folklore canario," *Anuario de estudios atlánticos*, XXI (1975), 570.

Towns such as Donaldsonville, Gonzales, Smoke Bend, and Sorrento have helped the Ascension Parish population grow to 50,000 in 1980. The more rural Assumption Parish has trailed behind, with only 22,000 inhabitants.[2]

A significant difference between the rural inhabitants of the past and the people who today choose to live in the countryside is that the latter are able to enjoy most urban conveniences—electricity, running water, and modern plumbing. Moreover, with highways, automobiles, and television antennae or satellite dishes, isolation belongs to the past, and country living can be favorably compared to life in the suburbs. Today's rural inhabitants of Louisiana, as most of those elsewhere in the nation, can take advantage of the best in both worlds. Much of the improvement in the quality of life has even penetrated into what remains of the brulees on Bayou Lafourche and down to Delacroix Island in St. Bernard Parish.

The mechanization of agriculture has served to drive Isleños as well as others from agriculture and into the towns and cities. Sugarcane, rice, cotton, corn, and soybeans are grown today on plantations, and the number of small farms and sharecroppers in the state has shrunk. Agriculture still enjoys importance in the state's economy, but fewer hands are now needed. The surplus labor has found employment in petroleum, natural gas, lumbering, manufacturing, salt, and sulphur industries. The expansion of these activities and of agriculture has increased state revenues and paid for modernization, especially in education. Education has become the single largest item in the state budget because of the great need: Louisiana continues to lead the nation in illiteracy.[3]

Another major change affecting life in Louisiana has been desegregation. Although there has been reluctance to accept black equality, the towns and cities began adjusting to the inevitable tide of desegregation in the 1960s and 1970s, while the countryside often lagged behind. Judge Leander Perez led the fight for segregation in Plaquemines Parish, blocking blacks from registering to vote and school integration in the 1950s and 1960s. St. Bernard Parish, too, resisted in a manner that recalled the Reconstruction era. In time, however, blacks in Louisiana won seats on the state legislature, in city governments, and on school and parish boards.[4]

2. Davis, *Louisiana: A Narrative History*, 354; recent statistical information is in *County and City Data Book* (Washington, D.C., 1983).
3. Taylor, *Louisiana: A Bicentennial History*, 180.
4. *Ibid.*, 174–76; Jeansonne, *Leander Perez*, 218–309.

The experiences of the Canary Islanders in Louisiana during the lasι four decades have paralleled those of the bulk of the state's inhabitants. A dual process seems to be at work in the second half of the twentieth century—modernization and the assimilation of the rural population. Schools, to a large degree, have promoted the assimilation of the Isleños. They have emphasized a knowledge of English over Spanish and the melting-pot process. Not without reason, Canary Islander parents have long lamented the effect of schools on their children. One Isleño has stated, "The schools made kids lose their pride in the language." In perhaps the strongest remaining center of the Isleños in Louisiana, Delacroix Island, the prevailing sentiment has been that an elementary education is good enough for their children. As the state lengthened compulsory education to age sixteen and for the first time in history made genuine efforts at combating truancy, schools continued to have a deleterious effect on Isleño identity.[5]

For the most part, rural Canary Islanders have shared many values with the rest of the state's rural population, particularly the Acadians. Being intensely Catholic, trusting in religious leaders, having a strong sense of family, teaching children to defer to parents, desiring families to live close together, using folk medicine, marrying early, often dropping out from school, and to a large degree adhering to traditional occupations have in the past been characteristic of the rural population.

In urban areas, the assimilation of Isleños into the American life-style has proceeded faster. Even within St. Bernard Parish, a distinction has long been drawn between the Delacroix inhabitants and those of the upper parish, the Torneros, named after the English Turn, a bend in the Mississippi River adjacent to the parish. Sometimes the attitude has existed that the Delacroix fishermen, hunters, and trappers are the genuine Isleños (those persons who still retain vestiges of Spanish culture) and that those who have farmed and entered other occupations are not. But the bulk of the Canary Islanders were brought to Louisiana as farmers and to be farmers. While some of them in St. Bernard Parish adjusted to their environment by becoming trappers, fishermen, and hunters, most of the Canary Islanders and their descendants in Louisiana did not take up those occupations.[6]

5. Taylor, *Louisiana: A Bicentennial History*, 180. The quotation is in Douglas Lee, "The Land of the River," *National Geographic*, CLXIV, No. 2 (August, 1983), 247.
6. Guillotte, "Masters of the Marsh," 88.

Those who have clung to the use of Spanish and a traditional way of life have lived in isolated and out-of-the-way places—brulees and the far reaches of St. Bernard Parish. The majority of the descendants of the Isleños in Louisiana have been assimilated. The use of Spanish, probably the most distinctive Isleño trait in rural Louisiana, has continued to decline. Thirty years ago Mark Anthony Quiñones (who is not Isleño) noted that almost all of the Delacroix Island inhabitants knew English although they spoke Spanish among themselves. The younger generation, however, preferred to use English and made little effort to speak Spanish. Quiñones observed that the greatest amount of education was possessed by the young and that older men scoffed at a need for schooling since they had long provided a home and food for their families with little or no education. Few Delacroix veterans of World War II took advantage of the GI Bill. Since the time of Quiñones' 1955 study, the use of the Spanish language has declined even further. In 1983 St. Bernard Parish historian Frank Fernandez estimated that of about ten thousand persons of Isleño descent in the parish no more than five hundred spoke Spanish. Although Spanish-speaking immigrants have continued to trickle into and settle in the parish and on Delacroix Island, they have not been sufficient to reverse the trend.[7]

The education levels in St. Bernard Parish are probably not much different from those in the other Isleño parishes in Louisiana. In 1950, 9.3 percent of the population had no schooling at all, only 5.5 percent had finished high school, and 4.2 percent had attended or graduated from college. By 1970 only 1.6 percent of the population had no schooling, 32.4 percent had finished high school, and 10.1 percent had some college credit or even a degree. In the last 15 years, the education levels of the parish have increased beyond the 1970 achievement. Isleño leaders in St. Bernard, in recognition that the trend to more schooling cannot be stopped, have encouraged the teaching of Spanish and other elements of their heritage to the children in order to try to preserve their ethnic identity. They have quarreled with school authorities who in 1978 received a grant to improve the English competency of the Spanish-speaking children. As a consequence, the Spanish Cultural and Heritage Society, founded in 1976, has developed classes in Spanish for both

7.   Mark Anthony Quiñones, "Delacroix Island: A Sociological Study of a Spanish American Community" (M.A. thesis, Louisiana State University, 1955), 89–95, 116; Lee, "The Land of the River," 247.

children and adults. They have been taught in the Isleño Museum on Terre-aux-Boeufs.[8]

But while some action can be taken in education, it continues to be difficult to fight against nature and man's own harm to the environment. On September 9, 1965, Hurricane Betsy hit the Louisiana coast. It started over land at the mouth of the Mississippi and reached up to Baton Rouge. Winds of more than 70 miles per hour, sometimes gusting to between 150 and 200 miles per hour, continued all night. The parishes most affected were St. Bernard, Plaquemines, and Orleans. The tidal surge was the worst in memory, rising up to 12 feet in some areas and flooding vast stretches of the low-lying lands. Half of St. Bernard's residences were damaged, and nearly all of the homes on Delacroix Island were destroyed. Only four years later, in 1969, Hurricane Camille struck lower St. Bernard and Plaquemines parishes. The island has never recovered from Hurricane Betsy, and not all of the people have rebuilt their homes. The Catholic Church also decided against reconstructing its Delacroix chapel. Those who returned to the island continue with a sense of nineteenth-century stoicism, accepting the ravages of nature as their fate. But while bowing to nature, many of the Isleños have been critical of the United States Army Corps of Engineers and the state conservation authorities.[9]

Since about the late 1920s, the corps of engineers has inadvertently brought about hardship for the residents of St. Bernard Parish. The construction of sturdier levees for the Mississippi River to prevent flooding has stopped the annual deposits of rich alluvial sediment that is essential for delta building. Moreover, the levees have prevented river waters from entering the marshes, which is necessary for freshwater wildlife and vegetation and to stop the encroachment of salt water. In addition, channels and canals have been dredged through the marshlands for the improvement of navigation and for the use of gas and oil companies. Perhaps the most serious damage was done between 1958 and 1965 with the building of the Mississippi River Gulf Outlet. The outlet destroyed thousands of acres of marshlands and disturbed thousands of acres more of shallow open water. Furthermore, the channels

8. Public Affairs Research Council of Louisiana, Inc., *Statistical Profile of St. Bernard Parish* (Baton Rouge, 1973), 3; Guillotte, "Masters of the Marsh," 83–84.

9. Kaiser Aluminum and Chemical Corporation, *They Now Call It the "Greatest Disaster in America" (or the Great Disaster . . . Hurricane "Betsy,") Sept. 9, 1965* (Chalmette, La., n.d.), 3; Guillotte, "Masters of the Marsh," 31.

have facilitated salt-water penetration, thereby accelerating the loss of additional marshlands. It is estimated that forty square miles of wetlands erode or sink into the gulf each year.[10]

The gulf outlet has had significant impact in St. Bernard Parish, affecting the yields that the gulf and marshes provide in fish, oysters, and pelts. An abundance of commercial and sports fishermen has also contributed to the decline in income. Conservation authorities only anger most of the Isleños because they enforce the law against the Canarians while looking the other way for vested interests. As early as the start of the twentieth century, pollution was occasionally a problem in the parish waterways, including Bayou Terre-aux-Boeufs. Since 1945, however, pollution has increased with the advancement of drilling in the marshes and offshore. The activity has had a negative impact on fishing and oystering and has reduced income from those occupations. Isleño complaints about contamination and the violation of laws by gas and petroleum companies have not attracted the attention of the authorities. Marsh buggies used in gas and oil exploration have helped to destroy the marshes and kill muskrats, thereby further reducing Isleño opportunities in their home environment. What the future holds in store for the Canary Islanders who make their living from trapping and fishing is difficult to predict, but decline seems evident.[11]

Observers of the customs of the Canary Islanders, mostly those living on Delacroix Island and a few more in Shell Beach and Yscloskey, have noted that they tend to live in single family units, with relatives occasionally residing nearby. Close family ties extend to first cousins, after which bloodlines become less certain. In lower St. Bernard Parish, endogamy (marrying within the group) has been the pattern in the majority of marriages, which no doubt has helped to preserve the Isleños' customs and identity. Male dominance in marriage is no longer as evident as it was in the past. In the division of labor, married women still tend to work at home, although there are notable exceptions. In child rearing, Canary Islanders have usually been stricter with girls than with boys. Girls often begin working at an earlier age than boys. Fishing, hunting, and trapping start as enjoyable experiences for boys before

10. Lee, "The Land of the River," 228–38. For additional information on the delta, see two studies by Coastal Environments, Inc., *Environmental Baseline Study, St. Bernard Parish, Louisiana* (Baton Rouge, 1972), and *Resource Management: The St. Bernard Wetlands, Louisiana* (Baton Rouge, 1976).

11. Guillotte, "Masters of the Marsh," 17–19, 36–38, 64–68.

becoming their livelihood, and sons are thus often seduced into following their fathers' occupation. Isleños frequently prefer to have relatives working with them on their boats rather than unrelated persons. The lower-parish Canary Islanders adhere to the work ethic and maintain the positive attitude that adversity can be overcome. Moreover, when they fall upon hard times, relatives and neighbors generally pull together to help one another. Theirs, for the most part, seems to be a classless society in which they move ahead together. Overall, the Isleños believe in paying their debts and in honesty. (These lower-parish Isleños should not be confused with the upper-parish gang—"the courthouse boys.")[12]

In lower St. Bernard Parish and probably along Bayou Lafourche, dancing for a long time was a popular form of diversion, and the Saturday night dances were a communal affair. Today, however, most of the dance halls no longer exist. Drinking seems to have gone along with having a good time for the men. On special occasions in St. Bernard Parish, *décimas*, a form of folk poetry, were sung to commemorate an event or a person. It was considered an honor to have a *décima* mention someone, even if in a negative way. Today, the singing of *décimas* is a dying art.[13]

Canary Islanders of St. Bernard Parish observe a number of celebrations through the year, most of which are typical of Catholics in lower Louisiana. All Souls' Day is the occasion for whitewashing tombs at the St. Bernard cemetery and decorating the graves of loved ones. Mardi Gras is a time for dressing up, festivities, and dancing. Christmas is celebrated with feasting within the family. The blessing of the fleet at Delacroix Island is a ceremony shared by many fishing communities in lower Louisiana. Besides a blessing for each boat, dancing, eating, and the naming of a queen mark the occasion. More peculiar to the Isleños is a custom that began during World War II—a walk from Yscloskey and

12. *Ibid.*, 95–109, 112, 119.
13. *Ibid.*, 122–24, 130–31. On the Isleño language, *décimas*, and folk literature, see the studies by Raymond R. MacCurdy, "Los Isleños de la Luisiana," 471–591; *The Spanish Dialect of St. Bernard Parish, Louisiana* (Albuquerque, 1950); "Un romance tradicional recogido en la Luisiana: 'Las señas del marido,'" *Revista hispánica*, XIII (1947), 164–66; "Spanish Riddles from St. Bernard Parish, Louisiana," *Southern Folklore Quarterly*, XII (1948), 129–35; "Spanish Folklore from St. Bernard Parish, Louisiana," *Southern Folklore Quarterly*, XIII (1949), 180–91; "Spanish Folklore from St. Bernard Parish, Louisiana: Part III, Folktales," *Southern Folklore Quarterly*, XVI (1952), 227–50; and by Calvin A. Claudel, "Spanish Folklore from Delacroix Island," *Journal of American Folklore*, LVIII (1945), 209–24; and "Louisiana Folktales and Their Background," *Louisiana Historical Quarterly*, XXXVIII (1955), 35–56.

Delacroix Island to the San Pedro church at Reggio on Good Friday. Each group carries a cross of two-by-fours and says prayers as it makes its way on the roads.[14]

While modernization has had a negative impact on many traditional customs, it seems not to have affected folk medicine on Delacroix Island. Canary Islanders probably brought a number of beliefs with them from their ancestral homeland two hundred years ago. Not until the twentieth century, however, was something written down about their beliefs in folk medicine. On Delacroix Island, techniques in folk medicine are passed down within families, often among women. The specialists want no compensation for their services and believe that their powers are God given. The secret prayers are passed on as the curer is about to retire or feels death approaching. Treating sunstroke, or "getting the heat out," appears to be one of the more common cures. Persons who suffer from the sun have symptoms of nausea, headache, eye irritation, and fever. Praying, using a small, water-filled jar, and "popping" of the scalp are techniques employed to "get the sun out." The sun is also blamed for other illnesses, including hepatitis, ulcers, and influenza. There are folk remedies for curing snakebite, upset stomachs, diarrhea, colds, toothaches, and much more. To a large degree, the elderly resort to folk medicine while the more assimilated Canary Islanders of St. Bernard Parish rely on modern medical practices.[15]

In diet, the Isleños of lower St. Bernard Parish resemble other lower Louisianians. In 1941 an observer noted that typical foods included beans, rice, potatoes, spaghetti, grits, and salt pork. The Isleños supplemented this basic diet with crabs, shrimp, fish, and game in season. They consumed enormous quantities of coffee, used condensed milk in the coffee, and ate canned vegetables. Deficiencies in their diet appeared to be fresh vegetables, milk, and fruit. At that time, electricity and refrigerators had just made their first appearance on Delacroix Island.[16]

Because the Canary Islanders along Bayou Lafourche were less isolated than those in St. Bernard Parish, beginning in the late eighteenth century the former were exposed to other cultural influences, mainly Acadian. Only in the brulees did they keep a large measure of their own culture, particularly the Spanish language. It, too, however, has experi-

14. Kammer, *A Socio-Economic Survey*, 44; Guillotte, "Masters of the Marsh," 123, 135–36.

15. Guillotte, "Masters of the Marsh," 136–41.

16. Kammer, *A Socio-Economic Survey*, 135.

enced a decline, especially in the twentieth century. Philologist Samuel G. Armistead, who visited the area in 1976, has called Spanish there a dying language confined overwhelmingly to the elderly. There are probably fewer Spanish speakers today in Ascension and Assumption parishes than in St. Bernard. Armistead noted that the Spanish language on Bayou Lafourche had incorporated many English and French words—a sign that it had lost its vitality since it lacked an infusion of Spanish-speaking immigrants to invigorate the language. Moreover, virtually all the Spanish speakers in the past and in the present have been illiterate in that language. The small Spanish brulees, enclaves of Isleño culture, for the most part have given way before the onslaught of modernization. The children of Canary Islanders, like many of the descendants of immigrants everywhere, have preferred to be assimilated into the mainstream of American life rather than retain the older culture that has often been depicted as ethnic and rustic.[17]

In several areas the Isleños on Bayou Lafourche adopted French material traits, particularly in house types, settlement patterns, recreation, and cuisine. They also learned the French, or Cajun, language and later even English, thus becoming trilingual. At least since the 1950s, television has helped to spread the use of English. The Isleños reserved Spanish for use at home, while they spoke French and especially English in the last several decades with the outside world. Their use of other languages prompted the erroneous assumption on the part of outsiders that Spanish-speaking inhabitants did not exist. Sometimes the local Acadians preferred to think that there were no Isleños. Discrimination against the Canary Islanders, particularly the brulee dwellers, appears to have been well entrenched for some time. In the 1970s, a local Isleño heatedly remarked, "Those damn French people think that we're not even here." A priest of French background, who had served Donaldsonville's main Catholic church for twenty years, denied the presence of any Spanish people in Ascension Parish.[18]

Hostility toward unassimilated brulee inhabitants has been the greatest. In the 1920s, V. M. Scramuzza called them unfit, half-savage, and of

17. Samuel G. Armistead, "Romances tradicionales entre los hispanohablantes del estado de Luisiana," *Nueva revista de filología hispánica,* XXVII (1978), 41–43; Raymond R. MacCurdy, "A Spanish Word-List of the 'Brulis' Dwellers of Louisiana," *Hispania,* XLII (1959), 547–54.

18. Francis Frederick Hawley, "Spanish Folk Healing in Ascension Parish, Louisiana" (M.A. thesis, Louisiana State University, 1976), 1–3, 8, 9; author's interview with an informant, Belle Rose, Louisiana, June 20, 1980.

inferior caliber. He praised instead assimilation and Americanization. Much the same attitude toward them has been the rule down to the present, especially in urban settlements such as Donaldsonville. Those who cling to an older way of life and to the Spanish language have been called ignorant, undereducated, or illiterate, but these opinions appear to be far from the truth. A 1976 visitor to the brulees who interviewed a number of Isleños found them to be trilingual and knowledgeable of local, state, national, and even international events. Radio and television in recent decades have provided them with a wider understanding of the world. The visitor added, "Furthermore, their graciousness and amiable sociability belied Acadian-French assertions that the *brule* was the abode of 'uncouth' and even 'savage' persons."[19]

In 1976 only Brulee Sacramento, six miles from Donaldsonville in Ascension Parish, remained as a Spanish enclave. Brulees Maurin and Longvue in neighboring Assumption Parish, which once contained sizable numbers of Isleños, were completely uninhabited. Sugarcane plantations have encroached on the brulees, and many inhabitants have preferred to move either to the towns or to the bayou front. The young in particular have favored abandoning rural life and accepting assimilation. The outward migration has resulted in the closing of neighborhood schools, stores, and chapels. Abandoned houses have often been torn down. Sometimes only a driveway denotes that once people lived in a particular spot. The houses that remain are usually small and wooden framed in the Acadian or Creole style. Occasionally, old houses are located next to trailers or new, modern ranch-style structures. In old yards, reminders of the past—butane tanks, water pumps, outhouses, and cars and trucks in various stages of decay—can sometimes be found.[20]

The lack of Spanish-speaking priests has changed the attitude of Isleños toward the Catholic Church, which has mainly French-speaking clergymen. The Church is no longer a vital institution that provides cultural cohesiveness for the Canary Islanders. The breakup of the Valenzuela Mission Church into several churches, which dispersed the Isleños among different Acadian congregations, appears to have been a turning point. Spanish efforts to reopen the Church of St. Joseph at Brulee Capite were met with indifference by the Catholic hierarchy,

---

19. Hawley, "Spanish Folk Healing in Ascension Parish, Louisiana," 5, 10.
20. *Ibid.*, 16–17, 20, 23–24, 29.

prompting several Isleños to remark that "the priests think that they're too good for us."[21]

Brulee residents also resent the bureaucracy in charge of social services that denies disabled cane workers welfare and social security benefits to which they are entitled. Disabled workers survive only through the charity of family members. The poor brulee residents do not wish to move into predominantly black housing projects in Donaldsonville as government agencies suggest they do. They choose instead to stay in poverty in their brulee homes. Furthermore, they resent environmental protection agencies and local lawyers who do not defend them against pollution by plantations. Beginning about the 1950s, sugarcane plantations began extensive aerial spraying of herbicides and pesticides. The spraying has harmed Isleño gardens of corn, okra, tomatoes, and other vegetables as well as killed the fish in the interior swamps and lakes. Protests to state and federal authorities have failed to bring the enforcement of the laws. This situation recalls the days when powerful interests ruled Louisiana. Not surprisingly, the brulee residents feel alienated from all levels of government. Several times in the 1970s, gunfire was aimed at low-flying crop dusters. One Isleño had his single-barrel shotgun confiscated. Although perhaps shaken by the "anti-aircraft fire," the crop dusters emerged unscathed.[22]

Pastimes of bygone years have changed on Bayou Lafourche. Hunting and fishing today are not as popular as they once were. Cane fields have expanded into the swamps, and many of the wooded areas have been cleared. Deer, rabbits, and other forms of game that were once abundant are no longer to be found. Baseball, a game immensely popular in the first half of the twentieth century, has also experienced decline. And as in St. Bernard Parish, many of the dance halls on Bayou Lafourche have closed their doors. The disappearance of former activities without finding new replacements has caused the young in particular to regard life in the brulees as dull. They have tended to flee from the boredom of country life to the lights of the towns and cities.[23]

Among the customs that Canary Islanders of Bayou Lafourche have retained are respect for the elders, women remaining silent while their men speak to outsiders, the oldest male acting as the head of the family, strict discipline for children while grandchildren are indulged, grown

21. *Ibid.*, 31–32.
22. *Ibid.*, 30–32.
23. *Ibid.*, 26–29.

male children not being corrected, women rarely working outside the home, the raising of their own vegetables, and owning most of the land on which they live. A practice observed on Good Friday until recently was to cover mirrors and to avoid looking at themselves. All Saints' Day was the time to visit cemeteries and place flowers on tombs. Another observance that seems to have survived until recently was to keep windows closed, even on the hottest days, to prevent "bad air" from entering the Isleños' homes. Furthermore, only in the last decade have Canary Islanders begun to use air conditioners.[24]

The folk medicine that has survived among Canarian brulee dwellers on Bayou Lafourche differs somewhat from that practiced in St. Bernard Parish. While there has been some Acadian influence, much of the tradition is purely Spanish. The *curandero*, or practitioner, regards himself as a recipient of divine power—*la gracia*. His ability emanates from God or the saints. Those who are pure Spanish and know the secret Spanish prayers have the greatest power. Prayers, not herbs, and talismans produce the cure. Contrary to the tradition on Delacroix Island, where the practitioners accept nothing, on Bayou Lafourche they take a small compensation for their services, but they never ask for it. Most brulee inhabitants know a few prayers; however, only the specialist knows fifty or sixty of them. Many of the practitioners are men, who pass down the prayers within families and sometimes to other men. Today the young seem disinclined to learn folk medicine and are skeptical of its ability to heal. They see it as a tradition of the unassimilated brulee dwellers. On the other hand, there are people who are not Isleños, living outside the brulees, who go there for healing.[25]

Folk medicine does not treat all diseases or ailments, only certain conditions. Serious illnesses are referred to modern medical doctors. "Evil eye" (*mal de ojo*) is one of the more common ailments that afflicts children. A non-immediate family member can cause it by fondling and kissing an infant or child; it produces a fever, and unless attended to, the child can die within twenty-four hours. *Mal aigre*, or "evil air," afflicts adults, producing red eyes, pains in the shoulder and back, and temporary paralysis. A way to guard against it is to keep house windows closed. *Golpe de sol* (heat stroke) strikes older men who labor too long in the hot sun without a hat. *Susto* is fright in children. Besides treating these ailments, folk medicine also cures minor dislocations of internal

24. *Ibid.*, 25, 40; information supplied by Juanita Harwell Sparks in 1980.
25. Hawley, "Spanish Folk Healing in Ascension Parish, Louisiana," 35–39.

organs—tongues, stomachs, and livers—by manipulation, prayers, and the sign of the cross over the affected organs. Ringworm and warts can only be healed during a full moon. Remedies also exist for stomach aches, constipation, and poison ivy. Once snakebites were treated by the *curanderos*, but not today. In the past, snake calling was practiced by the very few. Antonio Diez, now deceased, reputedly once summoned hundreds of snakes out of the swamps near Brulee St. Martin in the 1930s. Today there is widespread skepticism in the brulees about snake calling.

Other practices by specialists include making love potions, treating impotence, and improving one's blood, which can become "bad" or "weak." Eating "sour"—lemons, oranges, and vinegar—is thought to improve women's blood, and eating meats and blood-building foods helps to produce pregnancy. Now lost is the Prayer of St. Anthony, which reportedly had the ability to recover lost items. The *curandero* died without passing on his secret prayer. Finally, the more powerful special-ists claim the ability to turn aside hurricanes or to produce needed rain to end drought.[26]

While the number of persons seeking folk cures appears not to be decreasing, the need for the practitioner to know the prayers in Spanish and be pure Isleño will undoubtedly severely trim the number of *curanderos*. Assimilation is progressing rapidly on Bayou Lafourche, and those who today know the Spanish of their ancestors are probably the last. Intermarriage with people who are not Canarians also continues, and it promotes absorption into the mainstream of cultural life in Louisiana. Finally, abandonment of the brulees, the last holdouts of Canary Islander culture, will probably continue. Some hundred and fifty years after the editor of the New Orleans *Weekly Picayune* predicted that the "overwhelming tide of . . . Americanism" would obliterate the Isleños, it at last seems to be happening along Bayou Lafourche.

The Canary Islanders of St. Bernard Parish will probably not disap-pear so easily. While assimilation and decline in the use of Spanish have occurred in the last half century, today some efforts have been taken to reverse that trend and make the young aware of their cultural heritage. The opening of the Isleño Museum, which was donated to the National Park Service by Louise Molero O'Toole and Mable Molero Quatroy, daughters of Manuel Molero, is helping to preserve artifacts of the past.

26. *Ibid.*, 39–55.

Isleño parish leaders continue to strive to teach Spanish to the young and stimulate an interest in their past. Another factor that has helped in the last decade, albeit slightly, has been an awakening of interest in genealogy. While genealogy stresses kinship ties, perhaps it will also kindle an interest in other aspects of the Canary Islander experience in Louisiana: history, politics, folk culture, and language.

Today, rather than emphasizing the melting-pot theme in the United States, people recognize that it has been cultural diversity that has helped to make this nation strong. And many of them realize that ethnic identity does not imply cultural inferiority. In the past, certain groups of people haughtily asserted their superiority over other ethnic groups in Louisiana—Irishmen, Greeks, Yugoslavs, Italians, Acadians, and, of course, the Canary Islanders. But that attitude belongs to the past, and the various cultural groups of lower Louisiana now boast about their contribution to the development and diversity of their state. Fifty thousand or more people can trace their ancestry back to the Canarian immigrants of 1778 to 1783. Many of them are still in Louisiana, but others have spread throughout the nation, with substantial numbers in the Southeast as well as in Texas, Colorado, and California. For nearly two hundred years, the demise of the Canary Islanders as a separate ethnic group in Louisiana has been predicted. Despite their small numbers, those who retain vestiges of their cultural heritage continue to survive against the "overwhelming tide of . . . Americanism."

Passenger Lists of Canary Islanders Sailing to Louisiana 1778–1783

BACHELORS AND MARRIED RECRUITS WITH THEIR
FAMILIES WHO EMBARKED ON THE PACKET BOAT
SANTÍSIMO SACRAMENTO, SANTA CRUZ DE TENERIFE,
JULY 10, 1778

Ventura Perdomo y Quintana
  María Hernández, wife
  María, daughter, 8 months
Domingo Grillo
Domingo Antonio de Acosta
  Francisca Mauricia, wife
Domingo García
Sebastián García
Blas Díaz de Eneda
Antonio García
  Ana Gonzáles, wife
  Amaro, son, 16
  Lázaro, son, 14
  Félix, son, 18 months
  María, daughter, 3
Francisco Amado
Tomás de Silva
José Gonzáles

  María Candelaria, wife
José Antonio de la Cruz
  Josefa Martín, wife
  María, daughter, 3
Julián de Herrera
  María Sánchez, wife
Juan Rodríguez Suárez
  María Concepción Rodríguez,
    wife
  María, daughter, 15
Alejandro de los Santos
  Bernarda García, wife
  María, daughter, 4
  Domingo, son, 2
Manuel Núñez Villavicencio
  Josefa Suárez, wife
  María del Carmen, daughter, 12
  María, daughter, 4

Esteban, son, 7
Ignacio, son, 2
Josefa, daughter, 2
José Martín [first]
　Rita de León, wife
　María, daughter, 5
　Domingo, son, 2
Francisco Gonzáles Toledo
　Bernarda Hernández, wife
　María, daughter, 5
José Martín [second]
　María del Cristo León, wife
Juan Mederos
　Josefa Martínez Duende, wife
　Francisca, daughter, 5
Antonio de los Reyes
Agustín Pinto de León
　María Casañas, wife
　Juan, son, 13
　Bernarda, daughter, 11
　María, daughter, 7
　Martela, daughter, 5
Diego Lachhart
　Doña María Agustina Estevez,
　　wife
　Juana, daughter, 5
　María, daughter, 4
　Bárbara, daughter, 11 months
José Hernández López
　María del Carmen, wife
　María, daughter, 18
　María, daughter, 15
　Josefa, daughter, 13
Blas Antonio Montesino
　Agustina García Martel, wife
Andrés Padrino
　Inés María, wife
José Martín
　Micaela García, wife

Antonio José Rodríguez
Cristobal Antonio Gámez
Manuel Mateos
Matías Gonzáles
Marcos Francisco Labrador
　Andrea Francisca Abreu, wife
　Antonio Francisco, son, 17
　Antonia, daughter, 22
　Josef, daughter, 19
　José, son, 11
　María, daughter, 5
　Bárbara, daughter, 3
Julián Godoy
Pedro Santana
Juan Díaz
Francisco Berjoy
José Martín Cabrera
Mateo Méndez
Juan Francisco Pérez Blanco
Isidro Hernández
　Bárbara Gonzáles, wife
Patricio José García
Francisco Xavier Truxillo
　Manuela Antonia Martela, wife
　Gregorio, son, 17
　Juan, son, 6
　Cristobal, son, 6
　María, daughter, 16 months
Diego Yáñez
Josef García
Mateo Gonzáles Fajardo
　Lorenza de Acevedo de Fables,
　　wife
　María, daughter, 3
　José, son, 7 months
Antonio Quesada
　Melchora Cabral, wife
　José, son, 12
　María, daughter, 6

José Pablo de León
Lorenzo López
Francisco Antonio Mallorquín
Amaro García
Antonio Montesino Clemente
  María Estevez, wife
  Lorenzo, son, 11 months
Antonio José Morales
  Isabel María de Candelaria, wife
  Sebastiana, daughter, 3
  María, daughter, 2
José Placeres
Pedro Martín
José Francisco Sosa
Pedro Herrera
José Martel
Luis Betancurt
José López
Silvestre del Rivero
Juan Benítez
Andrés Díaz
Domingo Hernández
  Andrea Josefa de la Cruz, wife
  Vicente, son, 15
  Clemente, son, 5
  Antonia, daughter, 16
  Gerónimo, son, 4
José Quintero
  Antonia de Armas, wife
  Antonio, son, 10
  Antonia, daughter, 8
Ventura Gerónimo Guirola
Juan José de Herrera (widower)
  Pedro, son, 10
  Agustín, son, 5
Nicolás Hernández
  Catalina Liaz [Díaz?], wife
Pedro Torralva
Francisco Gonzáles

Domingo Díaz
  María Alonso, wife
  Salvador, son, 11
Joaquín de Páez
José Antonio Gonzáles
  María Pérez, wife
Bernardo Pedres
José Antonio Díaz
  Blasina Fajardo, wife
José Agustín Capitán
  Isabel García, wife
  Francisca García, mother
  Pablo, son, 5 months
Antonio Silva
  Clara Poscas de Arvelo, wife
José Hernández Montesino
  Polonia Rodríguez Correa, wife
  María Josefa, daughter, 21
Domingo García
  Ambrosia Montesino, wife
  Juan, son, 4
José Antonio Silverio
  María Pérez, wife
  Julián, son, 16
  Pascual, son, 4
  José, son, 7
  María, daughter, 5
  Rosalía, daughter, 2
Baltasar Martín
  Rosalía Perez, wife
  Antonia, daughter, 18
  María, daughter, 10
  Andrés, son, 9
  Leandro, son, 8
  Juan, son, 4
Juan Neris
Juan Gonzáles
Juan Francisco Gutiérrez
Francisco Gonzáles Corbo

Andrea Ruiz, wife
Cecilia, daughter, 25
Lorenza, daughter, 24
María, daughter, 17
Rita, daughter, 15
Andrea, daughter, 13
José, son, 9
Agustín, son, 8
Domingo, son, 3
Juana, daughter, 11
Juan Cabral
Andrés Domínguez (widower)
María, daughter, 14
Juan, son, 12
Petra, daughter, 1 month
Bárbara, daughter, 21
José Miranda
José Rodríguez Forme
María Agustina de Guerra, wife
Domingo, son, 14
Francisca, daughter, 10
Francisco Castañeda
Felipa Padrón, wife
Vicente Antonio Navarro
Pedro Martín
María García, wife
María Dorta, mother
Nicolás Rodríguez Forme [Forne?]
Francisco Melián
Silvestre de León
María Dionisia de las Nieves, wife
Luis Antonio de Vargas
Cristobal Vargas
Gregorio Gonzáles
María de la Encarnación, wife
Francisco Miranda
Antonio Alfonso

José Cava
Lorenzo Hernández Neda
Pablo Rodríguez Sierra
José Escobar
Francisco García
Blas García de Abreu
Diego Antonio Román
Antonia Rodríguez, wife
José García Grillo
Nicolás Pérez de Abreu
Ignacio Pérez Roque
Juan Candelaria Grillo
Juan Antonio Prieto
Antonio Agustín Hernández
Diego Hernández Truxillo
Antonio Gonzáles Gómez
Cristobal Simón
Antonio José Carrillo
Antonio del Castillo
Manuel Díaz
Francisco Pérez
Francisco Hernández
María Cherine, wife
José Antonio Rivero
Dominga Flores, wife
Tomasa, daughter, 4
Juan Cabrera
Lorenza Artiles, wife
Juan, son, 2
Francisco, son, 1
María, daughter, 12
Sebastiana, daughter, 4
Lorenzo José de Jesús
Juan Antonio Martín
Antonia María, wife
Nicolás de la Cruz
Juan María Robles

María de la O Morales, wife of recruit Nicolás Rodríguez Forme, married after the list was prepared.

Source: AGI, SD, leg. 2661.

BACHELORS AND MARRIED RECRUITS WITH THEIR FAMILIES WHO EMBARKED ON THE POLACRE *LA VICTORIA*, SANTA CRUZ DE TENERIFE, OCTOBER 22, 1778

Antonio Terry Palao
Andrés de Vega
   Constanza Lujan, wife
   Rosalía, daughter, 10
   Juana, daughter, 8
   Antonio, son, 12
   María, daughter, 6
   Josefa, daughter, 18 months
Juan Suárez
   Elvira Lorenza, wife
Juan Hernández
   Petrolina Sánchez, wife
Cristobal Ramírez
   Ana Caballero, wife
   José, son, 18
   Catalina, daughter, 15
   Fernando, son, 13
   Pedro, son, 11
   Francisco, son, 9
   María, daughter, 10
   Ana, daughter, 12
Pablo Suárez
   Teresa Santana, wife
Sebastián de Nis
   Ana del Toro, wife
   Cristobal, son, 12

Andrea, daughter, 7
Salvador Peraza
   Margarita Gutiérrez, wife
   Manuel, son, 11
   Antonio, son, 4
   María, daughter, 2
Salvador Ramírez
   Juana Pérez, wife (she fled)
   Diego, son, 13
Juan Medina
   Manuela Gonzáles, wife
   Fernando, son, 8 months
Ignacio Ramírez
Tomás Collado
   María Alemán, wife
   María Collado, sister, 12
Pedro Santana
Francisco Ortega Ramos
   Tomasa Suárez, wife
   Pedro, son, 18
   Bernardo, son, 10
   Josefa, daughter, 14
José Herrera
   Lucia Gonzáles, wife
   Ignacio, son, 8
Manuel Romano

María, sister, 17
Juan Antonio Sanchez
  Margarita Macías, wife
  Gaspar, son, 18 months
Pedro Jorge Callero [Caballero?]
  María Gonzáles, wife
  Andrea, daughter, 7
  Juana, daughter, 5
  Domingo, son, 4
  Miguel, son, 9 months
  Josefa, mother-in-law
Domingo López
  Francisca, sister, 26
Bartolomé López
  Catalina, sister, 10
Juan Alonso Romero
  María Jorge, wife
  Juan, son, 13
  Francisco, son, 4
  Antonio, son, 2
  Rosalía, daughter, 7
  Andrea, daughter, 5
  María, daughter, 7 months
Miguel José Rodríguez
Salvador Milán
  Antonia Alemán, wife
  María, daughter, 10 months
Gaspar Sánchez
  Beatriz Flores, wife
  Ana, daughter, 10
  Cristobal, son, 6
  Francisco, son, 4
  Josefa Pérez, mother-in-law
Bartolomé Díaz
  Josefa Pérez, wife
  Diego, son, 10
  Manuel, daughter, 8
  Juan, son, 6
  José, son, 4

Francisco, son, 2
Francisca, daughter, 13 months
Juan Sánchez Melián
  Catalina Navarro, wife
  Francisco, son, 5 months
Juan de León Rodríguez
  Josefa Rodríguez, wife
  José, son, 12
  Francisco, son, 9
  Juan, son, 7
  Antonio, son, 5
  Domingo, son, 4 months
  Catalina, daughter, 10
Antonio Gonzáles
  Rosalía Ortega, wife
  José, son, 8
  Francisco, son, 4
  María, daughter, 1
  Josefa Ortega, mother-in-law
Andrés Perera
  María del Rosario, wife
  Antonio, son, 4
  Domingo, son, 2
Antonio Cazorla
  Francisca Ruano, wife
  José, son, 14
  Diego, son, 11
  Diego Antonio, son, 9
  Josefa, daughter, 20
  María, daughter, 16
  Catalina, daughter, 4
  Rosalía, daughter, 4 months
Lorenzo Huerta
Ramón de Cubas
Domingo Melo
Melchor Díaz Donoso
Pedro de los Reyes
Sebastián López
Lucas Agustín Santana

Francisco López Machado
  Margarita Ramírez, wife
  María, daughter, 3 months
Fernando Rodríguez
  Rita Perdomo, wife
  Lucia Rodríguez, sister
  María, sister
Joaquín del Pino
  Catalina Espinosa, wife
  José, son, 3
  Cristobal, son, 10 months
José Sánchez Ramírez
José Agustín Enrique
Miguel Herrera
  Catalina Rodríguez, wife
  Antonio, son, 3
  Francisco, son, 6 months
Silvestre Ojeda
Blas Ramos
Cristobal Ventura
  Doña Josefa del Toro, wife
  Pedro, son, 4
  Joaquín, son, 2
  María, daughter, 2
Matías Gonzáles
  Isabel Rodríguez, wife
Miguel Sánchez
  Isabel Juana, wife
  Josefa Lujan, mother-in-law
Antonio Gonzáles
  Josefa Rivero, wife
Miguel Martín
  Josefa Medina, wife
  Miguel, son, 5
  Roque, son, 4
Miguel Quevedo
  María Saavedra, wife
  Tomasa, daughter, 5
  Ana, daughter, 2

José Tilano
  Micaela Reyes, wife
  Juan, son, 12
  José, son, 9
  Gaspar, son, 6
  Agustín, son, 3
  María, daughter 2
Alonso Cerdeña
  Francisca Ortega, wife
  Juan, son, 8
  Francisco, son, 2
  María, daughter, 2
  José, son, 4
  María Zavallos, mother-in-law
Melchor Ximénez
  Catalina Perdomo, wife
  Juan, son, 8
  Diego, son, 6
  Josefa, daughter, 7
  Francisco, son, 13 months
Antonio Santos
  María del Pino, wife
Juan Viera
  Dominga Ojeda, wife
  María, daughter, 17
  Rosalía, daughter, 13
  Isabel, daughter, 8
Felipe Sánchez Romero
  María Sánchez, wife
  Andrea, daughter, 5
Lucas Miguel Gonzáles
  Isabel Navarro, wife
  Manuela, daughter, 9
  José, son, 4
  Miguel, son, 4 months
Francisco Rodríguez
  Ana Romero, wife
  Agustina, daughter, 4
  Sebastiana, daughter, 10

Juana, mother-in-law
Vicente Sardina
  Rita Gabriela, wife
  María, daughter, 13
  José, son, 2 months
Matías Díaz Marino
  María Marrero, wife
  José, son, 12
  Francisca, daughter, 14
  Paula, daughter, 10
Gregorio Durán
  Ana Hidalgo, wife
  Francisco, son, 12
  Miguel, son, 7
  José, son, 6
  María, daughter, 13
  Antonia, daughter, 3
Antonio Acosta
  María Pérez, wife
  Andrea, daughter, 18
  Lorenzo, son, 14
  Domingo, son, 13
  Francisco, son, 10
  Blas, son, 8
  María, daughter, 15
Francisco Suárez
  Francisca Suárez, wife
  Pablo, son, 18
  Juana, daughter, 14
Bartolomé Marrero
  Josefa Sosa, wife
  Tomasa, daughter, 20
  María, daughter, 17
  Catalina, daughter, 14
Francisco Monzón
  Josefa de Castro, wife
Roque de Ávila Bordón
  José, son, 8
Sebastián Hernández

Teresa López, wife
  Sebastián, son, 17 (he fled)
  Manuel, son, 15
  Vicente, son, 10
  Lázaro, son, 7
  Bartolomé, son, 5
  Juan, son, 4
  Ana, daughter, 12
Francisco Cazorla
Manuel Melo
Patricio Melo
Pedro Guedes
  Isabel de Sosa, wife
  Sebastiana, daughter, 22
  José, son, 7
Juan Gonzáles Siverio
  Catalina Espino, wife
  Ana, daughter, 12
  Antonio, son, 4
Bartolomé Hernández Hidalgo
  Isabel Hidalgo, wife
Antonio Martel
  Francisca Antonia, wife
  Antonio, son, 6
  Domingo, son, 2
  Blasina, daughter, 11
Salvador Bermúdez
  María Ramos, wife
Miguel Espino
Joaquín Díaz
  Josefa Ana, wife
Juan Díaz
Joaquín del Pino
  Francisco, brother
José Mateo
Diego Gonzáles
José Gonzáles
  Catalina, sister, 18
Blas Alemán

Juan del Pino Rodríguez
Francisco Sánchez Melián
  Ana Espino, wife

Domingo Antonio Domínguez
  María Candelaria, wife

Juana Pérez, wife of Salvador Ramírez, fled the night before embarking; the same for Sebastián Hernández, son of the same name. Teresa López enlisted separately. Josefa María de las Nieves, mother-in-law of Andrés Perera, was forgotten in the enlistment.

Source: AGI, SD, leg. 2661.

BACHELORS AND MARRIED RECRUITS WITH THEIR FAMILIES WHO EMBARKED ON THE FRIGATE *SAN IGNACIO DE LOYOLA*, SANTA CRUZ DE TENERIFE, OCTOBER 29, 1778

Martín Terry Palao
  Doña Antonia Prast, wife
  Doña Olaya, daughter, 17
  Don Pedro, son, 6
  Doña María, daughter, 3
Don Ignacio Terry Palao
Don Martín Terry Palao
Juan Hernández Pestaño
  Jacinta de León, wife
Juan Antonio Alfonso
  María Marrero, wife
  Luis, son, 2
Pablo Estevez
  María Rodríguez, wife
Antonio Siverio Pimental
  María Jorge, wife
  Marcial, daughter, 15
  Francisca, daughter, 10
  Pedro Francisco, son, 9
  Isabel, daughter, 7
  Ana María Suárez, stepdaughter
  Bartolomé Suárez, stepson, 8

Antonio Esmeraldo
  Ángela Guerra, wife
  María, daughter, 2
José Antonio Alonso
  Manuela Delgado, wife
José Rodríguez Charnero
  María García, wife
  Domingo, son, 2
  Pedro, son, 7 months
Felipe Artiles
  Juana Ximénez, wife
  Juan, son, 11
  Antonio, son, 7
  María, daughter, 2
  Juan Cazorla, brother, 15
José Hidalgo
  Isabel Sambrana, wife
  Gregorio, son, 10
  Francisca, daughter, 9
  Juan, son, 10 months
José Antonio Rodríguez
  Juana de la Cruz, wife

María, daughter, 4
Sebastiana, daughter, 3
José Morales
    Antonia Viera, wife
    María, daughter, 6
    Catalina, daughter, 4
    Ignacia, daughter, 10 months
Francisco Sánchez
    María Caballero, wife
    Juan, son, 2
    Francisco, son, 1
Antonio Martín
Juan Ximénez
    Juana, daughter, 20
    María, daughter, 14
Lorenzo Hernández
    María Ximénez, wife
    Ana, daughter, 2
    María, daughter, 5 months
José Alejandro Pérez
    Nicolasa Cambaluz, wife
    María, daughter, 7
Vicente Delgado
    Felipa Ximénez, wife
    Isabel, daughter, 3
    Sebastiana, daughter, 3 months
Simón Casimiro
    Catalina González, wife
Matías Martín
    María Magdalena, wife
    Juan, son, 4
    María, daughter, 2
Bartolomé Fernández
    Catalina Mireles, wife
    Juan, son, 13
    Vicente, son, 5
Domingo Vicente Morales
    Gregoria Hidalgo, wife
José Bermúdez

María Ramírez, wife
Catalina, daughter, 3 months
Agustín Sánchez
    Francisca Ortiz, wife
    Lorenza, daughter, 7
    María, daughter, 2
Esteban Hernández
Gregorio Judas Ravelo
    Melchora de los Reyes, wife
    José, son, 3
    María, daughter, 8
Juan Melián
    María Ortiz, wife
Antonio de Fuentes
    Marcela Pérez, wife
    Juan, son, 11
    Francisco, son, 8
    Pedro, son, 6
    José, son, 4
    Ana, daughter, 2
Luis Macías
    Tomasa de Borges, wife
    Miguel, son, 17
    Francisco, son, 13
    José, son, 9
    Francisca, daughter, 3
Juan Sánchez
    Francisca Martel, wife
    María, daughter, 11
    José, son, 8
    Bartolomé, son, 5
Salvador Luis Ravelo
    Agustina Gonzáles, wife
    Domingo, son, 8
    José, son, 4
    Josefa, daughter, 12
    María, daughter, 9
Salvador Viera
    Antonia Viera, wife

Antonio, son, 8
Sebastián, son, 5
María, daughter, 12
Andrea, daughter, 10
María Leonor, daughter, 2
Lorenzo Rodríguez de León
María Espino, wife
Luis, son, 12
Antonio, son, 8
Sebastiana, daughter, 6
Juan Espino
Joaquina Solier, wife
Miguel, son, 1
Cristobal Ojeda
Josefa Figueroa, wife
Cristobal, son, 17
Antonio, son, 8
Francisca, daughter, 20
María, daughter, 12
José Antonio de la Santa
María Borge, wife
Antonio Rodríguez
María Jorge, wife
Juan, son, 12
José, son, 8
María, daughter, 3
Francisca, daughter, 2
Francisco, son, 2 months
Pedro Barrero
María Antonia, wife
Antonio, son, 4 months
Gabriel Hernández
Bárbara Melián, wife
Vicente, son, 17
Félix, son, 15
Domingo Antonio Ascano
María Hernández, wife
Pedro, son, 5
Juana, daughter, 7

María, daughter, 3
Micaela, daughter, 6 months
Agustín Romero
Polonia Rodríguez, wife
José, son, 12
Domingo, son, 10
Juan, son, 7
Agustín, son, 4
Diego Rafael de Barrios
Teresa Camacho, wife
Francisca, daughter, 2 months
Tomás Jorge Manzano
José María Truxillo
Juan Antonio García
Francisco Peña
María de los Santos, wife
Juan, son, 1
Francisca, daughter, 10
Catalina, daughter, 5
Antonia, daughter, 7
Gregoria, daughter, 2
Manuel Gonzáles
Josefa Sánchez, wife
Francisca Cabrera, wife of
recruit José Sosa, who
embarked July 10
Melchor García
Salvador Rodríguez
Juan Marrero
Bartolomé Romero
José Justo Díaz
Felipe Francisco
Bernarda Francisca, wife
Domingo, son, 18
Felipe, son, 12
José, son, 9
Lorenzo, son, 4
María, daughter, 23
Rosalía, daughter, 14

Andrea, daughter, 12
Matías Francisco
Tomás Mayor
  Gregoria Sánchez, wife
  Cristobal, son, 18
  José, son, 5
  Pedro, son, 3
  Catalina, daughter, 20
  Leonor, daughter, 12
  María, daughter, 6
Diego Morales
  Juana María, wife
  Nicolás, son, 1
Francisco Manuel Gómez
  María Perera, wife
  Juana, daughter, 6 months
Alonso Ruano
  Ignacia Casañas, wife
  José, son, 7
  María, daughter, 2
  Isabel, sister
Matías Hernández Neda
  Josefa Casalta, wife
  José, son, 6
  Domingo, son, 4
  María, daughter, 11
Antonio García de Abreu
  Agustina Sánchez, wife
  Rafaela García, sister-in-law
Antonio Suárez
  Juana Suárez, wife
  Francisco, son, 10 months
Guillermo Gonzáles Chocho
  María Gil, wife
  Sebastián, son, 3 months
Pablo Ruiz
  María Olivares, wife
  Juan, son, 4
Francisco Alvarado Machado

Domingo Hiedra
Antonio Hernández
  Sebastiana Montesdoca, wife
  Juan, son, 13
  Luis, son, 1
  María, daughter, 2
Antonio Sánchez
  Juana López, wife
  Andrea, daughter, 9 months
José Perera Sánchez
  María Santana, wife
  Francisco, son, 2
  Isabel Antonio, sister, 6
José Perera
  María Ramírez, wife
  María, daughter, 13
  Catalina, daughter, 11
  Josefa, daughter, 9
  Francisca, daughter, 7
  Luisa, daughter, 5
  Isabel, daughter, 3 months
Juan Alemán
  Juana Ramírez, wife
  Antonio, son, 14
  Baltasar, son, 5
  Pedro, son, 2
  Josefa, daughter, 9
  Sebastiana, daughter, 7
Bernardino Ginory
  Francisca Ana Polier, wife
Gaspar Ortiz López
  María Sánchez, wife
  Juan, son, 3
  María, daughter, 1
Cristobal Falcón
  Josefa Martín, wife
  Antonia, daughter, 9 months
  Catalina, daughter, 4
  Antonia Martina, sister-in-law

Cristobal Quintero
  María Ruano, wife
  Cristobal, son, 18
  María, daughter, 14
  Beatriz, daughter, 10
Antonio Ramírez
  Ana Santana
Gaspar Falcón
  Francisca Mateo, wife
  Juan, son, 4
  Miguel, son, 2
Gregorio Bermúdez
  Ana Navarro, wife
  Diego, son, 14
  Clemente, son, 4
  José, son, 6
  María, daughter, 16
José Antonio Ventura
  Antonia Pérez, wife
  José, son, 2
Antonio Alonso
  Rita Andrea, wife
  Antonia, daughter, 5
  Agustín, son, 2
Antonio Pérez Gordillo
  Francisca Gonzáles, wife
  Domingo, son, 13
  Lucas, son, 10
  Antonio, son, 5
  Francisco, son, 4
  Gonzalo, son, 2
  José, son, 11
Felipe Antonio de las Mercedes
  Rufina Francisca, wife
  María, daughter, 5
Salvador Sánchez
  Agüeda Domínguez, wife
  Felipe, son, 9 months
  María Ramírez, sister

José Espino
  María Acosta, wife
  Fernando, son, 3
José Juan de Barrios
  Bernarda Núñez, wife
  María, daughter, 4
  Bárbara, daughter, 1
Cristobal de Mesa
  Josefa Gonzáles, wife
  José, son, 1
Manuel Ojeda
  Francisca Medina, wife
  Juan, son, 8 months
  María, daughter, 3
Gregorio Ojeda
  María Suárez, wife
  María, daughter, 5
  Josefa, daughter, 3
  Rosalía, daughter, 1
  Catalina Quintana
Juan Alvarado
  María Suárez, wife
  Tomás, son, 4
  Isabel, daughter, 2
  Francisca Antonia, sister-in-law
José Ángel Quintana
  Agustina Monzón, wife
  María, daughter, 17
  Catalina, daughter
  Manuel, son, 10
  Diego, son, 8
José del Pino
  Rita Monzón, wife
  María, daughter, 7 months
  (died)
Antonio Guzmán
  Francisca Guerra, wife
Domingo Cabrera
  Rita Sánchez, wife

Felipe, son, 5
Bartolomé Díaz
  Josefa Aguilar, wife
  Fernando, son, 13
  Agustín, son, 5
  Francisca, daughter, 7
  Josefa, daughter, 4
Cristobal Rodríguez
  Catalina Arvelo, wife
  Francisco, son, 5 months
  Josefa Arvelo, mother-in-law
  Bernarda, daughter, 20
Gerónimo Quintana de Ávila
  María Manuela Matos, wife
  Esteban, son, 9 months
  María, daughter, 7
  Petrolina, daughter, 5
  Josefa, daughter, 5
Juan José Reverón
  Antonia de Gracía Delgado,
    wife
José Francisco Polo
  Ángela Regalada, wife
Manuel Francisco García
  María de San Pedro, wife
  Agustín, son, 10
  José, son, 5
José Gómez
  Juana Esmeralda, wife
Antonio Hernández
Francisco Montesdoca
Francisco de Orta
  Josefa López, wife
  Pedro, son, 8
  Antonia, daughter, 20

Josefa, daughter, 11
Isabel, daughter, 10
José Domínguez
  María Francisca, wife
  Felipa Domínguez, mother
  Fernando, son, 8
  Tomasa, daughter, 7
Juan Francisco Guzmán
  Antonia, sister, 30
Antonio Gonzáles Camacho
  Rita Blanco, wife
Francisco Verde
Cristobal Quintero
José Hernández Corvo
  Beatriz Francisca, wife
  Salvador, son, 8
  Antonia, daughter, 4
  Francisco, son, 14 months
Francisco Ramírez
  Ana Pérez, wife
  Francisco, son, 4
  Antonia, daughter, 5 months
Francisco Javier Xenera
  Isabel de Espino, mother
  Felipa, sister, 19
Bartolomé Hernández
  Josefa Ortega, wife
  María, daughter, 7
  Ana, daughter, 4
  Francisco, son, 14 months
Manuel Dominguez
  Juana Francisca, wife
  Antonio, son, 19
  Agustín, son, 18
  María Luisa, daughter, 12
  José, son, 5

Antonio Guzmán married after he enlisted. He takes his orphan sister-in-law Ana Guerra, and Catalina Espino, sister of José Espino. Antonio

Gonzáles Camacho is taking his mother-in-law, Francisca Bergara. Pedro Francisco, age nine, omitted earlier.

Source: AGI, SD, leg. 2661.

BACHELORS AND MARRIED RECRUITS WITH THEIR FAMILIES WHO EMBARKED ON THE PACKET BOAT *SAN JUAN NEPOMUCENO*, SANTA CRUZ DE TENERIFE, DECEMBER 9, 1778

José Antonio Herrera
José Gómez
  Catalina Peraza, wife
  Ana, daughter, 4
  Domingo, son, 3
  María, daughter, 2
Fernando Morales
  Bernarda Gonzáles, wife
  Isidro, son, 1 month
  Fernando, son, 2
José Enrique Almeyda
  Lázaro, son
  Francisca, daughter, 21
Antonio José de Armas
  María Delgado, wife
  Domingo, son, 2 months
Ignacio Antonio Martos
  Josefa Román, wife
Bernardo Nieves
  María Rodríguez, wife
  Juan, son, 2
  Brigida, daughter, 1 month
  Isabel, sister-in-law, 17
Antonio Pérez
  Catalina Pérez, wife
  Nicolás, son, 8
  María, daughter, 5

Juan de Ojeda
  Josefa Casimiro, wife
Bartolomé Monzón
  María Peñales, wife
  Francisco, son, 5
  Isabel, daughter, 4
  Juana, daughter, 2
  Juan, son, 13
  Josefa, daughter, 20
Juan Morales
  Teresa de Jesús, wife
  María, daughter, 2
Domingo Zaballos [Ceballos?]
  Rita María, wife
Estaban Cabrera
  María de las Nieves, wife
José Antonio Releva
  Ana del Carmen, wife
Miguel Suárez
  María de la Cruz, wife
  Domingo, son, 11
  Sebastián, son, 7
  Miguel, son, 1 month
Juan Rafael Truxillo
  María Teresa Cabrera, wife
Antonio Agustín Pérez
Mateo Rodríguez

María, sister, 23
Gabriela, sister, 18
José María de la Paz
  María Rebeca, wife
  Ramón, son, 13
  Antonia, daughter, 7
  Eugenia, daughter, 5
Domingo Truxillo
  Catalina María, wife
  Antonio, son, 14
  José, son, 6
  Juan, son, 3
  Marcelina, daughter, 7
Juan de Lugo Navarrete
  María de Arsola, wife
  Antonio, son, 3
  Rosa, daughter, 8
  María, daughter, 6
  Francisca, daughter, 2 months
Juan Antonio de Niebla
  Rosa, wife
  Juan, son, 15
  Antonio, son, 12
  Pedro, son, 16
  José, son, 7
  Domingo, son, 5
Blas Ríos
  Josefa Ledesma, wife
  Juana, daughter, 20
  Narcisa, daughter, 8
  Marcelina, daughter, 12
Manuel Rodríguez
  Lucía Brito, wife
Carlos Teodoro de Acevedo
  Ana Francisca Fernández, wife
  Rafaela, daughter, 16
  Margarita, daughter, 14
  Bárbara, daughter, 11

Carlos, son, 9
José, son, 7
María, daughter, 5
Juana, daughter, 2
Lucas Aguilar
  María del Castillo, wife
  Francisca, daughter, 18
Matías Cabrera
  María Brito, wife
José Suárez
  Francisca Rodríguez, wife
  María, daughter, 5
Luis Pérez
  Catalina de San Mateo, wife
Lorenzo Morales
  Josefa Rodríguez, wife
  Francisco, son, 15
  Vicente, son, 15
  Miguel, son, 2
  Inés, daughter, 17
  Sebastiana, daughter, 8
Pedro Sánchez
  María López, wife
  Andrés, son, 2
  María, daughter, 1
Bartolomé Caballero
  María Artiles, wife
  Diego, son, 17
  Antonio, son, 6
  Bartolomé, son,2
  María, daughter, 12
  Agustina, daughter, 3
  Andrea, daughter, 1 month
Miguel Padilla
  Lucía Enrique, wife
  María Padilla, mother
Francisco Alemán
  Tomasa Bordón, wife

Salvador, son, 1
María, daughter, 3
Catalina, daughter, 12
Sebastián Perera [Pereira]
María Moreno, wife
Pedro, son, 2
Francisco, son, 1 month
Ángel Gómez
Lázara María, wife
Antonio, son, 4
Diego, son, 2
Juan de Placencia
Josefa de Reyes, wife
Domingo, son, 9
Antonio, son, 6
Andrea, daughter, 11
Antonia, daughter, 2
Gaspar de Placencia
Melchora Barroso, wife
Francisco, son, 13
Baltasar, son, 2
María, daughter, 15
Leonor, daughter, 7
María, daughter, 6
José Suárez
José García Aguilar
Josefa María Guía, wife
José Antonio de la Paz
María de la Concepción, wife
Francisca, daughter, 3
Rita, daughter, 1
Domingo Francisco Estevez
Isabel García, wife
Fernando, son, 4
Manuel, son, 2
Antonia, daughter, 5 months

Alonso de Cubas
Antonia de Gracia, wife
Lorenzo, son, 6
José Vicente
María Mercedes, wife
Lorenzo de Cubas Romero
Lucía Sánchez, wife
Cristobal, son, 15
Lorenzo, son, 7
Antonio, son, 2
Pedro Cansiles
Sebastiana Moreno, wife
Antonia, daughter, 10
Juan, son, 7
María, daughter, 4
Catalina, daughter, 8 months
Simón Verde
Ana Sánchez, wife
Catalina, daughter, 16
Josefa, daughter, 13
Ramón López
María Verde, wife
Antonio López
Catalina Pena, wife
Juan, son, 3
Bernardo, son, 1
Tomás Lorenzo
María de Jesús Caballero, wife
Isidoro, son, 6
Estabana, daughter, 3
Francisca, daughter, 1 month
Pedro Espinosa
María Martel, wife
Luis, son, 8
Narcisa, daughter, 1 month
Juan Galán

Source: AGI, SD, leg. 2661.

BACHELORS AND MARRIED RECRUITS WITH THEIR FAMILIES WHO EMBARKED ON THE FRIGATE *LA SANTA FAZ*, SANTA CRUZ DE TENERIFE, FEBRUARY 17, 1779

Antonio Franqui
  Margarita Perera, wife
  Francisca, daughter, 20
  Nicolasa, daughter, 18
  María, daughter, 17
  Juan, son, 19
  Antonio, son, 8
Juan García Raimundo
  Catalina Rodríguez, wife
  Manuel, son, 2
  Antonia, daughter, 12
  María, daughter, 7
  Rosa, daughter, 4
  María, daughter, 3
Pedro José Alberto Negrón
  Francisca Antonia Machado, wife
  María de Campos, mother
  Pedro, son, 7 months
José Alberto Negrón
  Isabel Gómez, wife
  María, daughter, 2
  Pedro, son, 3 months
Juan Alonso Casanova
  Josefa Rodríguez, wife
Don Juan Segura
  Doña María León, wife
  Juan, son, 2
José Dávila
Ángel García
  Agustina Gonzáles, wife
José Viera (widower)
  Juan, son, 13
  Francisco, son, 10
  María, daughter, 23

Josefa, daughter, 22
Domingo Francisco Gutiérrez
  Josefa Hernández, wife
  José, son, 3
  José, son, 13 months
  Josefa Agustina, daughter, 6
Juan Diego Macías
José Hernández
  Francisca Josefa, sister, 3
  Juana María, sister, 25
Francisco Viera
  Ana Padrón, mother
Gabriel Alberto Negrón
  Beatriz Saa, wife
  María, daughter, 22
  Agustina, daughter, 18
  Lucía, daughter, 15
  Tomasa, daughter, 12
  María, daughter, 3
Francisco García Melchor
  (widower)
  Antonio, son, 15
  María, daughter, 23
Francisco Felipe
  María Hernández, wife
  José, son, 7
  Juan, son, 4
  Francisco, son, 2
Antonio de la Cruz
  Francisca Teresa, wife
  María del Rosario, daughter, 4
Bernabé de la Paz
  María de Aguilar, wife
  Juana, daughter, 5

Agustín Díaz de Noda
  María Serafín de Leonor, wife
  Agustín, son, 5 months
Antonio Barroso
  Feliciana Josefa de Cuba, wife
  Juan, son, 8
  Antonio, son, 5
  Pedro, son, 5
  Josefa, daughter, 18
Antonio José Hernández
  María del Carmen, wife
Juan Antonio Reyes
  Josefa Antonia, wife
  Laurencia, daughter, 8
  Francisca, daughter, 3
  Antonio, son, 1 month
José del Alamo
Pedro Mendoza
Ignacio Martín Morales
  Rafaela de Torres, wife
  Antonio, son, 8
  José, son, 4
  Mateo, son, 1 month
Benito Francisco Suárez
José Joaquín de Rojas
Felipe Juan Borges
  María Francisca, sister
Roque José Perera
  Josefa Hernández, wife
  Juana, daughter, 2
  Antonio, son, 1 month
Manuel Pérez
  Antonia del Rosario, wife
  Santiago, son, 8
  José, son, 6
  Agustina, daughter, 4
  Nicolasa, daughter, 2
Antonio Romo y Aguilar
  Catalina de Jesús, wife

Antonia, daughter, 12
Andrés, son, 10
Bernardino, son, 18
Josefa, daughter, 17
Catalina, daughter, 15
Francisca, daughter, 7
Antonia, daughter, 5
Juana, daughter, 2
Francisco Antonio Gonzales
  Antonia Francisca Álvarez, wife
  Francisco, son, 7
  Lorenzo, son, 3
  María, daughter, 2
  Felipe, son, 1 month
Cristobal de Vargas
  María Magdalena, wife
  José, son, 3
Roque Antonio Gonzáles
  María Francisca, wife
  Francisco, son, 9
  José, son, 4
  María, daughter, 1
Francisco Hernández Querido
  Bárbara Francisca, wife
  Bernabé, son, 9
  Alejandro, son, 5
  Josefa, daughter, 2
Domingo Miguel Rodríguez
  María de la Encarnación Quer-
    ido, wife
  Barnabé, son, 2
  Francisca, daughter, 3
  Antonio, son, 7
  Josefa, daughter, 1
Bernardo Luis Alfonso
  Bernarda Francisca Mansit, wife
  María, daughter, 2
  Bárbara, daughter, 1
José Luis Hernández

Clara Mendoza, wife
José, son, 6
Francisco, son, 4
Domingo, son, 2
María, daughter, 10
Josefa, daughter, 8
Agustín Martel de Vargas
María de Gracia (Carrera), wife
María, daughter, 6
Josefa, daughter, 1 month
Felipe Gómez
Isabel Francisca de Aguiar, wife
José, son, 3 months
María Francisca, daughter, 2
Josefa, daughter, 2
José Hernández
María Gerónima Marg.sa, wife
Bernabé, son, 4
José, son, 1
Cristobal Mendoza
Francisca Rodríguez de Guía,
wife
María, daughter, 3
Antonio Bello
Clara de Vargas, wife
Antonió, son, 2
José Díaz Domínguez
María Teresa, sister, 30
Bárbara, sister, 18
Bartolomé Medina
Josefa de Guía, wife
Cristobal Rodríguez
María Francisca Díaz, wife
Francisco, son, 8
Antonio, son, 5
Salvador, son, 1 month
Juan Pérez
Catalina López, wife
Juan, son, 14

Juan Antonio, son, 12
Domingo, son, 4
María, daughter, 20
Josefa, daughter, 10
Francisca, daughter, 6
Domingo Luis Ravelo
Josefa Francisca, wife
Miguel, son, 6
Domingo, son, 1
María, daughter, 5
José Hernández Socas
Francisca Márquez, wife
Ana Francisca, mother-in-law
José de Torres
María Benítez, mother
Beatriz, sister, 25
Lorenzo Agapito Hernández
Brigida María Montesinos, wife
Antonia, daughter, 30 months
Pedro López
Bernarda Perera, wife
José Antonio, son, 12
Estefana, daughter, 10
Agustina, daughter, 8
Diego, son, 3
Pedro, son, 3 months
Simón Antonio López
Isidro Rodríguez
María del Rosario, wife
José, son, 4
Gabriela, daughter, 8
María, daughter, 5
Antonia, daughter, 3 months
José de Xeres Cabeza
Josefa Fonte del Castillo, wife
Rosalía, daughter, 12
Mariana, daughter, 12
María Leonor, daughter, 8
Blasina, daughter, 2

Pedro Domínguez Gillama
   Catalina Francisca Negrón,
     wife
   Catalina, daughter, 18 months
Gregorio Monzón Peña
   Luisa Ortega, wife
   Juan, son, 14
   Francisco, son, 7
Salvador Gonzáles
   María Padrona, wife
   Pedro, son, 8
   José, son, 5
   Salvador, son, 3
   Francisco, son, 4 months
   María de la Concepción,
     daughter, 7
Nicolás Gonzáles
Mateo Henrríquez
   Josefa Vélez, wife
   Felipe, son, 15
   María, daughter, 2 months
Domingo Hernández Claro
   Bárbara Francisca, wife
   José, son, 13
   Nicolasa, daughter, 22
   María, daughter, 20
   Francisca, daughter, 10
Antonio García Pestaño
   Josefa Rodríguez, wife
Juan José García Melchor
   Josefa de los Santos, wife
Juan de Mendoza
   Francisca Rafaela, wife
   Antonia, daughter, 10
   María del Carmen, 2
Pedro Francisco Manuel Plasencia
   Beatriz Cabrera, wife
   María Rosalía, daughter, 9
Juan Perdomo

Sebastiana de Armas, wife
   Teresa, daughter, 19
Juan Manuel Plasencia
   María Mendoza, wife
   Antonio, son, 8
   Pedro, son, 2
   María, daughter, 5
Antonio Rafael de la Paz
   María del Rosario, wife
   Antonio, son, 12
   Francisco, son, 3
   Antonio, son, 8 months
Antonio Francisco de Vargas
   Gracia Francisca Acebedo, wife
   José, son, 7
   Francisco, son, 3
   María, daughter, 1 month
José Antonio Rojas
   Catalina Morales, wife
   Cristobal, son, 13
   Pedro Antonio, son, 10
   Catalina Gregoria, daughter, 6
   María, daughter, 6
   Francisca, daughter, 3
   Antonia, daughter, 5 months
Nicolás de Rojas
   Antonia de Rojas, wife
Don Hilarión de la Paz Barroso
   Doña Josefa Salazar, wife
   Hilarión, son, 3 months
   María, daughter, 7 months
Francisco José de Armas
   Ana Francisca, wife
Juan Rodríguez Mena
   Josefa de Orta, wife
   Francisca de Orta, mother-
     in-law
Antonio Rodríguez
   María Lorenza, sister

Antonio Díaz
  Ana Benítez, mother
  Ana, sister, 25
Antonio Meneses
  Teresa Vicenta, wife
  Antonio, son, 1
  Antonia, daughter, 5
Cayetano Méndez
Joaquín de Rojas
Felipe Gonzáles Mansit
  María Francisca, wife
  Domingo, son, 13 months
  Antonio, son, 3
Felipe Besa
  María del Carmen, wife
  Josefa, daughter, 18 months
Tomás Antonio Rodríguez
  Petra Pabla de Cháves, wife
  Vicente, son, 14
  Gregorio, son, 11
  Domingo, son, 7
  Bárbara, daughter, 17
  Antonia, daughter, 9
  Gertrudis, daughter, 1
Felipe Luis Alfonso
  María Marta Carrera, wife
  Diego, son, 3
Bernardo Antonio Rivero
  María Díaz, wife
  Rosalía, daughter, 18 months
Francisco Álvarez
  Josefa de Borges, wife
  José, son, 8
  Antonio, son, 5
  María, daughter, 18 months
Nicolás de Fornes
  María Delgado, wife
  José Nicolás, son
  María, daughter, 5

Beatriz, daughter, 3
Juan de Torres
  María de Abreu, wife
  Juan José, son, 7
  Bartolomé, son, 2
  María Josefa, daughter, 4
Domingo Hernández Socas
  Ángela Francisca Mansit, wife
  Domingo, son, 12
  María, daughter, 14
  Josefa, daughter, 10
Salvador Hernández
  Rita Antonia Parra Verde, wife
  Domingo, son, 10
  Pedro, son, 4
  María, daughter, 8 months
  José, son, 8
Salvador Díaz
  María Casana, wife
  María, daughter, 6
  Francisca, daughter, 4
  Ana, daughter, 2
Gaspar Antonio Alegría
  Ana Álvarez, wife
  Domingo, son, 4
  María, daughter, 2 months
José Gonzáles Ruiz
  Josefa Gonzáles Mansit, wife
  Bernardo, son, 11
  Domingo, son, 4
  Bárbara, daughter, 2
José Gonzáles Vicente
  Isabel María de la Luz, wife
  Gaspar, son, 4
José Gonzáles de la Cruz
  Juana Rodríguez Cháves, wife
  Antonio, son, 10
  Pedro, son, 6
  José, son, 4

Diego, son, 2
Pedro de Torres
 Josefa María Díaz, wife
 Pedro, son, 8
 Antonia de la Concepción,
  daughter, 23
 Antonia, daughter, 16
 María, daughter, 12
Cristobal Lorenzo Carrero
 Manuela Márquez, wife
Manuel Melián
 María Carrillo, wife
 Antonio, son, 8
 Antonio José, son, 5
 Paula María, daughter, 1
Domingo Manuel Hernández
Juan José Montesinos

María Felipa Morales, wife
Antonio Manuel Navarro
 Catalina de Cristo, wife
 Antonio, son, 4
 María, daughter, 8
 María del Rosario, daughter, 10
  months
Juan de Abreu
 Lugarda María Trujillo, wife
 Juan José, son, 11
 María, daughter, 6
 Ana Josefa, daughter, 3
Salvador de Torres
 Florencia Roque, wife
 Melchora, daughter, 20
 Josefa, daughter, 15
 Antonia, daughter, 10

Source: AGI, SD, leg. 2661.

PERSONS AND FAMILIES WHO CAME FROM THE
CANARY ISLANDS FOR LOUISIANA AND WHO ARE
NOW GOING ON THE FRIGATE *MARGARITA*, HAVANA,
JULY 28, 1783

Agustín de Zejas
 Luisa, daughter
 Francisca, daughter
Tomás de Zejas
 Catalina, wife
Manuel Ramos
 María, wife
 María, daughter
 Juan, son
 Josefa, daughter
 Tomás, son
Lorenza Marrero
 Juan, son
 Francisca, daughter

Diego Rodríguez
 María, wife
Juan Lorenzo Gonzales
 María, wife
 María, daughter
Patricio Gonzáles
 Tomasa, wife
 Luis, son
 Francisco, son
Antonio Gonzáles
 Isabel, wife
 Antonia, daughter
Juan Alonso de la Fuente
 Beatriz, wife

María, daughter
Antonia, daughter
Juan Quintana
  Isabel, wife
  María, daughter
Antonio de Flores
  Catalina, wife
  Margarita, mother-in-law
Francisco Truxillo
  Beatriz, wife
  Josefa, daughter
  Francisca, daughter
Domingo Machado
  Antonia, wife
  Antonio, son
  José, son
  Francisco, son
  Pedro, son
Juan Alonso Morales
  Antonia, wife
  María, daughter
Antonio Valentin Rodríguez
  Luisa, wife
  Santiago, son
Antonio Esteves
  Elena, wife
  María, daughter
José Marrero Luis, son [*sic*]
  Vizenta, daughter
  Luis, son
  Pedro, son
  Josefa, daughter
  Josefa [*sic*], daughter
María, widow of Antonio Infante
  María, daughter
  Antonia, daughter
  Francisca, daughter
  Dominga, daughter
Antonio Rodríguez

María, wife
María, daughter
Alonso, son
Francisco, son
Ana, daughter
Francisca, daughter
Julián López
  María, wife
Francisco de Campos
  María, wife
José Oleda [Ojeda?]
  Úrsula, wife
  Eugenio, son
Antonio Rubio
  Josefa, wife
  Nicolás, son
Antonio Machado
  María, wife
  Sebastián, son
  Josefa, daughter
  Andrea, daughter
  María, daughter
  Pedro, son
Manuel de la Caridad
  María, wife
  Antonia, daughter
Antonio Dupierrez
  Catalina, wife
  Juan, son
María, widow of José Lorenzo
    Juárez
  Antonio, son
  Juan, son
  Miguel, son
  Francisco, son
  José, son
  Francisca, daughter
  María, daughter
José Alemán

Antonia, wife
Juan, son
Matías, son
Santiago Hernández
  María, wife
  María, daughter
  Francisco, son
  Josefa, daughter
  Antonia, daughter
Felipe Gonzáles Fuentes
  Antonia, wife
José Antonio Quintana
  María, wife
  María, daughter
  José, son
  Rafael, son
Juan de Acosta
  Luisa, wife
  José, son
  José [sic], son
Manuel Hernández Claro
  Catalina, wife
  María, daughter
  Antonio, son
  Josefa, daughter
José Antonio Gonzáles

Antonia, wife
  María, daughter
Luis Martel
  Antonia, mother
Pedro Hernández
  Isabel, wife
  José, son
  María, daughter
Domingo Díaz Núñez—deserted
  on 16th
  María, wife
  Domingo, son
  María, daughter
  Luisa, daughter
  María [sic], daughter
  Domingo [sic], son
Antonio Bienes
  Manuela, wife
José Ramírez
  Diego, son
  María, daughter
  Isabel, daughter
Sebastián Carzola
  Isabel, wife
  Bartolomé, son
  Ángela, daughter
  Ángel, grandson

Source: AGI, PC, leg. 1393.

PERSONS AND FAMILIES WHO CAME FROM THE
CANARY ISLANDS FOR LOUISIANA AND WHO ARE
NOW GOING ON THE PACKET BOAT *SANTÍSIMA TRINI-
DAD*, HAVANA, AUGUST 7, 1783

Tomás Meneses
  Josefa, wife

Antonio, son
Juan Ramírez

Ana, wife
Cristobal Luis Molero
  Josefa, wife
  Bartolomé, son
  Juan, son
  Antonia, daughter
  Agustina, daughter
  María, daughter
  Catalina, daughter
  Francisco, son
Francisco Ramírez
  María, wife
  José, son
  Juan, son
  Bernardo, son
  María, daughter
Domingo Gonzáles
  Catarina, wife
  Juan, son
  Miguel, son
  Bartolomé, son
  Juan, son
  María, daughter
Domingo de Sosa
Antonio Pérez
  Josefa, wife
  María, daughter
  Juan, son
Nicolás Folentino
  Juana, wife
  José, son
  Ángela, daughter
  Antonia, daughter
  María, daughter
  Tomasa, mother-in-law
Nicolás Estrada (his wife and
  son deserted)
Domingo Ramos
  Gabriela, wife

Rosa, daughter
María, daughter
Juana, daughter
Antonia, daughter
María [*sic*], daughter
Marcos Sanabria
  Juana, daughter
Pirona [?], widow of Bartolomé
  Rodríguez
  Manuel, son
  Domingo, son
  Antonio, son
  María, daughter
José Agustín Martín
  María, wife
  Ana, daughter
Juan Alemán
Francisco García Oramas
  Francisca, wife
  José, son
  María, daughter
  Gerónimo, son
  Marcelina, daughter
Gaspar Zerpa
  Ana, mother
  Francisco, brother
José de Mesa
  Josefa, wife
  María, daughter
Francisco de la Mar
  Margarita, wife
  Francisco, son
  Sebastián, son
  Rosa, daughter
  Marcela, daughter
  Juana, daughter
  Domingo, son
Miguel Sanabria
  Catalina, wife

María, daughter
Pedro Hernández
 Tomasa, wife
 Francisca, daughter
 Josefa, daughter
 Pedro, son
 Francisco, son
 Juan, son
Pedro Gía
 Vicente, son
 Pedro, son
 Antonia, daughter
Antonio José de León

Francisco Luis Hernández
 Josefa, wife
 José, son
 Francisco, son
Juana Pérez
Domingo Amaro
 Isabel, wife
 José, son
 Luis, son
José Bayano
 Tomás, son
 María, daughter
 Ángela, daughter
Bartolomé Pérez
 Ana, wife
 José, son
 Francisco, son
 María, daughter

Agustina, wife
Catalina, daughter
Antonia, daughter
Leonardo Gonzáles
 Catalina, wife
 Antonio, son
 José, son
Domingo Masito
 Josefa, wife
 Felipe, son
Gerónimo Curbelo
 Eugenia, wife
 Ángel, Son
 Francisco, son

(This family stays in Havana
because the wife is
sick, and will go soon.)

(She stays because she is sick.)
(The same.)

(The same.)

(The same.)

Source: AGI, PC, leg. 1393.

Bibliography

ARCHIVES AND DOCUMENTARY COLLECTIONS

Archivo General de Indias, Seville
  Audiencia de Santo Domingo
    Legajos 2547, 2548, 2552, 2554, 2560, 2570, 2609, 2610, 2611, 2657,
    2661, 2662
  Mapas y Planos
    Luisiana y Florida
  Papeles Procedentes de la Isla de Cuba
    Legajos 1, 2, 9A, 11, 13, 14, 17, 25B, 27AB, 28, 29, 30, 33, 34, 44, 49,
    50, 51, 71A, 72, 73, 77B, 83, 85, 112, 113, 115, 117A, 119, 121, 122AB,
    129, 132, 134A, 139, 155B, 161A, 176B, 192, 193A, 194, 195, 196, 198B,
    199, 200, 201, 202, 203, 204, 206, 207AB, 208AB, 209, 211A, 212, 213,
    215A, 216A, 217A, 218, 260, 538B, 568, 595A, 603AB, 606, 608AB,
    689, 1232, 1425, 1443A, 2351, 2354, 2358, 2364
Archivo Histórico Nacional, Madrid
  Sección de Estado
    Legajo 3900
Louisiana State University Archives, Baton Rouge
  Archives of the Spanish Government of West Florida, 19th Judicial
    District Court, Baton Rouge, WPA Translation
  Pintado Papers
Louisiana Historical Center, New Orleans
  Spanish Judicial Records
  School Records for 1834 and 1835, St. Bernard Parish
  J. M. Lee Report of Saint Bernard Parish Riot, October 25–27, 1868,
    New Orleans, November 27, 1868
Orleans Parish Civil Court Building, New Orleans

Notarial Records: Carlos Ximénes, Volumes XV and XIX
Humanities Research Library, University of Texas, Austin
  Parsons Collection
Ascension Parish Courthouse, Donaldsonville, Louisiana
  Land, 1799
  Marriage Contracts, 1787–1809
United States Census Office
  American Census Records
    Fourth Census (1820), St. Bernard Parish
    Sixth Census (1840), Ascension and Assumption Parishes
    Seventh Census (1850), Ascension and Assumption Parishes
    Eighth Census (1860), Ascension and Assumption Parishes
    Twelfth Census (1900), Ascension, Assumption, and St. Bernard
      Parishes

NEWSPAPERS

Donaldsonville *Chief*, 1874–1945
Louisiana Gazette and Mercantile Adventurer (New Orleans), April 5, 1815
New Orleans *Times*, October–December, 1868
St. Bernard *Weekly Eagle*, March 16, 1882
St. Bernard *Voice*, 1892–1945

THESES, DISSERTATIONS, AND REPORTS

Alleman, Elise A. "The Legend and History of the Place-Names of Assumption Parish." M.A. thesis, Louisiana State University, 1936.
Allen, Frederick Stuart. "A Social and Economic History of Baton Rouge, 1850–1860." M.A. thesis, Louisiana State University, 1936.
Bowie, Helen M. "Bayou Lafourche." M.A. thesis, Louisiana State University, 1935.
Carmouche, Norman Edward. "The Development of Public Education in Assumption Parish from 1807–1943." M.A. thesis, Louisiana State University, 1944.
Guillotte, Joseph Valsin. "Masters of the Marsh: An Introduction to the Ethnography of the Isleños of Lower St. Bernard Parish, Louisiana, with an Annotated Bibliography." Report for the Jean Lafitte National Historical Park, n.p., *ca.* 1982.
Harris, Thomas H. "The History of Public Education in Louisiana." M.A. thesis, Louisiana State University, 1924.

Hawley, Francis Frederick. "Spanish Folk Healing in Ascension Parish, Louisiana." M.A. thesis, Louisiana State University, 1976.

Kaltenbaugh, Louise Pauline. "A Study of the Place-Names of St. Bernard Parish, Louisiana." M.A. thesis, Louisiana State University— University of New Orleans, 1970.

LeBreton, Marietta Marie. "A History of the Territory of Orleans, 1803–1812." Ph.D. dissertation, Louisiana State University, 1969.

Newton, Lewis William. "The Americanization of French Louisiana: A Study of the Process of Adjustment Between the French and the Anglo-American Population of Louisiana, 1803–1860." Ph.D. dissertation, University of Chicago, 1929.

Parenton, Vernon J. "The Rural French-Speaking People of Quebec and Louisiana." Ph.D. dissertation, Harvard University, 1948.

Quiñones, Marc Anthony. "Delacroix Island: A Sociological Study of a Spanish American Community." M.A. thesis, Louisiana State University, 1955.

Renauld, Marie Louise. "The History of the Public Schools in St. Bernard Parish to 1877." M.A. thesis, Tulane University, 1946.

Reynolds, Jack A. "Louisiana Place-Names of Romance Origin." Ph.D. dissertation, Louisiana State University, 1942.

Roland, Charles Pierre. "Louisiana Sugar Plantations During the Civil War." Ph.D. dissertation, Louisiana State University, 1951.

Savoy, Grace June. "Louisiana Parishes: Their People and Governments. A Developmental Analysis." Ph.D. dissertation, Louisiana State University, 1979.

Scramuzza, V. M. "Galveztown, a Spanish Settlement of Colonial Louisiana." M.A. thesis, Louisiana State University, 1924.

Suarez, Raleigh A. "Rural Life in Louisiana, 1850–1860." Ph.D. dissertation, Louisiana State University, 1954.

BOOKS

Acosta Rodríguez, Antonio. *La población de la Luisiana española (1763–1803)*. Madrid, 1979.

American State Papers: Public Lands. I–VIII. Washington, D.C., 1832–1861.

Arthur, Stanley Clisby. *The Fur Animals of Louisiana*. Department of Conservation Bulletin 18 (rev.). New Orleans, 1931.

———. *Louisiana Tours: A Guide to the Places of Historic and General Interest*. New Orleans, 1950.

Bartlett, Napier. *Military Record of Louisiana, Including Biographical and Historical Papers Relating to the Military Organizations of the State.* New Orleans, 1875; rpr. Baton Rouge, 1964.

Baudier, Roger. *The Catholic Church in Louisiana.* New Orleans, 1939.

Bemis, Samuel Flagg. *Pinckney's Treaty: America's Advantage from Europe's Distress, 1783–1800.* Rev. ed.: New Haven, Conn., 1960.

Biennial Report of the Secretary of State of the State of Louisiana, 1886–1887. Baton Rouge, 1888.

Biographical and Historical Memoirs of Louisiana. 3 vols.: Chicago, 1892; rpr. Baton Rouge, 1975.

Bolton, Herbert Eugene, and Thomas Maitland Marshall. *The Colonization of North America, 1492–1783.* New York, 1920.

Bonnet y Reverón, Buenaventura. *Las expediciones a las Canarias en el siglo XIV.* Madrid, 1946.

Brackenridge, Henry Marie. *Views of Louisiana, Together with a Journal of a Voyage up the Missouri River, in 1811.* Pittsburgh, 1811; rpr. Chicago, 1962.

Brading, David A. *Miners and Merchants in Bourbon Mexico, 1763–1810.* London, 1971.

Bravo, Telesforo. *Geografía general de las Islas Canarias.* Santa Cruz de Tenerife, 1964.

Brunner, E. *History of Louisiana, from Its Discovery and Settlement to the Present Time.* New York, 1841.

Burson, Caroline Maude. *The Stewardship of Don Esteban Miró, 1782–1792.* New Orleans, 1940.

Casey, Powell A. *Louisiana in the War of 1812.* Baton Rouge, 1963.

————. *Try Us: The Story of the Washington Artillery in World War II.* Baton Rouge, 1971.

Catholic Diocese of Baton Rouge. *Catholic Church Records, 1770–1803.* Baton Rouge, 1980.

Caughey, John Walton. *Bernardo de Gálvez in Spanish Louisiana, 1776–1783.* Berkeley, Calif., 1934; rpr. Gretna, La., 1972.

Chambers, Henry E. *A History of Louisiana, Wilderness—Colony—Province—Territory—State—People.* 3 vols.: Chicago, 1925.

Citizens of Louisiana from Whom U.S. Direct Tax Was Collected in 1865. Baton Rouge, 1892.

Claiborne, William C. C. *Official Letterbooks of W. C. C. Claiborne, 1801–1816.* Edited by Dunbar Rowland. 6 vols.: Jackson, Miss., 1917.

Cline, Isaac Monroe. *Storms, Floods, and Sunshine.* 3rd ed.: New York, 1951.

Coastal Environments, Inc. *Environmental Baseline Study, St. Bernard Parish, Louisiana*. Baton Rouge, 1972.

————. *Resource Management: The St. Bernard Wetlands, Louisiana*. Baton Rouge, 1976.

Coderch Figueroa, Mercedes. *Evolución de la población de La Laguna entre 1750–1860*. La Laguna, Tenerife, 1975.

Cohen's New Orleans and Southern Directory for 1856 . . . New Orleans, 1856.

Cohen's New Orleans Directory for 1855 . . . of the Cotton and Sugar Plantations of Louisiana and Mississippi. New Orleans, 1855.

County and City Data Book. Washington, D.C., 1983.

Crété, Lilian. *Daily Life in Louisiana, 1815–1830*. Baton Rouge, 1981.

Cunningham, Edward. *The Port Hudson Campaign, 1862–1863*. Baton Rouge, 1963.

Cuscoy, Luis Diego. *Los guanches*. Santa Cruz de Tenerife, 1968.

Dalrymple, Margaret Fisher, ed. *The Merchant of Manchac: The Letterbooks of John Fitzpatrick, 1768–1790*. Baton Rouge, 1978.

Daniel, Pete. *Deep'n as It Comes: The 1927 Mississippi River Flood*. New York, 1977.

Darby, William. *The Emigrant's Guide to the Western and Southwestern States and Territories*. New York, 1818.

————. *A Geographical Description of the State of Louisiana*. 2nd ed.: New York, 1817.

Dargo, George. *Jefferson's Louisiana: Politics and the Clash of Legal Traditions*. Cambridge, Mass., 1975.

Davis, Edwin Adam. *Louisiana: A Narrative History*. 3rd. ed.: Baton Rouge, 1971.

————, ed. *The Rivers and Bayous of Louisiana*. Baton Rouge, 1968.

Dawson, Joseph G., III. *Army Generals and Reconstruction: Louisiana, 1862–1877*. Baton Rouge, 1982.

De Vergas, Marie Cruzat (Mrs. Edwin X.). *American Forces at Chalmette, Veterans and Descendants of the Battle of New Orleans, 1814–1815*. N.p., 1966.

Din, Gilbert C., ed. and trans. *Louisiana in 1776: A Memoria of Francisco Bouligny*. New Orleans, 1977.

Duffy, John, ed. *The Rudolph Matas History of Medicine in Louisiana*. 2 vols.: Baton Rouge, 1958–62.

Dunn, Gordon E., and Banner I. Miller. *Atlantic Hurricanes*. Baton Rouge, 1960.

Edmonds, David C. *The River Campaign (February–May, 1863)*. Lafayette,

La., 1983. Vol. I of Edmonds, *The Guns of Port Hudson*.

Evans, Gen. Clement A. *Confederate Military History: A Library of Confederate States History*. 12 vols.: Atlanta, 1899.

Farragut, Loyall. *The Life of David Glasgow Farragut*. New York, 1882.

Flint, Timothy. *Recollections of the Last Ten Years in the Valley of the Mississippi*. Edited by George R. Brooks. Boston, 1826; rpr. Carbondale, Ill., 1968.

Fortier, Alcée. *Louisiana, Comprising Sketches of Parishes, Tombs, Events, Institutions, and Persons* . . . 3 vols.: N.p., 1914.

––––––. *Louisiana Studies: Literature, Customs and Dialects, History and Education*. New Orleans, 1894.

Freiberg, Edna B. *Bayou St. John in Colonial Louisiana, 1699–1803*. New Orleans, 1980.

Garon, Henry A., ed. *Donaldsonville, Its Businessmen, and Their Commerce at the Turn of the Century*. N.p., 1976.

Gayarré, Charles. *History of Louisiana*. 4 vols., 3rd ed.: New Orleans, 1885.

Gibson's Guide and Directory of the State of Louisiana, and the Cities of New Orleans and Lafayette. New Orleans, 1838.

Gilbert, Sam F. *History of the Town of Napoleonville*. Napoleonville, La., 1936.

Giraud, Marcel. *A History of French Louisiana*. Vol. I: *The Reign of Louis XIV (1698–1715)*. Translated by Joseph C. Lambert. Baton Rouge, 1974. Vol. II: *Années de transition (1715–1717)*. Paris, 1958. Vol. III: *L'Epoque de John Law (1717–1720)*. Paris, 1966. Vol. IV: *La Louisiane après le système de Law*. Paris, 1978.

Hair, William Ivy. *Bourbonism and Agrarian Protest: Louisiana Politics, 1877–1900*. Baton Rouge, 1969.

Harris, William H., ed. *Louisiana Products, Resources and Attractions, with a Sketch of the Parishes: A Hand Book of Reliable Information Concerning the State*. New Orleans, 1881.

Hatfield, Joseph T. *William Claiborne: Jeffersonian Centurion in the American Southwest*. Lafayette, La., 1976.

Henry, Adolphe, and Victor Gerodias. *The Louisiana Coast Directory of the Right and Left Banks of the Mississippi from Its Mouth to Baton Rouge*. New Orleans, 1857.

Hernández Hernández, Pedro, ed. *Natura y cultura de las Islas Canarias*. 4th ed.: Santa Cruz de Tenerife, 1982.

Hillgarth, Jocelyn Nigel. *The Spanish Kingdoms, 1250–1516*. London, 1978.

Historical Records Survey. *Inventory of the Parish Archives of Louisiana, St.*

Bernard Parish. Louisiana State University, Department of Archives, Baton Rouge, 1938.

Holmes, Jack D. L. *Gayoso: The Life and Times of a Spanish Governor on the Mississippi, 1789–1799*. Baton Rouge, 1965.

————, ed. *Honor and Fidelity*. Birmingham, Ala., 1965.

Hooton, Ernest A. *The Ancient Inhabitants of the Canary Islands*. Cambridge, Mass., 1925.

Howell, Roland Boatner, Sr. *Louisiana Sugar Plantations, Mardi Gras and Huey P. Long: Reminiscences of Roland Boatner, Sr.* Baton Rouge, 1969.

Hutchins, Thomas. *An Historical Narrative and Topographical Description of Louisiana and West Florida*. Facsimile of 1784 ed.; Gainesville, Fla., 1968.

Jeansonne, Glen. *Leander Perez, Boss of the Delta*. Baton Rouge, 1977.

Kaiser Aluminum and Chemical Corporation. *They Now Call It the "Greatest Disaster in America" (or the Great Disaster . . . Hurricane "Betsy,") Sept. 9, 1965*. Chalmette, La., n.d.

Kammer, Edward J. *A Socio-Economic Survey of the Marshdwellers of Four Southeastern Louisiana Parishes*. Washington, D.C., 1941.

Kane, Harnette T. *The Bayous of Louisiana*. New York, 1943.

————. *Deep Delta Country*. New York, 1946.

Kemp, John R. *New Orleans: An Illustrated History*. Woodland Hills, Calif., 1981.

Kinnaird, Lawrence, ed. *Spain in the Mississippi Valley, 1765–1794*. 3 parts. Washington, D.C., 1949.

Ladero Quesada, Miguel Angel. *Los primeros europeos en Canarias (Siglos XIV y XV)*. Las Palmas, Gran Canaria, 1979.

Latour, [Major] Arsene Lacarriere. *Historical Memoir of the War in West Florida and Louisiana in 1814–15*. 1816; rpr. Gainesville, Fla., 1964.

Leeper, Clare D'Artois, comp. *Louisiana Places: Collection of the Columns from the Baton Rouge "Sunday Advocate," 1960–1974*. Baton Rouge, 1976.

Lewis, Charles Lee. *David Glasgow Farragut*. 2 vols.: Annapolis, 1941–43.

López Herrera, Salvador. *Las Islas Canarias a través de la historia*. Madrid, 1971.

Louisiana Legislative Council. *Membership in the Legislature of Louisiana, 1880–1980*. Baton Rouge, 1979.

Ludlum, David M. *Early American Hurricanes, 1492–1870*. Boston, 1963.

MacCurdy, Raymond R. *The Spanish Dialect of St. Bernard Parish, Louisiana*. Albuquerque, 1950.

Maduell, Charles R., Jr. *Federal Land Grants in the Territory of Orleans: The Delta Parishes*. New Orleans, 1975.

Mahan, Alfred T. *Admiral Farragut*. New York, 1892.

Marchand, Sidney, Sr. *Across the Years*. Donaldsonville, La., 1949.

――――. *An Attempt to Reassemble the Old Settlers in Family Groups*. Baton Rouge, 1965.

――――. *The Chief in the Land of the Chetimachas*. Donaldsonville, La., 1959.

――――. *The Flight of a Century (1800–1900) in Ascension Parish, Louisiana*. Donaldsonville, La., 1936.

――――. *Forgotten Fighters, 1861–1865*. Donaldsonville, La., 1966.

――――. *The House of Marchand*. Donaldsonville, La., 1952.

――――. *Marchands on the Mississippi and on the St. Lawrence*. Donaldsonville, La., 1968.

――――. *The Story of Ascension Parish, Louisiana*. Baton Rouge, 1931.

Marrero Rodríguez, Manuela. *La esclavitud en Tenerife a raíz de la conquista*. La Laguna, Tenerife, 1966.

McCrary, Peyton. *Abraham Lincoln and Reconstruction: The Louisiana Experiment*. Princeton, 1978.

Menn, Joseph Karl. *The Large Slaveholders of Louisiana—1860*. New Orleans, 1964.

Mercer, John. *The Canary Islands: Their Prehistory, Conquest, and Survival*. London, 1980.

Morales Lezcano, Victor. *Relaciones mercantiles entre Inglaterra y los archipiélagos del Atlántico Ibérico, su estructura y su historia (1503–1783)*. La Laguna, Tenerife, 1970.

Morales Padrón, Francisco. *Canarias: crónicas de su conquista*. Seville, 1978.

――――. *Sevilla, Canaria y América*. Las Palmas, Gran Canaria, 1970.

New Orleans *Item. The Book of Louisiana: A Newspaper Reference Work*. New Orleans, 1916.

O'Callaghan, Joseph F. *A History of Medieval Spain*. Ithaca, N.Y., 1975.

Olmstead, Frederick Law. *A Journey in the Seaboard Slave States in the Years 1853–1854 with Remarks on Their Economy*. 2 vols.: New York, 1904.

Peraza de Ayala, José. *El régimen comercial de Canarias con Las Indias en los siglos XVI, XVII y XVIII*. Seville, 1977.

Perrin du Lac, François-Marie. *Voyage dans les deux Louisianes*. Paris, 1805.

Public Affairs Research Council of Louisiana, Inc. *Statistical Profile of St. Bernard Parish*. Baton Rouge, 1973.

Raphael, Morris. *The Battle in the Bayou Country*. Detroit, 1975.

Ripley, C. Peter. *Slaves and Freedmen in Civil War Louisiana*. Baton Rouge, 1976.

Robertson, James Alexander, ed. *Louisiana Under the Rule of Spain, France, and the United States, 1785–1807*. 2 vols.: Cleveland, 1911; rpr. New York, 1969.

Robichaux, Albert J., Jr., ed. *Colonial Settlers Along Bayou Lafourche, 1770–1778*. Vol. II: Harvey, La., n.d.

———. *Louisiana Censuses and Militia Lists, 1770–1789*. Harvey, La., n.d.

Robin, Claude Cesar. *Voyage to Louisiana*. Translated by Stuard O. Landry, Jr. Abridged ed.. New Orleans, 1966.

Rodriguez, Mrs. B. M. *Our Rodriguez Family*. N.p., ca. 1983.

Roland, Charles Pierre. *Louisiana Sugar Plantations During the American Civil War*. Leiden, 1957.

Romeu Palazuelos, Enrique *et al. Las Islas Canarias*. Madrid, 1981.

Rumeu de Armas, A. *España en el Africa atlántico*. 2 vols: Madrid, 1956.

———. *La política indigenista de Isabel la Católica*. Valladolid, Sp., 1969.

Schwidelzky, Ilse. *La población prehispánica de las Islas Canarias*. Santa Cruz de Tenerife, 1963.

Shugg, Roger W. *Origins of Class Struggle in Louisiana*. Baton Rouge, 1939.

Sitterson, J. Carlyle. *Sugar Country: The Cane Industry in the South, 1753–1950*. Lexington, Ky., 1953.

Smith, Rhea Marsh. *Spain: A Modern History*. Ann Arbor, 1965.

Southern Manufacturer. *Baton Rouge of Today: The Capital City as a Commercial, Railway, Financial and Industrial Centre*. New Orleans, 1908.

Souvenir Program [of] St. Maurice Church Fair . . . April 27–28–29, 1912. N.p., 1912.

Sparks, William Henry. *The Memoirs of Fifty Years*. Philadelphia, 1870.

State of Louisiana. *The Fur Animals of Louisiana*. Department of Conservation, Bulletin 18 (rev.). New Orleans, 1931.

Stoddard, Major Amos. *Sketches, Historical and Descriptive, of Louisiana*. Philadelphia, 1812.

Stubbs, William C. *A Hand-Book of Louisiana . . . giving Geographical and Agricultural features . . . together with . . . crops that can be grown*. New Orleans, 1895.

Tannehill, Ivan Ray. *Hurricanes: Their Nature and History*. Princeton, 1938.

Taylor, Joe Gray. *Louisiana: A Bicentennial History*. New York, 1976.

———. *Louisiana Reconstructed, 1863–1877*. Baton Rouge, 1974.

Thompson, James M. *Louisiana Today*. N.p., 1939.

Transcriptions of Parish Records of Louisiana: St. Bernard Parish. 3 vols.. Department of Archives, Louisiana State University, 1941.

Tunnel, Ted. *Crucible of Reconstruction—War, Radicalism and Race in Louisiana, 1862–1877.* Baton Rouge, 1984.

Verlinden, Charles. *The Beginnings of Modern Colonization.* Ithaca, N.Y., 1970.

Villeré, Sidney, comp. *The Canary Islands Migration to Louisiana, 1778–1783.* Baltimore, 1972.

Wall, Bennett H., ed. *Louisiana: A History.* Arlington Heights, Ill., 1984.

Whitaker, Arthur Preston, ed. *Documents Relating to the Commercial Policy of Spain in the Floridas.* Deland, Fla. 1931.

Winters, John D. *The Civil War in Louisiana.* Baton Rouge, 1963.

Winzerling, Oscar William. *Acadian Odyssey.* Baton Rouge, 1955.

Young and Co.'s Business and Professional Directory of 1908–Louisiana–1909. Atlanta, 1908–1909.

ARTICLES

Acosta Rodríguez, Antonio. "Overview of the Consumption of Food and Goods by Isleño Immigrants to Louisiana." Translated by Paul E. Hoffman. *Louisiana History,* XXI (1981), 299–306.

Armistead, Samuel G. "Romances tradicionales entre los hispanohablantes del estado de Luisiana." *Nueva Revista de filología hispánica,* XXVII (1978), 39–56.

"The Capture of Baton Rouge by Galvez, September 21st, 1779." *Louisiana Historical Quarterly,* XII (1929), 255–65.

Carrigan, Jo Ann. "The Pestilence of 1796—New Orleans' First Officially Recorded Yellow Fever Epidemic." *McNeese Review,* XIII (1962), 27–36.

Caughey, John Walton. "The Natchez Rebellion of 1781 and Its Aftermath." *Louisiana Historical Quarterly,* XVI (1933), 57–83.

Claudel, Calvin A. "Louisiana Folktales and Their Background." *Louisiana Historical Quarterly,* XXXVIII (1955), 35–56.

———. "Spanish Folklore from Delacroix Island." *Journal of American Folklore.* LVIII (1945), 209–24.

———. "Tombs of Historic Interest in the Saint Bernard Cemetery." *Louisiana Historical Quarterly,* XXIV (1941), 353–59.

Dethloff, Henry C., and Robert R. Jones. "Race Relations in Louisiana, 1887–1898." *Louisiana History,* XIV (1968), 301–23.

Din, Gilbert C. "*Cimarrones* and the San Malo Band in Spanish Louisiana." *Louisiana History,* XXI (1980), 237–62.

———. "Early Spanish Colonization Efforts in Louisiana." *Louisiana Studies,* XI (1972), 31–49.

———. "Protecting the '*Barrera*': Spain's Defenses in Louisiana, 1763–1779." *Louisiana History*, XVIII (1978), 183–211.

———. "Spain's Immigration Policy and Efforts in Louisiana During the American Revolution." *Louisiana Studies*, XIV (1975), 241–57.

Douglas, Lee. "The Mississippi's Delta: The Land of the River." *National Geographic*, CLXIV, No. 2 (August, 1983), 226–52.

Favrot, J. St. Clair. "Baton Rouge, the Historic Capital of Louisiana." *Louisiana Historical Quarterly*, XII (1929), 610–29.

Faye, Stanley, ed. "The Schism of 1805 in New Orleans." *Louisiana Historical Quarterly*, XXII (1934), 98–141.

Forsyth, William H. "A Memorial to Col. Pierre Denys de la Ronde." *L'Heritage*, III, No. 9 (January, 1980), 60–64.

Hennessy, Melinda Meek. "Race and Violence in Reconstruction New Orleans: The 1868 Riot." *Louisiana History*, XX (1979), 77–91.

Hernández Rodríguez, Germán. "La aportación de la isla de la Gomera al poblamiento de la Luisiana, 1777–78." In *IV Coloquio de historia canario-americana (1980)*. 2 vols.: Salamanca, 1982, II, 227–45.

Holmes, Jack D. L. "Pensacola: Spanish Dominion, 1781–1821." In *Colonial Pensacola*, edited by James R. McGovern. Pensacola, 1972.

Jiménez de Gregorio, Fernando. "La población de las Islas Canarias en la segunda mitad del siglo XVIII." *Anuario de estudios atlánticos*, XIV (1968), 127–301.

Liljegren, Ernest R. "Jacobinism in Spanish Louisiana, 1792–1797." *Louisiana Historical Quarterly*, XXII (1939), 47–97.

MacCurdy, Raymond R. "Los Isleños de la Luisiana. Supervivencia de la lengua y folklore canario." *Anuario de estudios atlánticos*, XXI (1975), 471–591.

———. "Spanish Folklore from St. Bernard Parish, Louisiana." *Southern Folklore Quarterly*, XIII (1949), 180–91.

———. "Spanish Folklore from St. Bernard Parish, Louisiana: Part III, Folktales." *Southern Folklore Quarterly*, XVI (1952), 227–50.

———. "Spanish Riddles from St. Bernard Parish, Louisiana." *Southern Folklore Quarterly*, XII (1948), 129–35.

———. "A Spanish Word-List of the 'Brulis' Dwellers of Louisiana." *Hispania*, XLII (1959), 547–54.

———. "Un romance tradicional recogido en la Luisiana: 'Las señas del marido.'" *Revista hispánica*, XIII (1947), 164–66.

Molina Martínez, Miguel. "La participación canaria en la formación y reclutamiento del batallón de Luisiana." In *IV Coloquio de historia canario-americana (1980)*. 2 vols. Salamanca, 1982, I, 135–58.

Morales Padrón, Francisco. "El desplazamiento a las Indias desde Canarias." *Revista Museo Canario*, XXXV–XXXVI (1950), 1–24.

———. "Las Canarias y la política emigratoria a Indias." In *I Coloquio de historia canario-americana (1976)*, Seville, 1977, pp. 212–30.

———. "Colonos canarios en Indias." *Anuario de estudios americanos*, VIII (1951), 399–441.

"Our Lady of Lourdes Catholic Church, Violet, Saint Bernard Parish, Louisiana." New Orleans *Genesis*, V. No. 7 (January, 1966), 42.

Porras Muñoz, Guillermo. "El fracaso de Guarico." *Anuario de estudios americanos*, XXVI (1969), 569–609.

Prichard, Walter, ed. "Some Interesting Glimpses of Louisiana a Century Ago." *Louisiana Historical Quarterly*, XXIV (1941), 43–48.

———, ed. "A Tourist's Description of Louisiana in 1860." *Louisiana Historical Quarterly*, XXI (1938), 15–17.

Pugh, W. W. "Bayou Lafourche from 1820 to 1825." *Louisiana Planter and Sugar Manufacturer*, September 29, 1888.

Scott, Priscilla. "The 1850 St. Bernard Census." *L'Heritage*, II, No. 7 (June, 1979) to V, No. 18 (March, 1982).

Scramuzza, V. M. "Galveztown, a Spanish Settlement of Colonial Louisiana." *Louisiana Historical Quarterly*, XIII (1930), 553–609.

Scroggs, William O. "Rural Life in the Lower Mississippi Valley About 1803." *Proceedings of the Mississippi Valley Historical Association for the Year 1914–15*, III (1916), 262–77.

Solano Costa, Fernando. "La emigración acadiana a la Luisiana española (1783–1785)." *Cuadernos de historia Jerónimo Zurita*, II (1954), 82–125.

"Statistical Collections of Louisiana: The Parish of Baton Rouge." *DeBow's Southern and Western Review*, XII (January, 1852) 3rd Ser., II, No. 1, 22–24.

Suarez, Raleigh A. "Chronicle of a Failure: Public Education in Antebellum Louisiana." *Louisiana History*, XII (1971), 109–22.

———. "Louisiana's Struggling Majority: The Ante-Bellum Farmer." *McNeese Review*, XIV (1963), 14–31.

Taylor, Ethel. "Discontent in Confederate Louisiana." *Louisiana History*, II (1961), 410–28.

Tornero Tinajero, Pablo. "Canarian Immigration to America: The Civil-Military Expedition of 1777–1779." Translated by Paul E. Hoffman. *Louisiana History*, XXI (1980), 377–86.

Warner, Charles Dudley. "The Acadian Land." *Harper's*, LXXIV (February, 1887), 354.

Whitehead, Leslie G. "Louisiana Place Names: Some Preliminary Considerations." *Louisiana Studies*, VII (1968), 228–51.

Wood, Minter. "Life in New Orleans in the Spanish Period." *Louisiana Historical Quarterly*, XXII (1939), 642–709.

Index

Acadians: entrance of, into Louisiana, 12; at Bayou Lafourche, 28; at Galveztown, 38; in St. Bernard, 55; settlement of, in Lafourche des Chetimachas, 64, 75; at Bayou Lafourche church, 75, 76–77; intermarriage of, with Canarians, 86, 137; in brulees, 89–90; in Civil War, 110; influence of, on Canarians, 201–203; mentioned, 99, 127, 207

Alleman, Elise A., 167, 170

Alleman, Lenesse J., 142

Alleman, Samuel A., 138

Amat de Tortosa, Andrés: and recruitment of Canary Islanders, 16–20; expenses of, 25–26; death of, 26

Anglo-Americans, 29, 33, 38, 92

Arabi, 87, 131, 157, 178, 194

Arazena, Josef, 77, 79

Ascension church: origins of, 64–65; priests at, 69–70, 73, 76, 77–78, 79; and celebration of war victory, 70; Canarian attendance at, 73, 77; new building for, 73; boundaries of, 77; records at, 82; settlement near, 87; mentioned, 166, 171

Ascension Parish: population in, 89, 168–69, 185, 195; wealth of Canarians in, 101; Civil War in, 107–109, 110; soldiers of, 110–12, 114; Canarian property in, 115–16; towns in, 136; eastern area of, 136; census in, 138; politics in, 139; conditions in, 166; economy of, 166–68; migration from, 169; education in, 169–70; and Canarians in military, 172–74, 186, 187–92; use of

Spanish in, 202

Assumption church, 78–80

Assumption Parish: education in, 95–96, 137–38, 170; religion in, 96–97; Canarians' wealth in, 101; 1900 census in, 138–39; occupations in, 138–39; conditions in, 140, 166; modernization in, 141; economy of, 166–69; migration from, 169; population in, 195; use of Spanish in, 202

Barataria: origins of, 47; departure of settlers from, 48–51; mentioned, 29, 37, 69

Baton Rouge: British trade from, 12; in war, 22, 67; British fort at, 33; Canarian settlement in, 45, 86; secession convention in, 103–104; mentioned, 191

Battle of New Orleans, 92

Bayagoulas, 48

Bayou Bienvenu, 91

Bayou Lafourche: Bernardo de Gálvez on, 29; Acadians on, 29; description of, 64, 88–89, 98–100, 135–36, 140, 141, 164–66; religion on, 95–96; religion on, 96–97; Civil War on, 107–109, 110, 115; and Canarians in war, 110–12, 114, 186, 187–192; economics on, 115–16, 166–68, 186; brulees on, 135–36, 164, 165; Canarian departure from, 136; census on, 138; labor force of, 186–87; and transition to peace, 192; changes on, 195, 202; Canarian customs on, 200, 201, 204–206

Bayou Manchac, 28, 29, 136

251